IDA KAMINSKA
MY LIFE, MY THEATER

IDA
KAMINSKA

MY LIFE,
MY THEATER

EDITED AND TRANSLATED BY
CURT LEVIANT

Macmillan Publishing Co., Inc.
NEW YORK

Collier Macmillan Publishers
LONDON

Contents

Illustrations following page 150

Preface

I BEGAN writing these memoirs in my native city, Warsaw. But my work was interrupted because the events in Poland in 1967 took such a turn that it was impossible to concentrate and take pen in hand. Besides, I was certain that, no matter how difficult it would be, I would have to leave the land to which I, my family, and all my father's ancestors were so strongly bound. Moreover, I was afraid that my departure would be thwarted because of the written material in my possession. I had also been informed that books and notebooks and even newspaper clippings were being inspected at the border.

In the atmosphere of attacks, hatred, and gossip that raged in Poland, it proved ever more difficult to breathe. It began with the condemnation of Israel after the Six-Day War in 1967, then developed into a hatred of the Zionists, directed against all those with the slightest sympathy for the defensive war of the Jews in Israel, and ended with the identification of Zionists with Jews in general. After all, the average man on the street did not understand the difference. He did not even know what a Zionist is.

From the highest levels of government a mistrust of Jews developed, and during the organized mass demonstrations people carried placards which insulted Jews. Protesting against this false propaganda was prohibited, hence emigration was the only course.

Nevertheless, we knew that there were Polish intellectuals who did not agree with the venomous propaganda, but no one dared to oppose it publicly. There were those who confidentially admitted, "We know we are cowards. We lack the strength we were so proud of during the last war. Perhaps we lack courage because everyone is afraid for his job. We envy the fact that you Jews can express your protest by leaving the country."

Indeed, behind the scenes there was a power struggle concerning ambition and pride. And the first victims—always the victims—were the Jews, and even some decent Poles.

I had often been asked to write my memoirs. However, my constant reply was that I didn't know if I was capable. After all, memoirs are neither novel nor narrative; fantasy and imagination are not part of the fabric. Memoirs must be truthful. They must contain concrete facts and be entirely objective. Moreover, the reader does not necessarily believe that the writer has been thoroughly objective. Yet the times in which we live, especially from the outbreak of the Second World War until today, are so rich in extraordinary events that every individual who personally experienced these events has the duty to write them down. However, a memoirist must be skillful enough to tell the story so that the reader should not doubt for a moment the truth of the tale whose contents often surpass pure fantasy. Even though the facts and events up to the Second World War are certainly worth writing down in detail, I will not expatiate upon them because, after the war and subsequent events, they have lost their significance.

I have begun my life anew several times, and with my move to the United States, I have begun life anew once more. Despite the fact that I do not work in the Yiddish theater as much as I would like, I do not feel lonely or neglected because, above all, I am surrounded by those persons who are nearest and dearest to me.

Even though I now reside in America, to a degree I consider

myself a citizen of the world. And with more intensity than before do I feel my sense of belonging to the Jewish people who, despite their suffering, continue to live and create.

I

The Beginning

"IDA, do you want to play Siomke?"

"And Regina?"

"Regina is already too big for the role. Siomke is just your age, between four and five."

That period is quite vague for me, but I distinctly remember the little dialogue between my mother and me and even the apartment where it took place.

Regina was my elder sister. She had already played all the children's roles of the existing Yiddish repertoire. She was nine then, but tall for her age; hence the younger children's roles were passed on to me. My stage debut took place in Warsaw in 1904, in David Pinski's play *The Mother*, in which I played the role of my mother's grandchild, Siomke. The performance was at the Jardin d'Hiver, the Winter Garden Theater, at 9 Chmielna Street. I don't know why the theater had a French name or why it was called "garden," for I have no recollection of any garden there. In contrast to my sister, I was able to play the children's roles for many, many years, for I was a "shrimp," as my mother used to call me.

In this simple fashion began my life in the theater, with all its joys and sorrows, its thorns and flowers, its high and low points, which everyone must experience, not only at the beginning but over the span of one's entire theatrical career.

My private life, for good and for ill, was colorful, too. Our family consisted of my mother, the famous actress Esther

Rachel Kaminska, known as the "Mother of the Yiddish Theater," my father, Abraham Isaac Kaminsky, my sister, Regina, and my younger brother, Yosef. We were a mixture of variegated temperaments and prsonalities. No one resembled anyone else, yet there were certain common characteristics: a feeling of close family unity, the ability to understand one another silently, and a wonderful sense of humor. Although such a combination should have yielded a quiet, happy life together, it was not that way all the time. There were great differences of opinion between my parents, who loved each other very much, and there was also the tragedy surrounding Regina and her untimely death. But my brother and I had memories of a home, which is significant in itself, for it leaves an imprint for the rest of one's life. The entire family worked: my mother, my father (who always attempted to make us more comfortable), Regina, I, and Yosef, who like me began his musical career at the age of five.

What I shall describe now preceded the beginning of my stage career. Yet it is this that I recall with greater clarity than subsequent events. I'm referring to our two-room apartment, which was long and not very well lighted. We had a large sofa, a dining room table with chairs, and a rather small credenza. I remember the dining room, for there the family gathered and changes in my life took place. But I can't recall the other rooms, even those in which I slept. Near the apartment was a park (still called Bagatella) that had a fountain and a playground. It's on a small street that now is one of the finest neighborhoods in the center of Warsaw, but in those days, when there were still no electric trolleys, it was considered a suburb. That street had a large theater that my father not only rented but moved into. My parents always tried to live as close as possible to their place of work. Several actors' families had settled in the small houses within the park.

When my parents rented the Elysium Theater on Karova Street, we moved to one of the main streets of Warsaw, a few steps away from the theater. There we had three rooms with a bathtub next to the kitchen. There was even a telephone in the foyer. During this period my parents decided to enroll me in the preparatory class of a grammar school, even though I already knew how to read and write. (I had a terrible handwriting and still do!) The studies certainly were not difficult for me, but the entire matter did not please me; it was light years away from the life of the theater. At school nobody sang your praises when the lessons were over. No curtain fell; no one applauded. In short, after six months I announced that I would not go to gymnasium (that is, high school) but study at home and continue to perform with my mother.

My parents were disappointed, but I know that, deep down, my mother was pleased. First of all, she felt that the performances in which someone substituted for me were inferior (that's a mother!). In addition to acting, I was also a stage manager who took care of everything: cues, lighting, curtain, prompting when somebody forgot a line (I knew all the roles by heart and, thank God, I remember them to this very day). In any case, my mother would always say that she had no worries when I was backstage.

I had begun all these activities in 1906, when I was almost seven years old. In the apartment near the Elysium Theater the great Yiddish writers Y. L. Peretz, Sholom Asch, Dinenson, Frischman, Mordecai Spector, Nomberg, and Mark Orenstein visited my parents. It's impossible for me to write about my impressions of these famous men, for I was too young at that time to recall them distinctly. But I do remember the courtesy with which Y. L. Peretz was received. He frightened me with his huge moustache and thick eyebrows, but we loved Dinenson, Frischman, and Spector, even though the latter also had a large moustache. They were all pleasant and amiable people.

In this apartment, too, Hershel Epelberg, the producer and playwright, read for the first time a play of Jacob Gordin, *The Stranger*. (Epelberg was also a partner in the Elysium Theater.) Here, too, Nomberg read his play *The Family* for the first time to a group of writers.

The tragedy surrounding Regina also began here. Although I remember her very well, it's difficult for me to talk about her precisely, for when she died in 1913 of a liver ailment, I was not quite fourteen, and one can't accurately evaluate anyone at that age. Only now do I realize that her behavior showed how naive she was. Beautiful, talented, successful, Regina was involved in various romances but chose for a husband Gershon Weissman, an actor in our theater, a man my father's age. Weissman had a son older than Regina from his first marriage. His second wife was also an actress, who, like many other theater people in those days, had only an elementary education. Weissman was not a bad actor, but he was no match for Regina. My parents suffered much because of this, but then suddenly my sister fell ill. When everyone suggested that this was caused by my parents' opposition to the marriage, they sadly and reluctantly gave their consent.

2

My First Tour as a Member of My Mother's Ensemble

DURING 1907, when I was almost eight, I had been performing with my mother both in Warsaw and on tour, in dozens of towns and villages in czarist Russia. One day in 1908, however, we were surprised to receive an invitation for my mother to perform in St. Petersburg, where not only Yiddish plays were forbidden but where residence without special permit was also taboo.

I don't know who exactly was responsible for our getting this permission to perform, but surely one of the prime reasons was my mother's success and fame. When we arrived in St. Petersburg—there were about fifteen in our company—and drove to the hotel reserved for us, we discovered to our dismay that we had the permit to perform but not the residence permit. The owner of the hotel was apologetic, but he didn't let us check in. When this became known, various Jews came and suggested that we stay with them temporarily. My mother, however, fearing that these people might suffer unpleasant consequences, decided that the troupe should hire horses and buggies and drive around town until the city administrator brought the residence permit. Only by nightfall were we able

to check into the hotel. We premiered with Jacob Gordin's*
The Slaughter and then continued with other plays, mostly
from the Gordin repertoire.

In Gordin's drama *The Kreutzer Sonata*, I played a young
boy (my mother's son). After the final curtain something unusual happened. The audience applauded enthusiastically
then made a rush for the stage to greet the actors who were
leaving via a nearby door. Someone snatched me offstage. I
heard my mother's voice: "The child!" She thought I had fallen
off the stage. The curtain rose. Then my mother saw that I
was almost at the other side of the hall. People had embraced
me, kissed me, and transferred me from hand to hand. Onstage, my mother stretched out her hands and, in the same
fashion, I was "transported" back to her.

We were an enormous success in St. Petersburg, both popular and critical, and we were reviewed by, among others,
Vladimir Jabotinsky, who was at that time a journalist in St.
Petersburg. The tour in St. Petersburg was decisive in establishing my mother's reputation as an actress, and it also prompted
the following: In 1908 an emissary came from America to
invite my mother to perform in the New York Yiddish theater
under the direction of David Kessler.

---

* Born in the Ukraine, Jacob Gordin (1835–1909) emigrated to the United
States in 1891 at the age of thirty-eight. Although he had never written
Yiddish before, he soon became one of the most popular and prolific playwrights of the Yiddish theater. Next to Abraham Goldfadden (1840–1908),
the father of Yiddish drama, Gordin is the most important influence on
modern Yiddish theater. His plays include *The Jewish King Lear* (1892),
the perennially successful *Mirele Efros* (1894), *The Slaughter* (1899), *God,
Man and Devil* (1900), and *The Kreutzer Sonata* (1902).

3

My Mother, Esther Rachel

ALTHOUGH decades have passed, I shall attempt to portray my mother, who during her lifetime was my dearest friend and after her death a source of longing.

I shall write as a daughter but still attempt to be objective. (I find it very painful and difficult to discuss the inept articles and monographs published about my mother.) "What sort of performer was Esther Rachel?" This is a question frequently asked of me by those who never saw her onstage. I am most embarrassed when I have to reply, for even the term *performing* is absolutely unfitting for Esther Rachel Kaminska. This doesn't mean that she couldn't make use of the entire arsenal of technical means, but when she did she was not thoroughly herself.

The first great actress I saw was my mother. At that time I was too small to visit other theaters, but I would come into our theater nearly every evening, for as a child I participated in almost every play in which Esther Rachel performed. Having been a witness to her great success, I never tried to analyze the cause of her greatness. It seemed perfectly natural. How else could one perform?

Years passed. I stopped my "theatrical career" and began to go to school. As a pupil I was not allowed to perform, so I began attending the Polish, Russian, and Ukrainian theaters that existed at that time in Warsaw. I also attended other Yiddish theaters and had the opportunity of seeing the plays of my mother's repertoire performed by other actors. Only then did I realize that the manner in which my mother achieved her stature was not typical for the theater.

Esther Rachel's path had begun in Porozovo, the little *shtetl* where she was born in 1870, and was linked to her poor home and the shop where she later worked. The poverty she saw with her clever eyes, the suffering her great heart empathized with, the injustice she noted with her enlightened mind, all became components of Esther Rachal Kaminska (her maiden name was Halpern.) When my mother suffered onstage, she felt that she suffered not only for herself; when she protested, she could clearly hear the protest of all those to whom injustice had been done. She raised the individual characteristic to the universal. That's why it is difficult to answer the question "What sort of performer was Esther Rachel?" One had to see her and hear her to sense the impact of her personality on an audience. To this day I don't cease wondering how her subtle and internal manner of performing was able to reach the then primitive Yiddish audience of so many years ago.

Unfortunately, Esther Rachel couldn't achieve her ultimate capacities on the stage. Conditions of the time did not create a suitable atmosphere. Dependency on the box office and concern for the continued viability of the ensemble were the restraints that prevented the development of the Yiddish theater.

My father always called her Mama. He never called her by her name. Her brothers and sisters called her Rachel, and when they spoke to her in Russian, they called her Esther Yefimovna (to which my mother would say, "Woe, if my father Hayim Yochanan heard that he was called Yefim!") But everyone else called her Esther Rachel. She never told anyone the date of her birth but only said she was born on the day before Purim, the Fast of Esther.

All names suited her: Rachel and Esther Rachel and even Esther Yefimovna. However, Mama was the best name for her. Regrettably, in the Yiddish theater the name Mama is inextricably linked with a certain level of theater, most frequently with cheap melodrama. However, this latter quality had nothing in common with Esther Rachel. She was Mama not only in feeling but also in her behavior and in her entire being.

Esther Rachel Kaminska had an abundantly good heart. It sufficed for a person to have one good quality for her to develop an affection for him. On occasions when she would take a liking to a person whom everyone denigrated, her justification would be "But he can tell a good joke."

Writers she admired she would praise: "God bless him, may no harm ever come to him." Talking of someone, she would refer to him as a "dear person." Often she would suffer from such "dear" persons, but when asked, "Do you still consider him a 'dear'?" she'd reply, "Of course! He's only lacking common sense; there are many fools in this world, but it's not their fault."

Actors are unfortunate, for when the generation that has seen them perform departs, there remain only words about them, and words can't convey the impression an actor or actress has made on an audience. More than a half a century has passed since my mother's death, but I still remember her every movement and gesture. All her vocal tones still ring in my ear, and I see before me every expression of her eyes.

During her youth her contemporaries on almost all the stages were nurtured by the so-called great repertoire that called for pathos and posing. Contemporary photographs of these actors tell us much about their manner of acting, but the pictures of my mother are very natural and simple, for she was free of pathos and posing.

Esther Rachel Kaminska's entire being was filled with a special homeliness and warmth. It is much easier to talk about her than to write about her. No first-rate monograph about her (sans fantasies) has yet been published. However, it seems to me that her personality could best be depicted by a collection of her *bon mots*, puns, and jokes.

My mother had a very hard life, full of work, worry, and suffering, yet her humor and lust for life never abandoned her. She joked in the most difficult situations (her granddaughter—my daughter—Ruth inherited this quality) and was able to withstand everything because of her health and strength, but seeing the suffering of those nearest to her caused my mother to break down. This wasn't visible on the outside, but we, her children, knew that despite her smile she had just shed tears in the next room.

Frequently away from home, my mother was often a guest in her own apartment. When she came home, tired from her journeys, my brother, Yosef, would play his violin and I would accompany him on the piano. My mother would sit on the sofa, wrapped in a shawl, listening to our playing. And then we knew that these minutes were the happiest in her life.

4

About My Parents

ABOUT the beginnings of my mother's stage career, I can only tell what I heard from her, for she began to act many years before I came into this world. She was thirty years older than me, but, though I knew she was the great mother and I the little daughter, this in no way diminished the fact that we both needed each other, onstage and in life. I would literally get sick with longing when she went on tour. And she, though she loved all three children equally, was bound more to me than to any of the others.

While my mother was in America in 1909 (my father later joined her), a visitor from Russia came to my mother's sister, Rivka. For as long as I could remember, Aunt Rivka managed the household and raised the children, for my mother had no time for this. The visitor was the Russian director Mikhael Chernoff, who invited me to play the child Serizha in Tolstoy's *Anna Karenina*. My aunt would probably not have permitted this, but seeing my great desire, she agreed. I was overjoyed, especially since I knew that I would have to play a scene with the then famous Russian actor Rafael Adelheim (his brother Robert was also a well-known actor). My sister had performed several times in this theater, and it was a great experience for us. But I suddenly fell ill with appendicitis and had to undergo an operation. My mother became aware of my illness only when it was all over, and when she read about it in a letter, an entire skein of her hair turned gray. When I recuperated, I decided to begin my studies, preparing for the second year of high school.

My mother's first appearance in America was in 1908, after her St. Petersburg tour; her second was in 1909. During her first tour she was unable to perform in plays of Jacob Gordin (for instance, *Mirele Efros*) because performance rights for Gordin's plays had been sold to another theater. On her second trip, however, she could appear in Gordin's plays, for she had been invited by the husband of actress Keni Lipzin, a theater manager named Michael Mintz. At that time people in the theater said that with this move Mintz wanted to discredit Esther Rachel Kaminska in the Gordin repertoire, especially in *Mirele Efros*.

Nevertheless, my mother was a great success, which is attested to by dozens of press notices. However, some maintained that Keni Lipzin was better in the role of Mirele. There was just a difference in the style of performance.

When my mother returned from America, she was asked to comment on her success in the United States. She replied, "I can't explain it, but I certainly could never act the way they do." After her death in 1925 an American writer remarked, "Esther Rachel came much too soon to us in America. Only now, after the Yiddish Art Theater has already been performing for several years, are they acting in the style that Esther Rachel utilized years ago."

With the money that my mother had brought from America, my father began to build his own theater. My father (1867-1918) was an interesting and remarkable man. Tall and good-looking, he had big gray eyes and was very successful with women, especially when he was manager of the theater. My father came from a poor home in Warsaw (his father had earned a living making spats). His sole education was the traditional *heder*, but since he had a progressive outlook, he had a tremendous desire to study and learn languages. I have memories of him always studying. He was constantly thirsty for knowledge. He couldn't bear the slightest falsehood and abhorred exaggeration, and when he mercilessly betrayed my mother, he also mercilessly reported this to her.

He built his theater, contrary to friends' advice, not in a Jewish neighborhood but in a non-Jewish section of Warsaw where rich, assimilated Jews lived. The construction took place during a period of unrest caused by the infamous blood libel trial of Mendel Beilis.

My father maintained, "I don't want a ghetto. Even the Jews with capotes and side curls should come to a fine, large theater in the center of town." It later turned out that this wasn't a happy idea, but I don't blame my father for this.

When we were in St. Petersburg, my father was attracted by a Russian theater called The Crooked Mirror, under the direction of A. Kugel and his wife Kholmskaya. It inspired him to write a play (it was not his first) in "The Crooked Mirror" style, that is, with the accent on irony and satire. It was an enormous failure; the audience's hoots and ridicule made an awful impression upon the actors and thoroughly depressed my father. The piece, of course, was removed from the repertoire.

Afterward, people he knew came to pour salt on his wounds. When everyone had gone, my father called me in and asked, "Do you also think I did a foolish thing?"

"I won't call it foolish," I answered, "but you overestimated our audience. They haven't yet seen good theater, so how could they judge bad theater?"

My father looked at me, called in my mother and my aunt, and said, "She's the first to clearly explain my failure."

I must admit that this made me proud.

When I was still very small, my parents left Regina with my mother's oldest sister, Chasya, because it was difficult for them to take two children on their tours. When I returned, Regina and I couldn't talk at length because I spoke Russian and she Polish. We both spoke Yiddish, but she had a heavy Warsaw dialect and we couldn't understand each other. My parents spoke Yiddish among themselves and to us, and while in Warsaw we spoke Polish.

When my parents realized that my sister's education was unsatisfactory, they decided to take her with them. At first Regina and I couldn't get along—Regina struck me as being very big and aggressive—but we soon became very fond of each other.

At that time my parents were touring the big cities (I remember only Odessa). Their financial state at that time, it seems to me, was not bad, because we were nicely dressed. My parents would say that there were times when the entire family had only one sour pickle to eat, but I don't recall any such situations. At home we lacked nothing—except money—for my parents, who worked very hard, were not miserly and were always trying to have a nicer home and live more comfortably. We were the first in our area with gas, electric light, central heating, and a telephone.

Generally speaking, people are not very subtle. They often make remarks in the presence of children that imprint themselves in a child's memory and have a deleterious effect on his psyche. The leitmotiv we always heard was "The older one is beautiful and the younger one is clever." I don't know how Regina took this, because she was already mature, but I interpreted it literally. When I was told, "What a beautiful little girl!" I would reply, "No, I'm not beautiful; Regina is beautiful. I'm clever," and thus display my foolishness. Despite the fact that during my youth I spoke and did many foolish things, the epithet "clever" followed me throughout my life.

As I grew older, I discovered that most people begrudge another person's attributes. They're likely to agree on one but not on two. If an actor (whether male or female) was beautiful, people would say, "But he's no good at acting"—and thereby do him an injustice.

Our entire family was musical in varying degrees. My mother's father was a cantor, but the most musical one of us was my brother, Yosef—until his retirement in 1969 the concert-master of the Israeli Philharmonic Orchestra—who began his musical career at the age of four.

Aunt Rivka's raising of the children was limited only to our physical development, not our spiritual one. My parents had little time for us, but they were not stingy with love, especially my mother. In later years, when I was performing opposite my mother, our frequent conversations influenced my way of reacting to events and people. But there were many events that I never understood, despite frequent explanation. I could easily comprehend the events of the year 1905 (the year of the first Russian revolution) and the demonstrations of people who fought for their existence, but no one could ever make me understand the reasons for anti-Semitism.

When I was a child, I would play with Polish children who regularly called for me (no game would take place without me). These same children, in talking about another Jewish girl, would use the insulting expression *zhyduva* (kike, yid). Frequently when I would walk through the streets, I would hear "Yids, go to Palestine" or "Yids, go to war." These Polish catcalls were directed mostly at Jews in the long gabardines or those with an obvious Jewish appearance. (Interestingly, both of these "insults" later became a reality.)

During my childhood and also somewhat later, the repertoire of the Yiddish theater was replete with the theme of Jewish persecution, and, understandably, justice triumphed in various ways. The dramas taught me that throughout their lives Jews were tormented and persecuted, but they did not explain why. Certainly the true reasons were difficult to explain to a child, and I developed a feeling of protest and a desire to discover the precise explanation. My father had some Polish friends (actually, very few), and I played with Polish children. We had nothing against one another, so what was the cause of Jewish persecution? That was one problem during my childhood.

The other problem was the unrest during the 1905 revolution. These events I could understand more readily: some people had too much, and others—the majority—had too little. Hence, on the first of May people paraded with banners covered with slogans about exploitation. But why were those carrying the banners beaten? That, too, I couldn't understand. Not only was their call not heeded, but they were beaten, too. This hurt me very deeply, and I would cry.

Throughout my entire life physical violence has repelled me. When a man was beaten, he was not only being hurt but humiliated as well. I always felt that an attack of a stronger person upon a weaker, or that of the many upon one, should be severely punished. Perhaps I felt this way because our parents never beat us. I could also never understand how anyone could get enthusiastic over boxing, and I have no sympathy for bull-fighting, where an innocent beast, teased before thousands of people, is stabbed and then killed. Why? Just because courage had to be spurred in one man, why did bloodthirstiness have to be developed in ten thousand others?

After all that has happened and still continues to happen, this attitude may seem naïve, but I still hold that civilization has always moved in the direction of exploiting man's mind, body, and strength without concurrently fighting jealousy and hatred in man. We have leaped up to the cosmos but still have not yet found how to properly cultivate the finer human attributes.

And now to Warsaw and Obozhna Street, where my father built his theater. The opening of the theater was a joyous celebration for everyone, especially for our family. The festive mood was broken by my sister's illness, but at that time it had not yet been taken too seriously. For the premiere we presented Jacob Gordin's classic drama *Mirele Efros*, starring my mother. I played the role of her grandchild, Shlomo. All the laborers knew me, for I had been a frequent visitor during the construction, but the new employees did not know me, so when I came to the entrance, the doorman asked for my ticket.

Humiliated, I didn't reply but went home and telephoned my father.

As I have already mentioned, my sister was seriously ill with a liver ailment that the doctors diagnosed in Berlin, where my parents had taken her a short while before her death. During their stay they learned that Mendel Beilis had just been acquitted in Russia from the ridiculous suspicion of blood libel. I recall this because it will have a connection with similar events in later years.

On the tragic day of my sister's death in 1913—which occurred several months after her marriage to the actor Weissman—we were supposed to play Jacob Gordin's *The Kreutzer Sonata*, starring my mother. My brother and I were to have played selections of Beethoven's *Kreutzer Sonata* backstage on violin and piano. We planned to rehearse before the performance, but not at home, where Regina lay struggling with death. The doctors knew this and requested my father to go with Yosef and me to my mother's sister Keyle Pulman, at Obozhna Street, No. 11. (The theater was at No. 1.) She had a piano and there we rehearsed, while my father sat and wept. My mother was already in the theater in her dressing room. The doctors, knowing that the catastrophe was near, didn't want my parents or the children to be present.

Suddenly we heard a great tumult: people returning from the theater. My father immediately understood the reason. He just barely managed to rise from the chair, leaning against my arm and the little hand of my brother. He said, "Come, children." On the street part of the huge crowd that streamed from the theater recognized my father. Many wept, and a woman he knew came up to my father and took him by the arm. I asked her what had happened and she said softly: "Regina Kaminska is dead." Had a fire suddenly broken out or a house caved in I would have more readily understood. I was almost fourteen and was considered quite mature. I knew that Regina was sick—but dying? At her age? It was something I couldn't consciously understand. I was so shocked I couldn't even cry, and seeing my state, my father became very frightened.

My poor mother had made plans to leave soon for guest appearances in Paris and London. Regina's illness had swallowed up all the resources of our household. The health of my father, who suffered from asthma, changed radically. Moreover, my parents feared I might succumb to depression. So it was decided that my father, my brother, and I should also leave Warsaw.

My mother went first, and we followed shortly thereafter. Accompanying us was my mother's impresario, Verite (Yosef Weissblatt), a very intelligent and beautiful man who, incidentally, also gave excellent readings of Sholom Aleichem. We were supposed to meet my mother in Paris, but in Berlin my father suffered a severe asthma attack. The doctors immediately sent him, accompanied by a nurse, to Meran, at that time a famous spa in the Austrian Tyrol. My brother and I went with my father, and Verite went to my mother. My father's health improved in Meran, and we met my mother in Warsaw after her return from Paris.

At Meran my father wrote to Warsaw instructing us to move into a newer, more beautiful apartment on Obozhna Street, No. 11, in order not to return to the house where Regina had died. This new apartment had five large rooms, with all the modern conveniences. It was easier to live there and let the deep wounds heal.

It was 1914 and time passed normally. My mother worked. My father was very busy with the theater, to which he had not been able to devote himself for a long time. I began to study with a tutor who said he could prepare me for the gymnasium exams in a year's time, and my brother, Yosef, studied music in the conservatory and also took private lessons with the famous violinist and theoretician Professor Henryk Heller.

However, we were still immersed in sorrow; my parents did not cease crying. We sought to tear them away from their mourning by performing for them on violin and piano. My brother was a *Wunderkind*. At eight Yosef already played like a seasoned, talented musician. I accompanied him often, but though my parents tried to convince me to fully develop my musical ability, I nevertheless thought only of acting. My mother didn't want me to be solely dependent upon the theater. She talked me into becoming a singer, if not a pianist (at that time I also had a fine voice). My mother used to say, "You understand, my child, that dealing with a piano is easier than a troupe of people and accessories, which are mandatory for a performance."

My parents thought of me very highly. I didn't hear this from my father but from others. Throughout her life, my mother regretted that I didn't go on to the university (I do, too, to this very day). "Had you continued your education, you could have become a prime minister," Mother would say. *That* I don't regret. My father would call me in to listen to him studying his roles and ask me for my opinion. At that time I was too young to appreciate such an expression of confidence in a child. I also had a good sense of enunciation. I would find my own way of speaking in children's roles and gradually would spot false intonation in other actors, which I would report to my parents, who, I later noted, took my remarks to heart. This had nothing to do with talent or wisdom but was simply a matter of logic; nevertheless, it strengthened the opinion that I was "clever."

5

The Outbreak of World War I

MY school friends convinced me to return to the gymnasium, and during the second semester I entered the sixth class. The attitude of my classmates in the gymnasium was a normal one. With the exception of two friends, no one knew my mother's profession, nor did they know about my acting, for few were Jewish. Later, however, when they did find out, they called me "the little actress."

My mother as usual was performing in Warsaw and traveling through the towns and villages of Poland. My hardworking father managed the theater on Obozhna Street and also performed from time to time. The children studied—until the famous shot in Sarajevo in 1914, when the Austrian Archduke Franz Ferdinand and his wife were assassinated.

In thinking about war between Russia and Germany, if one had to choose between Czar Nicholas and Kaiser Wilhelm, one would have frankly preferred the latter, for Germany was considered the more civilized nation. In Germany, after all, there were no pogroms, just *Kultur*. Nevertheless, people were very frightened, and that is why my mother accepted the invitation for guest appearances in Odessa and other cities deep in Russia. My father, Yosef, and I followed again. I once more interrupted my gymnasium studies. But in Odessa, too, the mood seemed to portend war, and the government forbade theatrical performances in Yiddish, as though that could have helped prevent the war or win it.

Various impresarios and Russian actors came to my mother, attempting to convince her to perform in Russian. Our financial situation was very difficult, for when my mother returned from guest appearances in London and Paris and brought with her a fully packed suitcase laden with golden pounds and francs, my father immediately changed them for czarist paper rubles. "This suitcase is too heavy to drag around," he said. "It will give me a hernia." The rubles, of course, immediately became valueless, and we later used them as stage money.

Although our situation was difficult and we were in debt for the hotel bill, it was still impossible to accept the offer to perform in Russian. Although she was only in her forties, Esther Rachel was even then called the "Mother of the Yiddish Theater." Moreover, my mother did not speak Russian well. Why should she have? Except for a *heder* education, she had not studied at all. Thanks to her musical ear, she had a good accent in all languages she spoke, but to master several roles of the Jacob Gordin repertoire in Russian was no small matter.

In Odessa lived many Yiddish writers, among them the grandfather of Yiddish literature, Mendele Mocher Seforim (1836-1917). My mother decided to visit him and seek his advice. She took me along. We met Mendele not far from his house, while he was on one of his daily strolls around the square. He wore a long black cloak with a black fur collar, to which his small white beard and white hair were a stark contrast. Mendele was a small man, but his high fur hat made his frame seem taller and thinner. He received us quite cordially and, realizing that we wanted to visit him, suggested that we join him during his walk. Meanwhile, my mother told him about our difficult situation and about the proposal to perform in Russian.

Mendele became angry. "Don't dare consider it!"

"How then can I help myself out of my impasse?" my mother asked.

Mendele replied, "Wait. Go to theaters and cinemas. Relax. Wait until everything passes."

Mother threw a quick look at me and told Mendele, "I have to leave now. People are waiting for me. Thank you."

As soon as we were alone, my mother said, with a sad smile, "You know what, my child? Unfortunately, I will have to perform in Russian."

My mother began diligently to learn the roles, including Mirele Efros, Ettie in *The Kreutzer Sonata*, and Esther in *The Slaughter*. She received money to pay for the hotel and for train tickets for our return to Warsaw. She remained two more months, however, in order to tour various towns in southern Russia.

It was late fall in 1914. Flames of war were already flickering in Europe, as well as on the borders of what were then Russia and Germany—that is, Poland. My home town, Warsaw, was not far from the front.

The mood in Warsaw was apprehensive. Transports of wounded soldiers were carried through the streets and from the ambulances one could hear cries of pain. Even passersby were asked to help bandage the soldiers' open wounds. All this made an awful impression. Still, in one's own apartment, calm reigned, as though nothing were happening. Aside from the fact that there was a lack of certain products, life proceeded normally, as though in peacetime.

I continued studying with my tutor, who still had the ambition of preparing me for the diploma exams. He said we would have to hurry because all the Russian educational institutions were being closed down, and the gymnasiums were mostly Russian.

No Yiddish theaters were operating at that time. My father had rented his theater to a Russian troupe managed by Arnoldov. Because of the prevailing atmosphere and the Russians' leaving Warsaw en masse, business declined. Arnoldov wanted to improve his financial condition, and so he left our theater, which was too large for him, and moved to a smaller once in one of the main streets. At that time Arnoldov's company was performing *The Women's Parliament*. One day, in early 1915, his leading actress, Dolinskaya, fell ill. This happened on a Sunday, the best day of the week and the manager asked my father to convince me to replace her, for he had heard that I was an actress and spoke Russian well.

My father was confident I would be able to learn the role in two or three hours, but he didn't know if I would accept. In fact, I was amazed when he set the proposal before me because occasionally he had forbidden me to go to that theater. Nevertheless, he assured me that this was a comedy, not a farce. I took the script two hours before curtain time, came into the theater before the play began, went through one rehearsal, and performed.

My father sat in the orchestra. Next to him was a Russian general who was very much charmed by my acting. He didn't realize that my father sat next to him. Suddenly the general called one of the ushers, scribbled a note, and ordered a box of chocolates brought to me. My father quickly understood, ran after the usher, and added a note of his own to me in Yiddish: "As soon as you finish, I'll be waiting for you by the doorway of the dressing room." The general's note stated that he would be waiting for me by the entrance to the theater. Of course, I left with my father.

Soon, however, this Russian theater, like all other Russian undertakings, hurriedly departed from Warsaw. Meanwhile, my mother returned from a very successful tour in Odessa. Her earnings had been good, but she commented, "Let's hope we don't have to go through that again."

A freshman at the university, my childhood friend Aaron (later Dr.) Irlicht had been preparing me for the diploma exams. He told me that even the Russian professors of the universities and gymnasiums were gradually fleeing. Irlicht discovered that the gymnasium for which I was about to stand for final exams was leaving, too. The exams were quite easy there, he said, and there was a tendency to pass everyone. So Irlicht registered me. Although most of the pupils were not sufficiently prepared, all of them were awarded diplomas, and not all the exams were given. My parents and Aaron were very pleased with my diploma. We now entered the phase of waiting for the Germans.

My father spent much time sitting in a café engaged in heated political discussions with his friends. Meanwhile, the Germans advanced closer and closer. They were expected to come in from the east, from the section of town called Praga. People said that the Russians would blow up the three bridges that spanned the Wisla River and that the shocks would damage the houses near the river. We removed everything from the walls, opened the windows, and in general prepared ourselves for going down to the cellars.

When the battles took place in the region of Warsaw, our relatives, who lived down by the Wisla River, spent a few days with us. During the night, when people expected the bridges to be blown up, many of the residents of our house gathered by the gate. They waited and waited and finally returned to their apartments. The next morning, while everyone was home, all three bridges were blown up. As we witnessed this through the windows, my mother began crying. When my father asked her why, she answered, "So much human effort was put into this. Strolling across the new bridge was so beautiful, and in one minute they turn everything to nothing. It's sheer cruelty." I wonder what my mother would have said during World War II, when in a short time dozens of cities and millions of people were annihilated and all of German *Kultur* came to naught.

Despite the blown-up bridges, the Germans entered Warsaw, and the Russians retreated through Praga. The armchair strategists had been dead wrong.

All night long we heard exchanges of firing. Since our relatives slept in our house, our immediate family slept in my parents' bedroom: my mother and I in one bed, my father in the second, and my brother Yosef on the sofa. Suddenly a bullet came crashing through our bedroom window. My father was the first to act and think clearly. Jumping off the bed, he stepped on the still warm bullet. He told us to bend down and to proceed thus to the kitchen, where the windows faced the yard, and sleep there. When we awoke in the morning, we expected to find our apartment destroyed. It turned out that we were hit only by one stray bullet and that everything in the apartment was perfectly in order.

It was a lovely summer's day. All over town people were saying that the Russians had been chased out of Praga, too, that Warsaw was full of Germans, and that the mood in the streets was calm and even joyous. My cousin Mina, daughter of my Aunt Rivka, came to take me for a trolley-car ride through Warsaw, to look at the Germans. Germans were sitting in the trolley and one of them even pointed at me and said loudly, "A beautiful Warsaw woman." That was my first success with the Germans.

When life had settled down somewhat, my friend and tutor, Aaron, submitted my diploma to the university and began to prepare me for entrance. He said it would be easy for me since I knew German. My father, meanwhile, was very busy, hurriedly organizing performances in Yiddish in his theater. There was a feeling in town that one could become rich from the Yiddish theater. The reasoning was that since the Germans had money and liked theater but did not understand Polish, they would go to the Yiddish theater. Hence several Yiddish theaters opened up in Warsaw. Everyone rushed about grabbing Yiddish actors and trying to open up his theater all the sooner.

I don't know why, but for the opening of his theater father chose Goldfaden's historic operetta, *The Binding of Isaac*. To raise the play's stature and ensure a bigger success, my father convinced my mother to play the role of Sarah, even though she had long since stopped performing in operettas. Unable to find an imposing enough actress for the role of Isaac, which was always played by the prima donna of the theater, my father decided to cast me in this role. I didn't have to be coaxed! And in this role I made my adult debut in 1916.

Aaron Irlicht strongly opposed my participation, for he held that it would be the end of my education. I replied that it would depend on the success of my debut. Despite the fact that acting onstage was nothing new for me, I felt a great sense of responsibility and was somewhat nervous. Although I was musically inclined and had a very nice voice and although I had known the role and the songs of Isaac ever since I'd been a little girl, this was the first time that I sang with an orchestra, directed by the fine conductor Isaac Schlossburg. His wife had always played the role of Isaac, and therefore I was very excited. To my great joy and Aaron's dejection, my debut was an unusual success; I was applauded by the Jewish audience and by the new German spectators.

In later years I tried to analyze this success. First of all was my youth. Then, various attributes, not necessarily the very best, were a bonus to success. I sang well and spoke clearly, especially beneficial in a theater with poor acoustics such as ours. Moreover, my acting wasn't too bad either.

After the role of Isaac came a long series of other roles. I played Hasidic and American boys and girls in banal but successful operettas. My greatest success was in the role of Itzik in *The Soul of My People*, an operetta by the famous American Yiddish actor and composer Boris Tomashevsky. On posters all over town the title was printed in Yiddish and in German, because the Germans—as expected—frequently attended the Yiddish theater.

One day my mother and I were riding in a trolley. At one of the stops one of the many Germans in the car read a corner poster and called, "*Die Seele Meine Folkes* [The Soul of My People]! *Ach! Das ist doch woh der Itzik ist* [Oh! That's where Itzik is]!" Yes, these were Germans of the First World War.

My popularity, with both the Jews and the Germans, grew from day to day. Jews greeted me, and German soldiers saluted as they met me.

I mention all this, not to speak about my successes, but simply to show how easy it is to swim to the top in a light, banal, and entertaining repertoire. Such a repertoire often contains senseless songs, which I would sing at home for my parents and cause salvos of laughter. Then I would rewrite the text and make the language more authentically Yiddish. My father, however, would say, "Leave the German words in. There are so many Germans coming." Father, after all, was the entrepreneur of the theater.

Even noted personalities of the time would attend, such as Mayor Almenreder of Warsaw and Mayor Zahm of Danzig, who used to send me bouquets of flowers. Once almost the entire contingent of a German military doctors' convention came to the Kaminsky Theater, including a nephew of Field Marshal Paul von Hindenburg. That evening we were performing *Pintele Yid*, in which I played Beynishl. After the performance Hindenburg's nephew expressed his appreciation. He gave me his card, with a recommendation to a film producer in Berlin. "Promise me that in Berlin you'll study theatrical arts," he said and he kissed me on the forehead and departed.

Generally speaking, the period of the first German occupation (1915-18) was very colorful, if one may label it thus. Although food supplies diminished, we didn't feel it at home. On the one hand, Jewish dealers sold us everything we needed; their attention alone was an expression of sympathy and recognition. On the other hand, German admirers would also bring us various products. After Hitler's bestial occupation of Poland during World War II, the near idyll of the first occupation is hard to comprehend.

One day the German authorities ordered all citizens to bring everything metallic from their homes; metal was needed for the manufacture of weapons. Some German acquaintances informed us that this order did not apply to us. Nevertheless, my father removed everything, even the joints of the doors, and brought it to the authorities. He said he didn't want to be an exception. Father had a rare sense of loyalty.

Warsaw during that period had four, sometimes five, Yiddish

theaters that prospered fairly well. Then the economic situation of the Jews gradually worsened, as did business for theaters. We began touring the provinces. From time to time my mother would present pieces from her famous repertoire, and I would joyfully perform with her. The roles were not important because I was still too young then to play opposite my mother. Part of the ensemble traveled, whether with my father or with my mother, but the Kaminsky Theater functioned without interruption until the end of the first occupation.

My activities as an actress were broadened when I began working as a director in the beginning of 1916; I was hardly seventeen. At that time the Yiddish theater had no standard operating procedures and no regular director. My activities as a director stemmed from the fact that I analyzed texts and frequently pointed out absurd situations or words in various performed plays. Actors who had been in these pieces for years reacted somewhat scornfully; others, however, wondered why they had not noticed these flaws before and agreed to the suggested changes. Gradually my scattered remarks developed into direction.

With all due credit to the old-time actors, most of whom knew me from my childhood and literally had carried me on their hands, I must say that they listened to me. Of course, some considered it a personal affront and comedown that "the little baby" had the nerve to teach them. But for most of the troupe I soon became an authority.

My great success in the operettas notwithstanding, I felt that I couldn't develop artistically with this repertoire. I had to make a break with it. The opportunity presented itself when my father came up with a sensational plan to stage *Uriel Acosta*, by Karl Goodskov, starring my mother in the role of a man. I was given the main feminine lead, Yehudis.

We were not used to seeing my mother in a man's role, but she performed intelligently. My father was an excellent De Silva, and Shmuel Landau played Vanderstratten. The well-acted main roles and the fine text (even though it was not a poetic translation) elicited a soul-stirring performance.

Hitherto, the most vocal opponent to my remaining in the theater had been Aaron Irlicht. He hoped I would cast away the theater and begin studies in the faculty of medicine, where he had enrolled as a student. He would spend hours sitting with me in the dressing room, arguing that I was not even performing for money. (At that time I wasn't getting any wages from my father. The thought wouldn't even have occurred to me.) He maintained that I was forcing myself to do something unimportant just for the sake of success.

The morning after the premiere of *Uriel Acosta*, Irlicht came to me. After a short silence he said, "If you continue to act in such plays, I won't regret your acting abilities, and I'll no longer try to tear you away from the theater." He decided I was Yehudis and gave me his photograph inscribed with a popular remark of the time: "If I forget you, Yehudis, may my right hand wither!" (A paraphrase of the famous verse in the Psalms: "If I forget you, Jerusalem, may my right hand wither!")

The role of Yehudis was a turning point in my life. It was at this time that I decided to discontinue working in operettas. The decision came about the following way. While still in my father's theater, I translated from the French a play by Henri Bataille, *The Misunderstood Girl*, in which I saw two fine roles, one for my mother, one for myself.

This play also marked the beginning of my steady activity in directing. For this my parents were responsible. I had never imagined that I would show my mother and father, both seasoned actors, what to do onstage. I would never have dreamed of teaching them how to act. However, they expressed such faith in me, following my every instruction, that it only enhanced my feeling of responsibility. Thereafter, I negotiated with an artist regarding proper decorations and costumes. I sought out suitable furniture and props. In brief, I did my best to make *The Misunderstood Girl* better than it ever had been, and it proved to be a great success.

I decided that one could not be a fully competent director with only a gymnasium diploma and some practical experience but without an education in theater arts. I began reading books about the theater and specifically about directing. Unfortunately, very little of what I read was applicable to our theater at the time. The books referred to normal theaters with a permanent place of residence and with subventions from the government or local authorities. (In Europe during World War I, most of the serious theaters were already subsidized.) But what I gained from my self-education proved useful to me in my later work in directing.

6

In My Mother's Ensemble

NOW that my career in operetta had ended, I went on tour with my mother for the first time as her partner. My name was already well known, and the posters advertised "Esther Rachel and Ida Kaminska." In contrast to the ensemble of the old Kaminsky Theater, where most of the people had been old and had a primitive education, our new ensemble consisted of young, intelligent people. One of them was the twenty-year-old Sigmund Turkov, a graduate of the Polish School of Theater, directed by the famous Alexander Zelverovitch. I knew Turkov and had even gone to see him in a small Polish theater where he performed with a group from his school. He was playing leading roles there and even then had demonstrated his maturity as an actor.

Sigmund had come from a traditional Jewish home. Although his father did not wear a gabardine and sidecurls, he was an observant Jew. Sigmund came away from his home with Yiddishkeit but at the same time loved the Polish national poets like Adam Mickiewicz, Stanislaw Wyspianski, and Julius Slowacki. Sigmund's father did not want him to become an actor. Despite this, Sigmund continued on his destined path and his father had no choice but to consent. Interestingly enough, two other sons also became actors: Jonas and Isaac (Itche) Turkov. A fourth brother, Mark, became a well-known journalist and community leader, and there were twin sisters, Rachel and Leah. The shining light of the Turkovs was the mother, a wonderful paradigm of Jewish motherhood. (She died in 1928, and her grave, near my mother's, was attended by us and decorated with flowers as long as we remained in Warsaw.) To make a long story short, in time I, too, became a member of that family.

The repertoire of our ensemble was quite a rich one for the time and included almost all the Jacob Gordin plays, in most of which I played my mother's rival. We also staged Bataille's *The Misunderstood Girl*, Andreyev's *Days of Our Life*, Artsybashev's *Jealousy*, Ibsen's *A Doll's House* and *Ghosts*, Leon Kobrin's *A Village Youth*, Peretz Hirshbein's *The Empty Inn*, A. Zuderman's *Homeland*, and L. Fulda's *Twin Sisters*. I should also note that in those years (1916-18) the occupied Russian-Polish territories contained towns such as Vilna, Bialystok, Lublin, and Rovno, where, owing to the vast Jewish population, one could perform for weeks and even months on end.

It's very difficult to write about one's successes, both on stage and in life. I include them only to clarify other events. For instance, there was a saying in the theater world: "Falling in love with Ida is as inevitable as the measles. One's case is mild, another's more difficult, but everyone succumbs." Nevertheless, this illness was catastrophic for no one, and when it was over, the "victim" and I remained best of friends.

Sigmund Turkov's measles began in epidemic fashion, but since this did not impress me, he chose the worst possible way to attract my attention. He began drinking (one and a half tumblers of whisky sufficed for him), indulging in frivolous affairs, literally wallowing in the gutters. He even made unsuccessful attempts at suicide. His friend Henekh Heldenberg, also a member of our ensemble, who lived with him, came to me as his advocate and became infected, too. But here the matter was more complicated; Heldenberg had a wife and a child.

In such a romantic atmosphere we performed every night, traveling about frequently, not in the most comfortable conditions. However, we were very successful and the earnings were not bad. Constantly in the company of my wise and humorous mother, time passed quickly. My father didn't like the idea of being the manager of only one company, so he toured with another, playing Nomberg's *The Family*, in which he excelled as the leading character. He fell ill and, knowing we were nearby, ceased his tour and came to us. We were then in Köningshütte (in Polish, Chorzow). The theater was in the same building as the hotel. Sigmund Turkov spent the entire day at my father's bedside, and each made an impression on the other. Since we had to move on to another town, our assistant administrator, Arnold Ginsberg, remained with my father. (Ginsberg later became a popular personality in Yiddish theater life in prewar Poland.) After resting several days, my father returned home.

Performing with my mother was both pleasant and important for me, but it was even better just to be with her. The romantic entanglements grew: Aaron Irlicht in Warsaw and Sigmund and Heldenberg in the troupe. So I decided to go to Berlin to study theatrical arts and perhaps acting as well, assuming that the passing of time would solve all problems. My mother understood and agreed.

When we returned home from our tour, I discovered that arranging the trip to Berlin was very complicated. It was difficult to obtain a passport. I was advised to go to Vienna, for which travel arrangements were easier. There the economic situation was not good either, but it was better than in Berlin. Moreover, I was told that Vienna was a much livelier city than stiff Berlin. As a young girl, I found this a point of attraction.

By Yom Kippur my father felt better, and I remained with him while my mother went to the synagogue. My father and I had a long, intimate discussion. I lectured him about

how he was hurting my mother. He wept and admitted that
he felt guilty toward her. I cried too, and my father tried
to convince me to marry Sigmund.

This was my last talk with my father.

7

Vienna 1917-18

IN Vienna I wanted to acquaint myself with film production, which interested me very much. Unfortunately, I discovered that because of a shortage in raw materials there was a crisis in the film industry and that there were hardly any productions. The Viennese said that they had nothing; the Germans had everything, even the raw materials. I received packages from home containing butter, salami, and sugar, which at that time were considered treasures. This put me in a better mood. I felt quite well. I made interesting friendships: actors, painters, sculptors, a circle of artists. I would get many letters from Poland: from my parents, Sigmund, Heldenberg, and Irlicht. Such a correspondence made it more pleasant being abroad, where I acclimated myself very swiftly. Since I knew German, I went to the Viennese theater almost every evening.

I even attempted to get a job in a theater, but because of the long war the theaters had few actors and a plethora of actresses. And as if that were not enough, there also an abundance of widows who had already left the theater but who, after the death of their husbands on the front, were given first preference for work. I applied to one of the most famous film producers, who happened to be in a depressed state. However, I must have made a good impression on him, for he took my address and told me that he would notify me as soon as production began.

Meanwhile, I was seeing various repertoires in the theaters. This period was the golden age of the Viennese operetta. Indeed, the operetta was the greatest attraction, although I saw various genres: drama, comedy, and revue. Because of the difficult situation in Austria, there was a tendency to give preference to light entertainment. I met good actors everywhere, and this was a great joy for me. I still remember some names: in opera, Maria Jeritza; in operetta, Gerta Miller, Kartouche, Totenheim, Hubert Marichke, Berta Fischer; in comedy, Constantine; in drama, Rudolph Schildkraut. Some of these names may have an unfamiliar ring today to someone who does not know the theater, but these were rare figures in the great age of the Viennese stage. Seeing such a mighty actor as Max Paulenberg was a pure joy, and Fritz Greenbaum was even then already famous as a star in revues.

I also made frequent visits to art galleries, acquainting myself with the masterpieces of painting and sculpture that were located in the capital city of the Hapsburg empire. And thanks to my cousin Heinrich Kaminsky, I was able to hear a series of lectures at the University of Vienna.

Contrasting the beauty of art were the streets of Vienna. War invalids were visible en masse, most of them on crutches. Seeing these young, smiling men distressed me greatly. Such sights were rather rare in Warsaw, an occupied city, but the Viennese were already inured to them, and lost none of their *Gemütlichkeit* and affability.

I also attended the Yiddish theater located in the Second Bezirk (district), mostly a Jewish district. After seeing the fine theaters of Vienna and even those in Warsaw, this was a painful experience for me. Here was a dirty hall without even a separation between buffet and stage and people sat at the buffet, speaking loudly during the performance. One could hear the continuing spritz of soda water from the siphons. The stage was a small one, and behind the curtain one could see the prompter, who, poor man, spoke louder than the actors. I was told that there were talented people in the group. Among them Leah Weintraub should be singled out for praise, but who could have noticed her in that entourage? I went home from that Yiddish theater in a gloomy state of mind.

8

The Second Loss in Our Family

SIX weeks later the telephone suddenly rang. It was the film producer I had met, asking to see me the following morning. I had an apartment in a beautiful house. Several floors above me was the studio of the famous sculptor Alexander Farbman, who shared his quarters with the young painter Misha Adler, today well-known in Paris by the name of Adlan. I used to visit them and there I got to know many other artists. There, too, my portrait was painted.

On the day I was called for a film interview, I was in Farbman's studio where I received a telegram with the tragic news: "Father seriously ill. Come immediately. Mother." It was 1918. Traveling from Vienna was not easy. Needed were a visa, permission to travel by train, and, moreover, the good luck of securing a train ticket to Warsaw. Getting all this would have taken several days, but seeing my situation, my cousin and several of my Viennese friends performed a miracle and arranged everything in two hours.

Several hours after receiving the telegram, I was sitting in the train, leaving most of my possessions with my cousin. Train trips in those days were awful. The train stood more than it moved, and one frequently had to change trains. In a station not far from Sosnovitz (we were now in occupied territory in Poland) a charming young man sat next to me. He wore a long gabardine and sidecurls and held a Warsaw Yiddish newspaper. With trembling hands I took the first

page, on which obituaries were generally printed. Not seeing what I had feared, I engaged the young man in conversation to feel him out. He was from Warsaw. He kept asking
me if I was ill and added that I looked very familiar to
him. When I told him who I was, he grew frightened and
fled with the newspaper. I ran after him and tore the paper
from his hands. In the center page I found the awful news:
an article about Abraham Isaac Kaminsky, of blessed memory, who had died at the age of fifty-one.

From that point the journey lasted another twenty-four
hours. For me it was an eternity. I didn't eat or sleep for
the rest of the trip.

As soon as I arrived in Warsaw, I hired a carriage to
take me home. At the door I met the porter, who, coin-
cidentally, was also named Kaminsky; he was a Pole, and I
requested the key to the elevator. At that point the porter's
wife turned to me and asked, "Does mademoiselle know
about her brother?" I grabbed the key and ran, and she cried
after me, "But everything's all right now!"

I learned that during the days my father lay ill with a
severe attack of asthma in the town of Lomzha, Yosef suffered from abdominal pains, typhus, and, to top it off, a
lung infection. Now he was on the mend after the crisis.
As Yosef lay in bed, he looked like a small child, even
though he was already fourteen. After both my mother and
I had cried each other's eyes out, I said I wanted to go to
the cemetery. She then told me that my father had been
buried in Lomzha. The local Jews had considered it an
honor that Abraham Isaac Kaminsky would remain in their
cemetery. I felt as though I had lost my father for a second
time. One could not easily make frequent visits to a distant
cemetery.

On the thirtieth day after his death, we traveled to
Lomzha, taking with us a tombstone. Only then did my
mother tell me what had happened. My father's death had
come at the critical period of my brother's illness. Mother

did not leave my brother's bedside; her sister, my aunt Rivka, went to my ill father. My mother was not even able to be present at the funeral. She also told me that the only person who, disregarding the danger of contagion, constantly remained at her side was Sigmund. "You won't recognize him, my child," my mother said. "He has changed. He's a quieter, more devoted man." I understood.

Meanwhile, Yosef grew stronger from day to day. Once again we all sat around the table. But the place at the head of the table remained empty. Every time we sat down to eat, Mother looked at the empty chair and began crying until, one time, I decided to take that place so that it would not remain unoccupied. This seemed to help because Mother stopped crying. This seating order remained for many years.

Ever since my childhood, some people would say that I was not beautiful, but clever. When I look at pictures taken in those days, I don't see a beautiful woman but certainly not an ugly one. But when people speak about a child, they habitually manage to add one fault to every good attribute. When I grew older and had much success with men, people stopped calling me "ugly" and began to say "bad." No one was ever to offer one concrete example of my badness, and so my words would be twisted, taken out of context, or even concocted.

For example, we had some poor relatives on both sides of the family, whom my mother systematically helped to the best of her ability. She always felt compassion for them and pitied their ill luck. As a child I remember my mother once spoke about our impoverished relatives to some people visiting us. I interrupted and asked, "What? Don't they earn anything?"

"No, my child," my mother answered.

"Then what do they do?" I asked again.

Mother answered with a sigh, "Nothing."

And then I, a child of a household where everyone, including myself, worked, asked, "Then why don't they go to work?"

This dialogue was distorted and given a bizarre ending. I was supposed to have said, "Mother, don't give them any money. Let them go to work."

In like fashion, the dramatic moment when I assumed the place at the head of the table was also distorted and misinterpreted. I supposedly announced, "Now *I'll* sit at the head of the table!" Even if I had had such a thought (so tactless a move never even entered my mind), I would not have mentioned it to anyone. Many years have passed and regrettably there are no longer any witnesses to that event. But I recall this now only to show the unwarranted injustice that ill-intentioned people often cause one another. Such incidents were frequent in my life.

Of course, I can't say that I never told a lie or mistreated anyone, especially in my youth. Still, unmitigated lies were told about me and intrigues woven about me at a time when I was completely innocent. I could not understand what people gained from this. Perhaps I have a naïve approach to all these incidents, for I take an opposite stance. Certain bitter experiences in my life notwithstanding, I still have confidence in everyone. When people come to me with gossip about others, I pay no heed to it and always want to see only good qualities. Even if I don't see them immediately, I make the attempt to search them out. In line with this I recall the following incident.

I had a friend, a Russian student, who used to drop into our house for breakfast (we lived near the university). He once said that one of the eggs he was eating was stale. I assured him that it was most definitely fresh. A short while later my friend Aaron Irlicht accused me, in the company of this student, of befriending suspicious girls. I became very angry and heatedly defended the girls. At this point the Russian student spoke up and said, "Don't argue with

Ida. For her, all stale eggs are fresh and all prostitutes, fine young girls."

I sought to see the good side, and that's the way I have remained. I am very careful about prejudging people.

In the summer of 1918 we again made a tour of the Polish provinces with my mother. Sigmund Turkov also traveled with us. During our journey my mother constantly pointed out Sigmund's good qualities, both onstage and off. Indeed, he had really changed for the good. My indifference gradually turned to affection. There was a man missing at home, and in a short while marriage was impending.

In *Mirele Efros*, I played the role of Sheyndele; Sigmund played Yosele. In the first act this young couple marries onstage. During one of the performances all the actors wished us a real *mazeltov*. We drank real wine, and Mother was happy. But I still didn't want to marry. First I wanted to travel to Vienna with Sigmund so that he might see theater there. I thought perhaps something would come of my earlier contacts with the movies. But Sigmund's father did not permit us to travel before the wedding, and so the wedding date was set for June 16, 1918.

9

Wandering During the Revolution

SEVERAL days after the wedding, our troupe began another tour, temporarily without my mother. The first stop on our June 1918 honeymoon was the town of Mezeritch. My mother soon joined us, and we began a lengthy tour eastward through towns under Austrian occupation. We did excellent business in the town of Ludmir (Vladimir Valinsk), and remained until the end of October. People in Ludmir were saying that the Austrian army was falling apart. We would be unable to return to Warsaw and were advised to travel to Rovno.

In Rovno the great chaos had already begun which, eventually, kept us away from home for two and a half years and made naught of all our plans. The German and Austrian armies had left the province of Volhyn, and for a time nationalist Ukrainians ruled. We moved on to Odessa; we couldn't even dream of returning to Warsaw. A period of confusion had already set in. Poles were battling Ukrainians. The latter, in turn, had to retreat in the face of the Bolsheviks. When we reached Odessa, the Allies were in power.

At first we even performed in Odessa to a moderately successful box office until an outbreak of fighting in town caused us to stop. Various military factions representing differing ideologies were struggling among themselves. The underworld exploited this by brazenly committing robberies on the streets in broad daylight. Trenches were dug in front of the beautiful hotel where we stayed, and wounded soldiers and officers were brought into the hotel.

At such a time I happened to become pregnant.

In Odessa I met my schoolmate and old friend Doba Taubin. Her family had left Warsaw for Russia in 1914, when Doba was preparing for her wedding. (My life was to become linked up with hers some thirty years later.) The military situation kept changing in Odessa, and with it the regime. People were afraid of the White Guard and of the bands of the various leaders. We decided the safest thing to do was to go with the Reds. Along the way we performed in every village.

Then something happened that still puzzles me. The members of the troupe, who owed their jobs primarily to my mother, began to treat her, me, and Sigmund as exploiters. Their first deed was to appropriate—simply take away—personal property that we had brought from Warsaw. Included were manuscripts, costumes, wigs, props. We took no money from the troupe for the use of this property, but they maintained that all of it should be nationalized. The troupe operated on a share basis—that is, profits were divided—and so the differences were very small.

In one Ukrainian village, Smila, the troupe even went to the Cheka, the notorious political security corps, and informed on us. We, too, went to the Cheka to complain. Fortunately, we found a young, intelligent, Jewish man there who advised us how to leave in the quickest possible fashion. He said, "You could have met another official and possibly come to a sad end." We took his advice seriously and decided to flee by night—Sigmund, his brother Jonas, and I. My poor mother couldn't leave, for without her the troupe could not perform, and she feared, moreover, that they would chase us and take revenge.

At night a horse and wagon came to take us to the train station. My mother stood in the hotel doorway. All of us were crying. That day happened to be my mother's birthday—the Fast of Esther, 1919.

All night long we stayed at the train station. Only at dawn did we begin our journey to Kharkov. Incidentally, this was the last train from that point. Sigmund had a cousin in Kharkov, and we also hoped to join the Yiddish theater that was to open there. Indeed, we were immediately accepted into it, but we lived under miserable conditions.

I had to stop performing because my pregnancy was already showing. Sigmund was dissatisfied with the Kharkov Yiddish theater, which he considered weak, but since the city had an interesting Russian avant-garde theater, directed by the famous Glagolin, Sigmund joined them. The leadership even promised that after I gave birth they would also take me into the troupe. However, at that time we were not destined to sit in one place long enough to make it warm.

A message came from my mother—from Poltave, where she was making a guest appearance—asking us to come to her immediately. The note was brought by my aunt Rivka's son, Ele. I was terribly homesick for my mother, and seeing each other again was a great joy. We had hardly unpacked when she showed us an ad in a Kiev Yiddish paper: a Yiddish state theater would be opening there, and they were looking for Esther Rachel, Ida Kaminska, and Sigmund Turkov, whom they wanted for the company. (In the course of the civil war, one town was cut off from another, and no one knew anyone else's whereabouts.) We packed our belongings again and made our way to Kiev, the capital of the Ukraine.

The ensemble in Kiev was a good one. Most of the actors knew me. Among them were my mother's old friends Yaakov Liebert and Gershon Weissman, who had married my sister, Regina. We also made the acquaintance of a new actor, Grisha Epstein, who immediately made a big impression on us all.

In Kiev, on July 20, 1919, I gave birth to my daughter,

Ruth. That very evening my mother and my husband performed onstage. I remained alone in a private clinic.

Times again were tumultuous and we thought about moving away from Kiev and going with the Red Army. We feared the Petlura bands and other gangs of pogromists that were made up of equal parts anarchists and hooligans. However, I was calm because I was happy. My love for the newly born little soul was unbounded. I talked to Ruth and promised that throughout her life I would protect her from all harm. Unfortunately, I could not keep my promise.

Meanwhile, my brother-in-law Jonas was drafted by the Red Army. All summer long we didn't know his whereabouts. Suddenly one day he came from the front, looking terrible but healthy. He spent a short while with us and then returned to the army. We departed from Kiev in 1919 in a ship that sailed along the Dnieper River to Gomel, in White Russia. Here, too, we remained only briefly, and in order not to continue running and fleeing, we decided to go to Moscow.

The trip by train, which should have taken ten to twelve hours, lasted three weeks. With a tiny baby in our hands, we traveled in a freight car. With us were a group of actors, among them Grisha Epstein, with his wife and little son. The train also carried soldiers, who did not know to which front they were going. Eventually we finally arrived at Moscow for the first time.

At the Moscow station we saw thousands of people, masses of beggars. Some of them were sprawled over the floor and tugged at our skirts. We wanted to flee as quickly as possible, but we had to wait until our baggage was unloaded from the freight cars. After a long while we finally left the hellish station and found a clean, even well-appointed hotel. The doors were open. Not only was there no manager, there were not even any servants or keys. There was nothing there. We only saw rats running about.

Nevertheless, we found people who arranged performances for us in the Zierkalny Theater (The Theater of Mirrors).

The shows were poorly advertised and hurriedly organized so that, along with the reigning confusion, even the debut of Esther Rachel Kaminska in Moscow caused little stir. The people had their own problems.

In addition to all the other difficulties, there had been a recent bomb attack on the Kremlin. The bomb had only partially exploded, but the attack resulted in a curfew. Evening performances were forbidden, so we played during the day. These performances didn't do too well either.

During those days I wouldn't sleep for nights on end. I was afraid that the rats might harm the tiny baby. I would remain awake until Sigmund rose and only then fall asleep. Then a friend of my mother's took compassion on me. Abraham Halpern, formerly an editor in Vilna, took me to his home. Here I slept with Ruth in a crib, but at least without fear.

Amid all these hardships and the war mood was a bright spot—my visit to the Moscow Art Theater. My mother came to watch the baby, and Sigmund and I went with trembling hearts to see Gorky's *The Lower Depths*, directed by Stanislavsky. How great was our surprise when, in addition to Vasily Kachalov, I. M. Moskvin, and an entire host of great actors, the founder of the Moscow Art Theater himself, the great Stanislavsky, also appeared. And as if any bonus were needed, in a loge to my left sat the great Russian basso, Fyodor Chaliapin.

I had already seen the Moscow Art Theater as a child, when my mother had made guest appearances in St. Petersburg. But this was my first time as an adult in this theater, and Sigmund's first time ever. It's easy, then, to imagine what two young theater-lovers experienced.

Nevertheless, I was deprived of enjoying this special event. A short while after the curtain went up, I fell asleep. I tried to pry my eyes open, cried out of despair, but nothing helped. I was thoroughly exhausted and lacking in sleep because of my perpetual watchfulness over the baby. (I even used to take Ruth with me when I performed and place her on a table or a chair, to which I would intermittently run.) Silence reigned in Stanislavsky's theater, and onstage it was dark, all of which helped put me to sleep. Only for the third act, when the stage was well-lighted and the action tumultuous, was I fully awake. Sigmund felt sorry for me, but he understood.

Just before we left Moscow, in 1920, people told my mother, "Esther Rachel, pretend that your current visit to Moscow never took place. When you return during normal times, you will be received with all the admiration due you, the way you are admired all over the world." Unfortunately, my mother was not fated to return to Moscow. Years later I returned to Moscow, but times again were not normal, and I didn't perform there.

10

On the Way Home

O UR common wish was to go home to Warsaw. First we had to get to territory from where we could more easily return to Poland. So once again we embarked on a long and difficult journey to Vitebsk, west of Moscow, in White Russia. We no longer thought of performing. We wanted to sell our theater baggage in order to make the crossing of the frontier easier. The only ones in our group who did not hail from Poland were Epstein and his wife and child. We tried to convince him to come with us to Warsaw. "The Yiddish theater of Warsaw needs an actor like you."

We arrived in Vitebsk late at night and had to sleep at the train station. There we attempted to sell our belongings, but it was very difficult. We then decided to check into a hotel near the station and look for buyers. But the "buyers" we found were just waiting for victims who had to travel without luggage. They were in league not to give higher prices. Had we sold to them we would have given away all our valuable property for a song.

Meanwhile, people in town had learned that Esther Rachel and her troupe were in Vitebsk, ready to travel on. Representatives of the municipal culture council ran over and asked us to perform at least twice in the Vitebsk Russian State Theater. Luckily we had not yet sold our props, or we would not have been able to stage a play. We presented Gordin's *Mirele Efros* and *The Slaughter*, which were unusually successful.

So, instead of staying several days, we settled down and performed in Vitebsk for an entire season. We moved into another theater and another hotel and became residents of the city. Business was good. In addition to the old repertoire, we introduced new plays, among them pieces that Sigmund and I translated from other languages. My mother, too, added another role in Oscar Wilde's *A Woman of No Importance.*

I directed most of the plays, while Sigmund directed two or three. In his work one could immediately see a great directorial talent, a view that was later fully justified. After all, he was the only one among us who had a specialized higher education in theater arts. Frankly, in those days direction was limited to technical remarks and advice regarding vocal tone. There was no sophisticated analysis of text.

During the few months we played in Vitebsk, there were several trials of pogromists who had been brought in from surrounding villages where pogroms had taken place. Often they had murdered the entire Jewish population of a village. In the courthouses one could see heart-rending scenes of witnesses who happened to be sole survivors. Despite the punishments meted out, reports still persisted about pogroms in villages where various bands ruled. In towns and villages there were frequent changes of "regime" and their military support. Tumult and tension reigned among the population. People feared and hated one another. Since there was no strongly organized central authority, bands committed pogroms and looted the Jews, ostensibly as part of the anti-Bolshevik struggle but actually out of simple hooliganistic anarchism. The Reds often had untrained primitive leaders who were unable to discriminate between supporters and antagonists. Meanwhile, the Jews, the universal scapegoat, suffered the most.

As our season drew to a close, our thoughts once again returned to Warsaw, where we had left our dear ones and our homes. Our friend Epstein, whom we wanted to take home with us, decided not to go. He feared the Poles. We didn't share his views, but we did not want to talk him into it. And so we left Vitebsk without Epstein.

In compensation for our separation with Epstein was the news that in Polotsk, the nearest town, Sigmund's brother Jonas would meet us and return home with us. In Polotsk, we were told, one could easily cross the frontier to the Polish side. On our way we came to the village of Nevel where we were unable to continue because all the roads had been taken by military transports. Civilian traffic was temporarily prohibited, we were told, but we would be informed as soon as it was possible to continue farther. Fortunately, Nevel turned out to be a pleasant place, for they had a fine dramatic circle that they asked us to direct and play in.

As soon as word came that we could ride on a military train to Polotsk, we jumped at the opportunity. As we were approaching Polotsk, we were ordered to barricade both sides of the wagon walls with all our possessions, chests, and bedding, and lie down on the floor. Immediately thereafter we heard a hail of bullets over our heads. Perhaps it didn't last too long, but for our family, who with their bodies protected little seven-month-old Ruth, it was an eternity.

Coming into Polotsk, we saw one vast ruin. Only in Poland in 1917, when we visited Kolish, which the Germans had bombed during the first days of the war, had we seen a city in such a state. The residents of Polotsk had been dwelling in the cellars for a year, but they grew sick of this and returned to their destroyed homes, living as best they could. In those days the armies used mostly light weapons, and the exchange of rifle fire between the Russians on one side and the Poles on the other was almost continuous. Occasionally, there was a cease-fire in this Ping-Pong game. Then the streets would fill with people. They met, joked, and did business as though nothing at all had happened.

During the hours of the cease-fire, for which we waited longingly, a white flag would be raised by the river, and then one could cross to the other side. From there, with the aid of binoculars, one could quite clearly see the Poles. Occasionally a deal would be made with them to send over a few Polish citizens, and later the shooting began again. That's how strange the war was then. As our ill luck would have it, the transfer of Polish citizens had ceased, and we had to sit and wait from day to day.

Meanwhile, people asked us, "If you're already waiting, why don't you perform?" We couldn't believe our ears. In such a tumult, in such a bullet-riddled town, the population was requesting theater! Of course, the performances had to take place by day, for no one was permitted to leave their homes at night. Heedless of the constant shooting, people filled the theater; even during the performance we heard the echoes of shots. To this very day I consider both the actors and the Polotsk audience heroic.

Once, in Polotsk, we left the baby with a woman we knew in the quiet outskirts of town. After the performance Sigmund quickly ran to get her. My mother and I took somewhat longer to dress after the show, but as soon as we were finished, we followed. Suddenly from a distance we saw a bomb exploding in front of Sigmund, who was carrying Ruth. Black smoke obscured them both. My mother and I stood petrified. We pressed close to each other and remained silent. Gradually the smoke dispersed, and we saw Sigmund approaching us, carrying a smiling baby.

Since we couldn't wait for a transport that would take us over to the other side, we decided to return to Nevel. It was impossible to live under the conditions in Polotsk with a tiny baby. The return trip was no small matter either. In the wagon we once again had to protect little Ruth against bullets aimed at the train. Traveling with us were soldiers who had typhus. We gave some of them water and tried to help them as best we could.

Jonas had not come to Polotsk because he had succumbed to typhus. However, before we left Polotsk, he sent a message stating that he was already well and would come to Nevel. My mother, who didn't want me to travel about with the baby, went with the troupe to perform in Moghilev and other towns. She decided that Sigmund and I should remain in Nevel.

In Nevel we lived in a small apartment (Jonas lived alone) under primitive conditions. Still, we didn't have to travel, we had pleasant work, and the fresh air calmed our souls and strengthened our bodies. Our new work was in the field of teaching: Sigmund in a drama circle and I in a children's school. In addition, we participated with Jonas in the performances of the drama circle, which we directed. I produced Hirshbein's *The Empty Inn*, and the three of us also performed in several plays. All of this brought us much joy. It endeared us to the local population and afforded us some income, paid mostly in commodities—flour, sugar, and the like. However, I yearned for my mother, corresponded regularly, and counted the days till her return to us.

Actually, I had never before been separated from my mother for an extended period of time, which is why I missed her wherever I went. Sigmund and Jonas missed her, too. When she finally returned, all of us began our journey. Besides pleasant memories we brought with us from Nevel several newly translated plays, some of which we later performed quite successfully. Among them were Sofiia Byela's *When Does the Devil Laugh?* (not great literature, but some magnificent roles), Leonid Andreyev's *The Thought*, Henry Bernstein's *Samson*, and Simeon Yushkeyvitz's *Sonkin's Luck*. I directed all these pieces except *The Thought*, which Sigmund staged. In Nevel both of us were invited to perform in Russian. A Russian actor, for whom we had arranged a benefit performance, chose *The Slaughter*, by Jacob Gordin, and we were to be the chief attraction. I played the role of Estherke, and Sigmund was Zissel Kroines. We had played these roles so often in Yiddish we almost didn't have to learn them in Russian but merely translated as we went along.

From Nevel we came to the little village of Lyady (made popular by the famous Hasidic rebbe of Lyady, Shneur Zalman Schneersohn. My mother was born in a little village called Porozovo. To my regret I have never been there, and

I can never forgive myself for this. When we were in various small villages, I used to ask her, "Mama, is this village like Porozovo?" She would reply, "Compared to Porozovo, this village is a metropolis." However, when we arrived in Lyády, my mother said, "Do you see, my child? This village is almost like Porozovo." In Lyady we performed in the Schneersohn residence, in which a theater and a stage had been constructed. Here, in 1920, my little daughter celebrated her first birthday.

The year 1920 was difficult. At that time the greatest battles were taking place between the Poles and the Russians. We heard horrible reports concerning towns and villages that were taken over in turn by the opposing armies. Frequently nothing was left of a village except the railway station, and as a consequence, the innocent population suffered tremendous anguish. Despite all this, we proceeded in the direction of home.

On the way to Minsk we saw several battle-scarred villages and all the ensuing misfortune that war brings. At that time I knew very little about politics, but events drew me in. We became followers of those who preached freedom, equality, and brotherhood, a world without exploitation. Of course, we also had to oppose those who robbed and committed pogroms. Like most of the Russian people, we, too, held in awe the names of Lenin and Trotsky—men who would free the world from injustice.

In Minsk, the capital of White Russia, where there was a large Jewish population, something happened that caused our family tears of joy. In a display window we saw a photograph of my brother, Yosef, holding his violin. It turned out that quite recently, when the Poles were ruling, my brother had come to Minsk for a concert. People who had attended told us about its great success. This merely strengthened our longing for home.

While waiting in Minsk, we performed again. We had a large audience, which was very restless throughout the performance. We were presenting Émile Zola's *Thérèse*

Raquin, in which my mother played the role of Mme. Raquin, and I, Thérèse. Unable to bear the tumult in the hall any longer, I halted the action and ordered the curtain to be lowered. (At that moment my mother was not onstage.) I cried out, "I can't go on. Those are beasts out there, not people." When the curtain was raised again, quiet reigned in the theater, but I couldn't forgive myself for that outcry.

In Minsk we also received horrible news that jolted all of us. At the Kazyatin terminal, before the eyes of their wives and children, our friends Epstein, Boymvol, and Liebert were shot by the Polish military. Epstein had not wanted to travel with us to Warsaw because he unconsciously feared the Poles. Now his premonition had come true, and he died at the hands of the Poles. Later we discovered that Liebert had only been wounded. He had dragged himself off to a hut and thus saved himself.

In Minsk we encountered a Yiddish troupe that included actors from Poland. Among them were Vladek Godik and the singer Mekhl Klein. They wanted to go home, too, and joined us. Just then we learned that troop trains were going to Molodetchno, on the Polish border. At that time a cease-fire was in effect, but no one could tell us when the train would leave. We could only sit at the train station and wait patiently, which is exactly what we did.

I don't remember how long we waited, perhaps a day or two. Finally a troop train arrived and we boarded it, along with our baggage. It was about twenty kilometers to Molo-detchno. Two kilometers outside the town, however, the train stopped, and we were told to leave. The train couldn't continue its journey because farther on the rails had been destroyed. In addition to us, there were several other families from Poland.

We left the train with all our belongings and remained in a desolate area. Then, just as it happens in the movies, it began to rain. We looked about and found a field hut. Our friend Klein continued walking until he reached the Lithu-anian border. (During that period the territory belonged to

Lithuania.) There he secured a horse and wagon, which came to pick us up. The baggage was placed aboard, the women and children climbed in, and the men followed on foot until we came to a village populated by Lithuanians.

In the village, after much pleading and running around, we were finally given another horse and wagon, which crawled along for forty-eight hours until it came to Vilna. How did we find this transportation? When people in Vilna discovered that Esther Rachel Kaminska, her children, and her troupe were nearby, they made a telephone call to the village.

In Vilna, Jews began streaming to my mother. A feeling of warmth, which we had not experienced for a long time, enveloped us. It was a new world for us. Under the Red regime, during our wandering we had assumed the mood of the region, but in Vilna, where Yom Kippur overtook us, my mother went to the synagogue. A couple of hours later I joined her in the women's section. The humidity there was suffocating. Knowing how difficult the enervating journey had been for her, I wanted her to go and have a bite to eat, but she refused, saying, "I can't do it, because the Jews of Vilna have placed so much trust in me. Why should I deceive them? Besides, today I feel a need for fasting."

When Mother returned home toward evening, she asked us if we had eaten, and where. I replied that we had eaten in Podolsky's hotel—a bad, watery soup.

"Why didn't you have the borsht?" my mother said. "The borsht was excellent."

It turned out that the very Jews for whose sake my mother wanted to fast took her to eat on their own. They asserted she had fasted enough during her long wanderings.

Vilna, under Lithuanian-rule, was in a gray mood. One could feel an impending political change in the air. People said that the Poles would drive the Lithuanians from the city. As usual, one didn't know whether this would be good or bad, especially for the Jews. Heedless of the atmosphere, we began performing and did excellent business. Soon it was forbidden to go out in the streets at night, and we performed only during the day.

Meanwhile, my mother had been invited to Kovno and Riga. This second separation from her, especially in such unsettled times, affected me greatly. Although the separation was to have been a short one, I felt depressed and gloomy. We communicated regularly until the Polish army, led by General Zheligovsky, marched into Vilna. This elicited mixed feelings—on the one hand, joy and hope that we might be able to return to Warsaw, but on the other hand I was cut off from my mother.

The atmosphere in town worsened. Soldiers looted, attacked innocent citizens—most of them Jews—and raped women. Perhaps these actions didn't have the approval of General Zheligovsky, because after a delegation of Jews had intervened with him (among them were several of our friends, including Dr. Yaakov Wigodsky and Dr. Tsemakh Shabad), the anti-Jewish excesses actually ceased.

Normal conditions returned to Vilna. Regular theatrical performances were not yet possible, but sporadic matinees were permitted. There was a proliferation of cheap (in the artistic sense) little theaters. Actors worked in the movies, and jobs were available for those Jewish actors who knew Polish. The soldiers greatly enjoyed the burlesques and vaudeville shows. Indeed, certain actors who forced themselves to make such appearances were able to earn some money.

To our surprise, one day we received a letter from my mother in Warsaw, where she had traveled from Riga. Because of our long absence from Warsaw, my mother provided details on our relatives, our home, and our city. She even wrote about those men whose condition worried me (those who had been heartbroken when I married Sigmund more than two years ago). As it turned out, no one had committed suicide, God forbid. The age of sentimental youth was over,

and the romances we read in those days had no tragic influence. They were all healthy, my mother wrote, married,
and fathers of children.

Meanwhile, our material situation in Vilna grew worse.
Our Vilna friends arranged a benefit performance for me
and produced Ibsen's *A Doll's House*. Despite the matinee and
despite the lackluster mood in town, our friends maintained
that the benefit would be a success. We agreed, and as it
turned out, we had a huge audience. This somewhat improved our financial situation. Unfortunately, however, we
couldn't travel to Warsaw, for men of military age were not
permitted to leave Vilna, and Sigmund was one of them.

At this point, in 1920, Sigmund's father, Naphtali, came
to Vilna and obtained special permission for Sigmund to
leave the city. We bade good-bye to our good friends in
Vilna and made our way home with our eighteen-month-
old child. After two and a half years we were finally on our
way to Warsaw.

The trip by train, lasting twenty-four hours, was one of
the worst we had ever had. We were squeezed in so tightly
we couldn't even move. At one station Sigmund wanted to
get out of the car and buy some milk for the baby. With
superhuman effort he pressed his way out of the car but then
couldn't make his way back to us. He just barely re-entered
the train. Riding on an outside step, his hands freezing, he
held on to an ice-cold iron handle. He continued in this
fashion for several stations. Of course, he had to drop the
milk bottle.

Finally we reached our destination and saw Warsaw, glit-
tering and huge. Once in the city we had been longing for,
our hearts began to pound with excitement. At the station we
were met by my dear brother, Yosef, and one of Sigmund's
twin sisters. The family had been waiting in shifts, for a
period of twenty-four hours, for no one knew exactly when
the train would arrive.

II

Back in Warsaw

WHEN we saw our city, our home, our friends and relatives after such a long absence and after so many hardships, we walked about in a state of confusion, heads spinning and in a fog. The baby couldn't walk on the polished floors. She almost stopped making sounds, not to mention talking. Nevertheless, we quickly got used to good conditions, and it was difficult to believe that we could have tolerated such misery for two and a half years.

My mother had returned from Riga and Kovno exhausted and took a well-deserved rest. Since we had to make a living, Sigmund and I went on tour. This was easy to arrange thanks to the fact that we now had several plays and a small ensemble, which consisted of Sigmund and me, two other actors, a technician, and an administrator. We traveled to Lodz, where business was not too good. But because of the smallness of our group, the trip was worthwhile and the artistic success great.

My longing for my little daughter, Ruth, with whom I had parted for the first time, was so immense that I wept day and night and became sick with yearning. I stopped performing and returned home. Sigmund remained behind; he engaged several actors and continued the tour. Seeing the baby was a horrifying experience. Ruth trembled, stared at me with tear-filled eyes, avoided me, and then burst into bitter tears. Later, when she began to talk, Ruth would cry that she had parents who wandered about, but I always longed for my mother and little Ruth. My daughter developed nicely, both physically and spiritually, and she was the apple of her grandmother's eye and of her mother's as well.

In Warsaw there was a small, ugly structure owned by a Yiddish theater in the best part of town. The troupe of actors who rented this theater on Lezhne Street asked all three of us to join their ensemble. This pleased us, especially after our wanderings. Now we were able to stay in our comfortable apartment and be with my mother in the theater and with our baby at home.

In our Kaminsky Theater we had occasionally staged an operetta or a melodrama and had also invited performers from America. Nevertheless, our theater on Lezhne Street, the Central Theater, was very successful. In addition to my mother's repertoire were several new plays that I had translated. The first successful drama that had a long run was Andreyev's *The Seven Who Were Hanged*, directed by Sigmund. He also directed and starred in Molière's *The Miser*; it was his greatest achievement. We had other interesting productions, but intrigues, jealousy, and hatred had begun to appear in the troupe, and the artistic level of the theater declined.

In 1922 I went for a short visit to Berlin, where Yosef was studying music. There I attended the theater and saw many first-rate actors. Among them was the German Jewish actor Alexander Granach, who in the early twenties was considered one of the most accomplished actors in Berlin. From Berlin I brought back several plays, one of which, *The Sinful Mr. Chew*, by Julius Berstl, was produced in the Central Theater. Another, Romain Rolland's *Wolves*, was produced in a later season by the Warsaw Yiddish Art Theater.

The first few years of Polish independence saw an efflorescence of Jewish culture. There also seemed to be a more tolerant attitude toward Jews. Unfortunately, this optimism vanished after the first few years. Various groups, and especially anti-Semitic newspapers, began a campaign of anti-Jewish agitation that particularly expressed itself later during the infamous Steiger trial in 1924-25. A Jewish student, Stanislaw Steiger, was falsely accused of attempting to assassinate the Polish president, S. Wojciechowski, while the latter was on a visit to Lemberg. During the Beilis trial in the czarist era, there had been pogroms. Regimes change, but hooligans remain the same. Hence, during the time of the Steiger trial the atmosphere was uneasy; luckily, however, there were no pogroms.

After Sigmund and I left the Central Theater, we organized in 1923 a new ensemble called the Warsaw Yiddish Art Theater, directed by both of us. This ensemble, in several phases, lasted for several years. At first my mother toured with us, but since there were no fitting roles for her artistry in the repertoire, she joined my brother in Vienna, where he had gone to continue his studies.

We then toured without my mother, who was vacationing in Baden bei Wien, and visited cities we had never seen before, such as Cracow and Lemberg, as well as other towns in eastern and western Galicia. Besides enjoying a successful tour, we were also pleased to see new regions and become acquainted with a new audience, the majority of which was intelligent. Among our many new friends in Lemberg were the painters Sigmund Menkes (now in New York) and Fritz Kleinman, who was also a stage designer who worked with us until 1941 and perished in Lemberg. We also befriended the musical and talented Gimpel family, grandchildren of the founders of the Lemberg Yiddish Theater in the 1880s. Of this family, Jacob, the pianist, and Bronislav, the violinist, are in America today. Unfortunately, almost all our Lemberg friends were victims of the murderous hand of Hitler.

In the town of Pshemishl, not far from Lemberg, we became acquainted with a magnificent man of harmonious disposition, the famous attorney Leib Landau, who was one of

Steiger's defense counsels. Tall, intelligent, and witty, with a fine profile and full face, he had the forehead of a Talmud scholar. After Steiger's acquittal, Landau became a hero. In his youth he had led a Yiddish dramatic circle, which accounted for his close links with the theater. We met him often through the years. Our last meetings were in Lemberg, from 1939 to 1941, but more of that later.

Between the two world wars in Galicia there developed an unusual kinship between the assimilated intelligentsia and Jewish culture; its chief expression was their attitude toward Yiddish theater. Many towns had their own dramatic circles, which in addition to average citizens included doctors, lawyers, engineers, and teachers. Unfortunately, this renascence was cut off by Hitler's angel of death.

In mentioning Galicia one must also write about the Cracow Yiddish Theater Society, which supported theaters with their own budget, and the Stanislav "Goldfaden Society," with its artistic productions staged by the finest directors. During our first tour of Cracow we befriended a group of wonderful people: the folksinger and poet Mordecai Gebirtig; Rachel Holzer, a charming woman and fine actress (today in Australia); and my present husband and colleague, Meir Melman, then a student at the Cracow University and in the dramatic school, who in his *shtetl* of Zholkiev—he is a Galitzianer—had organized a Jewish cultural society with a drama circle.

There was a difference between the towns and villages in Galicia and those we knew in Crown Poland (formerly under Russian rule) and Lithuania. Galicia had nicer hotels, better restaurants, more elegant cafés. But the Yiddish theatergoers, although externally different, remained the same warm, folksy, enthusiastic audience as in the other towns of Poland and Lithuania. They were simple, lovable Jews who were annihilated by the bestiality of the Germans and their local supporters.

Mother had never visited these towns, and people wanted

her to come. We imagined how she would be received and what an imprssion she would make when she came. Unfortunately, this was not to be.

Despite its successes, our first Warsaw Yiddish Art Theater failed, and Sigmund himself lent a hand to its downfall. This was part of his nature, exactly as it had been my father's—building and destroying. However, the burden of it fell on me, for he didn't mix into administrative matters and left everything to me.

Once again we organized a small ensemble whose repertoire was not as extensive as that of the Warsaw Yiddish Art Theater. Our tours were artistic and financial successes.

During one of our journeys my mother returned from Baden with Yosef, who had to report for an induction physical. She was very worried for him and couldn't find a place for herself. Nothing good was ever heard about military service; moreover, my brother was a very delicate and pampered only son, and the army would have had ill effects upon his musical career.

Several factors came to my brother's aid. After his bout with typhus, he developed a weak heart and some problems with his ear. Also, the authorities were not too eager to take Jews into the army. All this helped to free my brother from military service. Once Yosef was declared unfit for military duty, however, my mother again feared that perhaps he was really sick, so she had another reason to cry. A Jewish mother! As it turned out, my brother was perfectly healthy.

Only when we had all calmed down did my mother admit that *she* did not feel too well. She had been bleeding ever since her vacation in Baden. The doctor who had treated her there told her it was the onset of menopause. Now, after the aggravations concerning Yosef, the bleeding had become more intense. Her Warsaw doctor felt it was a tumor in the uterus and suggested a smear for lab examination. I accompanied my mother to Dr. Frishberg (he perished in the Warsaw Ghetto), where for the first time I heard her scream. I couldn't recognize her voice, but when I realized it was she screaming, I felt I would burst into the doctor's office and tear my mother away from his hands or jump out the window; but I restrained myself. Finally my mother was brought back into the waiting room. When she saw me and realized what I had experienced, she immediately smiled to me. The doctor asserted it was nothing dangerous but suggested an operation in Vienna as soon as possible.

In a carriage on our way home from the doctor, my mother said, "It's cancer, my child." I assured her that it was not true, and, to calm her, swore by the life of my child. (Since I knew nothing, I did not swear falsely.) But it was she who attempted to calm me.

We immediately began preparations for the journey, which were concluded in two or three days. My mother was calm, even joyful. She called a hairdresser to the house, manicured her nails, and even played cards with me. At night Sigmund told me the horrible news. It *was* cancer. It is hard to describe what I lived through. Here was another of those incidents that I simply could not comprehend.

When we arrived at the train station, the noted operetta star Clara Young was already waiting for us. On short notice we couldn't get accommodations in sleeping cars, and Clara had ordered two first-class seats for my mother and my mother's older sister, Keyle Pulman. Aunt Keyle had a son, Shimon, in Vienna, who was a professor in the music conservatory. (In 1939 Shimon and his wife went on a holiday from Paris to Warsaw. They were unable to return. Shimon then played with a symphony orchestra in the Warsaw Ghetto, where he perished with his wife.)

The train began to move. Through the window we saw two beautiful middle-aged women. One was unaware of her dangerous illness, and the other, like the rest of us, pretended she was not worried at all. So both smiled to us and to each other. My mother's radiant smile lingered before my eyes even after the train had departed. Then a cry tore out of my throat, half sob, half scream, which no one could stop.

With trembling hearts we all waited for news from my mother in Vienna. We only received telegrams signed by my cousin Shimon Pulman. After several informative telegrams, finally one came saying, "Operation successful. Shimon." After this, Sigmund left for Vienna. I wasn't permitted to leave home, for my family thought that my condition would not help my mother's.

Only after several days, when Sigmund returned with the news that my mother was in satisfactory condition, did I leave for Vienna. I was warned not to excite her with my behavior. Nevertheless, when I arrived, none of the warnings did any good. My mother's usual restraint in expressing her feelings were of no avail either. We fell upon each other's necks and cried. We spent a long time together.

After my mother was released from the hospital, she moved into a hotel, for she still had to be examined several times by her surgeon, the noted Professor Dr. Weibel. My mother had visits from friends and strangers who had discovered that she had just undergone a serious operation. I was always worried that someone would blurt out the truth about her illness, for she was still unaware of it.

From outward appearances Esther Rachel Kaminska looked well. She also made attempts to calm both myself and her, but she was very weakened. The look in her eyes seemed to be extinguished. Gone was her radiant motherly glance.

I went alone to see Dr. Weibel several times and he told me that the operation had been performed in order to avoid, as far as possible, further consequences. However, the operation should have come sooner. In any case, she was to avoid hard work and excitement and should see him again in six months. When my mother and I later bade the professor farewell, he told us, "Don't worry. This won't happen again to you."

Of course, he wanted to set her mind completely at ease, but he explicitly told me to watch her, for my mother was attempting to resume her usual pace and activity, even though I saw that it was difficult for her.

Meanwhile, in Vilna the new theater season had begun with excellent actors and Sigmund had been invited to join them. I, too, was expected in Vilna, as was the biggest attraction —my mother after her operation.

Upon our return home to Warsaw, we surrounded my mother with the greatest warmth and attention. A short while later I left for Vilna, a city with a great Jewish intelligentsia that always warmly responded to serious Yiddish theater. The Kaminsky family, beginning with my mother, who soon joined us, was especially enveloped with love. No wonder, then, that my mother's first appearance after her operation took place in Vilna. When she came onstage as Mirele Efros, the entire audience stood and gave Esther Rachel Kaminska an ovation that lasted several minutes. I stood backstage, dressed in my wedding gown for the role of Sheyndele, my heart beating like a hammer and tears streaming from my eyes. My mother's performance was magnificent, and it was hard to believe that she was struggling with an awful illness.

During the second act I had to say to Mirele (that is, to my mother), "Do you think a person can live forever?" but I could not utter the final part of the question. I got as far as "Do you think . . ." but the rest of the line remained stuck in my throat. Seeing this, my mother did not let me finish and replied, "I know what you mean. Don't worry. I know that a person cannot live forever." At the end of the act my mother embraced me: "My poor sweetheart, you couldn't say those words. But don't worry. Everything is all right, and I feel well."

Acting had an excellent effect upon her psychological state, but unfortunately the operation was indeed too late, and the ravaging illness gradually attacked her lungs. She performed for a full year, however, and even went on tour. She would joke with us, but occasionally her smile bore witness to her sadness. I knew every nuance of her face. My heart would begin to pound, and with assumed indifference I would say, "What's wrong, Mama?"

"Nothing," she would reply.

"Then what is it?"

"I don't know," she would say, smiling. "I'm not myself."

We continued touring, and she attempted to hide her feelings from us. One day, in the town of Baranovitch, she felt quite ill. We called the doctor, who told her that it was an abdominal pain. However, to us he revealed that it was the cancer affecting the liver. As it later turned out, he erred slightly, for it was her lungs. Unfortunately, this was the beginning of the end. We broke off our performances and brought Mother home. We thought she would soon recover, and so Sigmund and I went on tour again because of the expenses at home and the bills for my mother's illness.

We took my mother to a sanitarium in Otvotsk, on the outskirts of Warsaw, concluded our tour several days early, and returned home and to my mother. We met her on the balcony of her room. She looked well.

"What are you doing here?" I joked.

"I don't know," she replied. "I don't feel bad. I'm not being cured here. I'm so bored, I'm thinking of returning home."

Sigmund and I returned to Warsaw in the evening and came back to the sanitarium the following morning. We discovered that my mother had passed a terrible night. She had breathing difficulties that were relieved by oxygen. My mother said if this recurred, she would go home.

With heavy hearts we rejoined the troupe. My mother left the sanitarium. Soon after, we received a telegram to cease performing and come home immediately.

When my mother saw us, she called out merrily, "Now I shall be well! Believe it or not, children, I have your father's illness: asthma. Imagine that! Now I understand how much he suffered, poor man." The doctors had convinced her of this, and it made us happy.

Every day became more difficult. She could not lie down; she gazed sad-eyed at the pillow. Oxygen was used several times a day. The pharmacist who had provided it was amazed at her strength.

Heedless of her condition, my mother avidly followed the Steiger trial, the sensation of the day, and regularly blessed the attorney Leib Landau. Though she did not believe that her end was so near, nevertheless when she was told that Steiger had been acquitted, she exclaimed, "Thank God," then added, "When Beilis was freed, Regina died." I berated her but she calmed me: "No, no, my child, I'm not thinking of dying. I must live. I have such wonderful children."

Various doctors came to her without even being summoned, but only to pay her homage with their last services. Since I couldn't watch her suffering, I ran to a *zinachar*—an unlicensed folk doctor—about whom various miracle stories had been told. A host of people were waiting to see him. When he opened the door, I fell at his feet and cried, pleading with him to save my mother. He was touched and answered in German, "I will save your mother." I seized his hand and kissed it.

All of this was so unlike me, but still I don't wonder at what I did. I simply couldn't accept the thought of losing my mother. I was like a drowning person who grabs at any straw. After several visits the *zinachar* told me, "Had I come earlier, I would have saved her."

Up to the last minute my mother did not look like a seriously ill person. Morphine injections made her sleep much during her last days, but when she opened her eyes, she was fully conscious. Several hours before her death a midwife visited her. She was the first to mention her illness. When my mother opened her eyes, the midwife asked her in Polish, "Madame Kaminska, don't you recognize me?"

"Why shouldn't I recognize you?" my mother replied.

And then to me she added wonderingly in Yiddish, "Look, her hair has turned yellow." Only then did I notice that the midwife had dyed her hair blond.

The next morning the attending nurse called attention to the drops of perspiration on my mother's forehead, a sign that the end was near. With trembling legs, hardly able to move, I came to my mother. She sat up in bed. Her eyes were unusually large and shining, her lips blue. She looked at me with a smile. I noticed that she appeared to have seen several people, because she shook her head as though she wanted to free herself of this vision.

Unable to restrain myself, I ran to the telephone and called our relative, Dr. Owsiej Bielinky. My mother's two sisters arrived, as did Sigmund and my aunt Rivka's son-in-law, also an actor. I approached the door of the next room and saw my mother's image in a huge mirror. She had reclined on the pillow. There was a calm smile on her face. Her facial wrinkles had become smoothed out. I ran to the phone again. Just then Sigmund ran over to me. "No need to call any more."

Although toward the end of her life we knew how incurably ill my mother was, we never dreamed that the final sentence had been imposed. During her illness I wept much, but when the catastrophe came, I didn't shed a tear. About an hour after her death I requested to be admitted to her with no one else present. The members of my family exchanged glances, but seeing that I was perfectly rational, they acquiesced. I came up to her bed, looked at her face, and spoke to her. It seemed she was breathing, but this didn't frighten me. On the contrary, I was almost certain that everyone had made a mistake, and I said, "Speak, Mama. Don't be afraid. I won't be frightened." When she didn't reply, I was certain that this was a deep sleep. Again it appeared she was breathing. I bent over to her and kissed her forehead, and then I sensed the awful truth for the first time—my mother was cold.

The relatives at her bedside stated that her last words were "Soon, soon the curtain will fall." And so in December 1925 ended the chapter called Esther Rachel Kaminska.

Certainly it was far too short. A comprehensive and precise monograph about her phenomenal personality is needed, but this must be a separate volume, devoted to her alone. Esther Rachel's death in 1925 at the age of fifty-six saddened all Jews who saw her and knew her and all those who had only heard of her. The funeral was a demonstration of Warsaw and Polish Jewry's affection for her, and news stories were full of amazement at the simple Jews of Warsaw.

I at twenty-six and my brother, Yosef, at twenty-two had now become full-fledged orphans.

12

The Second Warsaw
Yiddish Art Theater and
Events in My Private Life

BETWEEN 1926 and 1931 we noted a fine growth in
our theater. The renewed Warsaw Yiddish Art Theater
flourished. Among its finest productions that helped secure its
fame were plays like *The Wolves* by Romain Rolland, the
dramatization of Dostoevsky's *The Brothers Karamazov*, *The
Treasure* by David Pinski, and *The Tenth Commandment* by
Abraham Goldfaden, edited by Sigmund.

Good actors of the former Warsaw Yiddish Art Theater
joined our ensemble, as did a new generation of actors,
among whom was my present husband, Meir Melman. In
1930 the perpetually restless and innovative Sigmund Turkov
decided to study film direction. When he was denied the opportunity to go to Moscow to the famous director, Sergei Eis-
enstein, he went to Berlin, not even knowing to whom and
whether or not he would be successful.

For the first time in twelve years I went on tour with a
troupe without Sigmund. Now I had to assume the burden
of the great moral and material responsibilities. I assembled
a good company and toured dozens of Polish towns that had
sizable Jewish populations. Fortunately, the tour was successful artistically and financially.

Meanwhile, Sigmund succeeded in entering the famous
prewar film production company UFA as voluntary assistant
director to the Russian director Shtrizhevsky. Thanks to his

great talents and long stage experience, Sigmund soon became indispensable and was much admired.

From Berlin, Sigmund began to ask me categorically to stop the tour and come to him.

I gave in. Under other circumstances perhaps I would not have, since it was financially damaging. (From my earnings Sigmund was also able to support himself in Berlin.) Nevertheless, I assented, for I felt somewhat guilty toward Sigmund. Since his departure I found myself drawn closer and closer to Meir Melman, who was in the troupe and who—it was no secret to anyone and not to Sigmund—had fallen in love with me from the first day he joined our ensemble.

My permission to leave for Berlin, received after much difficulty, was good for only ten days. During his stay in Berlin, Sigmund had learned much. Compared to the Polish film productions, Berlin films at that time were on a much higher level. Since Sigmund had to sign a declaration that he would not work professionally in Berlin, we decided to return home together. After coming back to Warsaw, we reformed our troupe and went out on tour.

Sigmund received various offers for film direction. Not one scenario pleased him. He also received offers in the theater; one was to play Robespierre in Büchner's *Danton's Death*. While I was on tour, he translated Verneuil's two-character drama *Monsieur Lamberthier*. Afterward he convinced me to leave the ensemble and travel with him, performing the Verneille play. Since my conscience wasn't too clear toward Sigmund, I agreed, even though it was difficult for me to part with my colleagues, with whom I had been working for years and with whom I got along harmoniously.

The tour was a brilliant one. In addition to succeeding artistically, we earned more money than ever before. Then something happened that came as a shock to our friends and acquaintances. For me, too, it was unexpected. In 1931 Sigmund and I divorced. Meir Melman (whom I always called Mel) was not the cause of it, perhaps just one of many reasons that I will not discuss. Actually it is not worth seeking reasons why one marries and why one divorces.

The uncertainty of our situation lasted a long time. Sigmund and I continued performing and living together in Belgium and in Paris. We came home and remained together until Sigmund went to Argentina. I rejoined my ensemble and produced several new plays. Sigmund remarried, and in 1936 I married Meir Melman.

13

The Ida Kaminska Ensemble

YEARS passed, years of wanderings, new forms in my theatrical activity, and new personal shocks.

In 1936 I was able to perform in Vilna, the "Jerusalem of Lithuania." While we were in Vilna, friends of mine and my mother's noted that it had been twenty years since I had made my adult debut. A committee composed of writers, artists, and communal leaders undertook to organize a twentieth jubilee. They also issued a brochure concerning my theatrical activity, to which many well-known writers and cultural figures contributed.

The times, however, were not tranquil. Hitler's agitation infected a great part of the Polish people. Especially excelling in this anti-Jewish activity was the academic youth. It was painful to see the participation of these young people, who should have been in the front line of the democratic movement and who should have understood that the anti-Jewish poison came from the outside. It was painful, too, to see them attacking poor innocent Jews. Jewish students and some —albeit too few—Polish students resisted, but the mood of brutality swept the streets.

When the question was then asked whether a jubilee celebration should be held in such an oppressive atmosphere, the overriding opinion was that it should be—that there should be a celebration to spite the enemies. The organizers carried it out in low key, with love and dignity, in a small theater far from the center of town. We had assumed people would be afraid to come, but in demonstrative fashion Vilna Jews came en masse. A building that normally held six hundred people now accommodated more than a thousand.

Many stood outside and were told what was happening within, for at that time there was no loudspeaker system. Among the speakers were Dr. Wigodsky and the white-haired Dr. Shabad, who spoke with profound nationalistic fervor. When my daughter, Ruth, who was onstage, heard Dr. Shabad saying, "I bow my head before you," then saw him incline his proud white head, she could not restrain herself, ran up to me, embraced me, and began to cry. Others spoke that evening, too, and I remember them with awe. They all became martyrs of Hitler. There were no tears of complaint in their speeches, just Jewish and universal pride. That's how they were, the Jews of Vilna. Blessed be their memory.

In 1936 I also traveled with my ensemble to Lithuania, then called Kovno Lithuania, since Kovno, not Vilna, was then the capital of Lithuania. To get to Lithuania we had to use a circuitous route through Latvia instead of the more direct route, which was closer to Poland. We did this because nearly twenty years after the First World War, after Poland and Lithuania had become independent, there were no diplomatic or any other relations between these two countries. This cost both nations dearly in later years.

In Lithuania we performed our standard repertoire. We met very warm-hearted Jews, nationalists who had pride in their Yiddish language. We traveled about in various towns of the small country, where there was no lack of poverty. In one town, Maviapol, I received a rare gift, brought to me onstage—a deluxe edition of Jacob Gordin's plays, with the following inscription: "For the beloved, authentically Jewish artist, from those who cannot afford to buy theater tickets." For several days I pondered how we could give free performances for these theater lovers, but my impresarios could not agree.

In Kovno, where we had performed so successfully, several of my colleagues and I experienced a great disappointment. At that time leaders of the Russian Revolution—Rikoff, Bukharin, and others—were brought to trial. Although we were not communists, in certain respects we saw in the Soviet Union a newly born world. Then this monstrous trial came as such a blow to simple logic that it confused us. Was this the authentic justice? Even the communists in Kovno felt ashamed and couldn't justify what was taking place. In 1936 the concept of Stalinism was still not understood. The naïve justifications of those who wanted to explain current happenings only succeeded in making nonbelievers of those who had believed in the system.

In Kovno I received word from Warsaw that both my mother's sisters had died—Aunt Rivka, who had brought us up during our youth, when mother used to travel about on tour, and Aunt Keyle Pulman, the main partner in the Kaminsky Theater. For many years Aunt Keyle had been the manager of the theater and attempted to make it a profitable enterprise. A beautiful, majestic woman, even in old age she was an imposing figure whom everyone admired. She had struggled for a long time with the owners of the property on which the theater stood. They attempted to remove the cultural edifice that my father had built. The trial was a very lengthy one, and we lost the theater.

When we returned to Poland in 1937, my brother Yosef and his family were preparing to emigrate to Palestine. Yosef was a violinist of the first order, as well as a composer. He composed music for the Warsaw Yiddish Art Theater, for the Vilna troupe, and songs for Polish revues. He was concertmaster of the Radio Philharmonic and appeared on the Polish radio with a quartet that had won first prize at a competition.

At that time Bronislaw Huberman was organizing the Palestine Philharmonic Orchestra. (After 1948 it became known as the Israel Philharmonic Orchestra.) He offered Yosef the position of concertmaster. My brother hesitated. It was difficult for him to part with his home town, with me, and with his famous quartet. However, he came to me and said, "You know what, Idele? I think I will go after all." He had been attacked in anti-Semitic newspapers which "revealed" that his real name was not Kaminsky, a Polish name, but Yoshe Kalb, after the hero of I. J. Singer's novel and drama, just then being presented by Maurice Schwartz in the Kaminsky Theater. The ignoramuses of the anti-Semitic newspapers could not tell whether Kaminsky was the name of the drama or the owner of the theater.

In general, the anti-Semitic newspapers busied themselves with "unmasking" Jews who were considered Poles. They would write the following: "Who do you think Bronislaw Huberman, Paul Kletsky, and Yosef Kaminsky are?" These newspapers concentrated one day on musicians, another on doctors, a third time on lawyers. Indeed, in those times there were plenty of such people to enumerate.

Once my brother told me that his conductor, Gregor Fitelberg, came over to him, patted his shoulder, and said (in Polish, of course), "Things are not too good for us, friend Kaminsky."

Fitelberg, one of the most famous Polish conductors, a luminary of Polish music, had never admitted that he was a Jew. Now, two years prior to the Hitler attack on Poland, he, too, felt the poison with which Nazism wanted to weaken the opposition of the Polish people.

It was after this episode that my brother said to me, "In other words, Idele, it's time to go." He wrote to Huberman that he would go to Palestine. It was now the summer of 1937. I was exhausted and went with my husband on a deserved two-week vacation to the beautiful resort of Krinitz. I was accompanied to the station by Yosef, his wife, and their beautiful four-year-old son, all of whom were to leave for Palestine in a few days. Standing by the window of the sleeping car and looking at them, I had an intuitive feeling that we were saying good-bye for a long time. A strange fear enveloped me, and I cried the whole night.

When I returned from vacation to Warsaw, I once again

harnessed myself to work. The economic state of most of the Jews worsened because of the boycott of Jews and their businesses. Nevertheless, the cultural activity of the folk masses grew, along with their cultural needs. Indeed, the Yiddish theater in Poland from 1936 to 1939 reached a very high level.

Political clouds covered the skies of Poland. The events in Hitlerland dragged up to the surface the entire rotten stench that had only been a dream of the reactionary elements. Unfortunately, however, it was not only the latter. The university youth demanded a quota system for Jews and supported these demands with riots and demonstrations against the universities and even on the streets.

In those prewar years a man named Boleslaw Piasetsky led a group called the Organization of Radical Nationalists. These extremely nationalistic youths would attack Jews. (Today Piasetsky is well-known in Poland as the leader of the Conformist Catholics, who even now are linked with the regime.) The government of Poland closed an eye to these events. The land was in a somnolent state, unaware of the great danger that came upon it in 1939.

Restrictions were imposed upon the Yiddish theater. Of the eighteen licenses granted for Yiddish theaters, half were revoked, yet the artistic activity of my theater and other theaters grew. In 1938 I succeeded in renting a theater in the center of town—the Novostchy Theater, located in a partly Jewish neighborhood. There were produced Max Bauman's *Glückel Hameln Demands Justice*, in which I played the title role. (I also produced this play in 1972 in New York.) This drama was based on the memoirs of Glückel, written in the seventeenth century, the first extant Yiddish autobiography. The play, Bauman's first, written when he was sixty, was not very theatrical, and so I reworked it. The reception accorded to it by the audience was extraordinary.

Glückel was premiered in Lodz. The sets were designed by the famous Polish artist and theater director Ivo Gal. A non-Jew, he donated his services as a tribute to the Yiddish theater. The play dealt with events in the life of seventeenth-century Jews in Hamburg, but it had strong allusions to the current persecutions of Jews in Germany. The heroine's demand for justice before the mayor of Hamburg rang out like the demand of Jews everywhere, especially in the Hitler orbit.

In addition to *Glückel* we performed my dramatization of Yehoshua Perl's novel *Flame* and Verneuil's French comedy *Attorney Balbec*. Of course, no season was complete without *Mirele Efros*.

I rented the Novostchy Theater for a full year. People came from both the Jewish and the non-Jewish sections of town. We experienced a renascence and I was pleased that finally I would be able to remain at one place in Warsaw for a long while. There was a community-wide response, and organized support was envisioned for the theater so that it could remain independent in artistic planning. The owners of the theater even gave me an option to rent the building for ten years. I tried to enhance the public's good impression of our theater, which was considered among the leading ones of Poland. (Polish theater, in turn, had a high reputation in Europe.) I succeeded in this especially with two new productions that raised the rank of the theater.

One was Joseph Lateiner's late nineteenth-century play, *Sara Sheyndl of Yehupetz*, which, with the assistance of poet Moshe Broderson, I adapted into an artistic musical. Set design was done by the Lemberg painter Fritz Kleinman, an innovator in the theater. (He perished in a German concentration camp in 1942.) My young daughter made her debut onstage in a man's role and was very successful in it. One evening during the run of the play, she met the famous jazz trumpeter Addy Rosner, who sent her a bouquet of flowers the following morning. And so the romance began. He fell in love with Ruth and later married her.

Our second big hit was my staging of Lope de Vega's

The Sheep Well in Aaron Kuzhnirov's translation, with sets designed by Ivo Gal. Special lyrics were written by the famous Yiddish poet Alter Katzizne, with music by the young, unusually talented Israel Shayevitch. These two productions were extremely expensive, but nevertheless we broke even.

The society that was to organize aid for us did not materialize. There was an air of crisis about that portended war. Hitler demanded the territories of Poland while concurrently instigating the German minority in Poland to revolt. People did not believe in the outbreak of war. "Clever and seasoned" politicians declared: "Hitler won't dare to start a war which he'd soon lose." However, the atmosphere continually thickened. Critical days approached.

The season in the Novostchy Theater ended, but still the theater remained mine. I rented it to Sigmund Turkov, who had come to Warsaw from Lemberg for two months with his newly organized Warsaw Yiddish Art Theater. He intended to produce Goldfaden's *Shulamis*, as well as *Bar Kochba*, which he had successfully presented in a new version in Lemberg.

In July 1939 I went with my troupe to Lodz. Subsequent plans included visits to Vilna and Lemberg, and after a short vacation we were to return to our Warsaw theater.

The atmosphere in Lodz was far more jittery than in Warsaw. People often spoke of war. The air of panic was especially bolstered by the 40,000 Germans who lived in Lodz. There were a quarter of a million Jews in the city, which had a population of 750,000. People were already beginning to hoard food. Gradually mobilization began. Of course, all of this affected the theater, but still we continued performing. I must admit that I, too, succumbed to panic, although I didn't show it. My intuition told me that a catastrophe was approaching. I could give no rational explanation for my feelings, full of visions of apocalypse.

It was in such a time that the owner of the Novostchy Theater in Warsaw came to me and signed a ten-year contract. Today this sounds grotesque. The theater owner received a twenty-thousand-zloty deposit, which my administrator, David Helfman, raised. Since neither of us had this sum, a friend of the theater from the city of Drohobitch paid the money. He was going to be our future partner. Both he and Helfman perished in the ghettos.

Once my family and I visited our Lodz friend, Dr. Goodstat, and his wife to play cards. Suddenly I heard the familiar, frightful voice of Hitler: "The Jews and the Polish swine want the war, so they'll have it." I could not comprehend how my card partners considered my fear naïve. We continued playing.

Then one day, like a thunderclap, came the news of the treaty between Hitler and Stalin—the Ribbentrop-Molotov Pact. Even the hopes of avoiding war didn't soften this blow. It was another incident that I could not understand rationally. How could governments of such opposing ideologies, who hated each other, sign such an agreement? "This is at the expense of Poland," said my husband.

At that very time Addy Rosner was also performing in Lodz. The war atmosphere affected the theater, as well as Addy's club. Quite simply, no one came. My daughter drew closer to Rosner. Meir Melman sat all day long reading newspapers and listening to the radio from all over the world. One day, while we were sitting in the Astoria, a restaurant where writers and artists would meet, a painter who had come from Germany told us something interesting. A German had shown him a mobilization card ordering him to Lodz in anticipation of the coming war. We were amazed at such organization. Among the Germans in Lodz, leaflets were already being distributed with the precise date when the German army would march in and "liberate" the suffering Germans.

Once, before we went to sleep, I asked Mel, "Why are you studying the map so diligently?"

He pointed to Gdansk/Danzig with a pen and said, "Do

you see? This is where the Germans will strike. They'll be here in Lodz the first day, and a week later they will be behind Warsaw, coming from the south and from the north [from Amtpreisen]. Two weeks later the Russians will enter from the east and occupy Rovno, Lemberg, and so on."

"In that case," I said, "perhaps we should discontinue the performances and go immediately to Lemberg. As long as the trains are still running, we'll be able to take both personal and theater baggage." (This still had a great value in those days.)

My husband replied, "I think so, too. That's the logical outcome of the German-Soviet pact. Yet I'm not fully certain of it."

Three days later it was already too late.

14

World War II

GENERAL mobilization was now proclaimed. Within a day rail travel became almost impossible because of military transports. People spoke with certitude of the German attack on Poland.

On August 31, 1939, one day before the outbreak, Ruth, Mel, David Helfman, and I traveled to Warsaw with two small valises. We left all our personal belongings with Palewski, the director of the Savoy Hotel—he was a German, incidentally—and all the theater properties had been left in the theater.

The trip from Lodz to Warsaw, usually a two-and-a-half-hour ride, took nine hours with an express train that made many stops. We encountered troop trains. In the eyes of the soldiers one could see their farewell to life.

In Warsaw, Helfman went to his relatives, while Mel and I went to Helfman's apartment, and Ruth went to her father, Sigmund Turkov. Then we discovered that Addy Rosner was also in Warsaw.

That night we went to sleep heavy-hearted. Earlier in the evening we were in a café whose windows were already blackened. There we heard "authoritative" opinions that the Germans "wouldn't dare" and that "we and France and England are stronger." At four that morning we heard the sirens.

Then a call from the courtyard: "Down to the cellars!" We on the fifth floor decided to go down to our acquaintance

Dr. Berlis, who lived on the second floor. Still sleepy-eyed, he opened the door for us and, realizing what had brought us down to him, laughed. "Aren't you ashamed? Intelligent people should realize that these are simply antiaircraft maneuvers. Go back to sleep!"

Meanwhile, the radio carried an announcement of how many houses had been bombed out and how many people killed. Dr. Berlis ceased being an optimist. We went out on the streets. Tumult, confusion. Police and soldiers were running here and there. From the loudspeakers on the streets we heard Mayor Stefan Starzynski proclaim that he hoped "we will not succumb and force the enemy to retreat." We returned to our apartment and heard Hitler's speech on the German station. "Today is the first day of the new thousand-year Reich!"

So began the first day of the World War, a war that radically changed our way of life. Meanwhile, the radio had begun to report the first news about the German attack upon Poland. The broadcast told of the number of houses and people destroyed and stated that on the fronts "we are pushing back the despicable enemy."

The people in Warsaw were relatively calm. During the first few days the coffeehouses were full. Everyone knew that Hitler's deed was one that violated all human and international morality, and they had faith in France and England.

So, despite the bad news from the fronts (we learned much from the German radio), when the report came that the two great powers had declared war against Hitler, joy and optimism reigned in Warsaw. We went to Gertner's restaurant to celebrate with others. There we met Addy Rosner, who had been looking for Ruth. While we were in the café, German airplanes flew over Warsaw, but no one left because no one thought of hiding in shelters. Moreover, the bombing was especially light.

The next morning people learned that much of Poland had been occupied by the Germans and that German tanks were approaching from all sides. A slight panic began, which intensified from hour to hour. It was September 4, my birthday, and my friend David Helfman brought a bottle of wine and we drank to my health. I was forty years old. That evening we went to the café again. People sought the opportunity not to be alone. The mood, however, was different from the previous night and nothing remained of last night's optimism. People related what the Germans had said, and everybody wondered what to do next.

On September 5, 1939, my husband sought a permit for a train ticket to Lemberg, but permits were not given anymore. He was told that the railroad tracks had been destroyed by German bombings. Rumors spread that some civil servants and ministries were being evacuated to the east. German planes appeared with greater frequency in the skies. On the night of September 8 a radio call came ordering all men of mobilization age to leave Warsaw for the east. Now the real panic began. Thousands of people dashed over the bridges of the Wisla River on their way eastward. Our men joined this human stream. David Helfman remained because of his mother, and Addy Rosner did not want to leave Ruth.

We found ourselves in the house of the parents of David's former wife. (He still loved her even though she had remarried.) In the evening—it was a Friday, just after the Sabbath candles had been lit—we suddenly heard a loud explosion. The Germans had begun firing artillery against Warsaw. We ran down the stairs to the gate. Some went down to the cellars, others ran into the street. Nothing was yet organized. A military patrol came up the steps to us and took Helfman and Rosner for some military work.

Tumult was so great that no one could hear anyone else. Added to this were the cannon noises. Ruth pressed close to me and whispered, "Mama, I know you're thinking of me now but remember your sister who died at the age of nineteen. No one lives forever. The main thing is that we are together."

After that, it quieted down somewhat. Ruth sang into my ear: "To life, fellow Jews, be merry; don't cry and don't complain. We'll yet hear joyful news." It was the refrain of a song I sang in our recent production of *Sara Sheyndl of Yehupetz.*

Just then Addy and David arrived. They had been taken to put up barricades in front of destroyed houses, but the work was broken off. Both now shouted, "Let's run from here!" I don't know where Ruth got such energy. She held me by the hand, cried, "Let's go!" and pushed her way through the mass of people. Everyone had been waiting for the first initiative. Now all followed. The road became dangerous. Shells were flying overhead. The smoke from burning houses was suffocating. We stepped over broken window glass and continued running. The mass of people gradually dispersed.

We came to 6 Kreditova Street, Warsaw's newest and most modern apartment house, managed by my cousin's husband. Ruth thought there would be good shelters there. As we entered our cousin's apartment, the maid told us, "The master has gone away and the mistress is in the cellar with her children."

We went downstairs, followed by the several people who had come with us. Upon entering the shelter we were warned to be still because people were sleeping. This seemed strange, but we, too, dropped to the earth and immediately fell asleep.

When we waked up, we saw that this was indeed a regular shelter with light, water, toilets. The residents of the large house had brought down beds, bedding, and provisions.

However, there was no room to turn around. The residents of the house looked at us suspiciously, especially when they heard that Rosner was speaking German. On the radio Mayor Starzynski announced that Warsaw was almost completely surrounded but that the people would fight to the last man. Mayor Starzynski behaved and died like a hero—shot by the Germans.

Our young people went into town and returned with some food. Rosner told of a much better bunker he had discovered. We went out into the street and, ironically, it was a quiet, sunny, beautiful day; because of the weather, reports stated, the German tanks were able to move forward quickly. Unfortunately, soon the artillery began again. We pressed to the walls and finally came to the Café Esplanade, where Addy and his orchestra had once performed. In the rear of the café there was a big, beautiful bar. One flight down, below ground, there were comfortable sofas, chairs, soft electric lights, and water. The kitchen was still working, and one could get coffee and tea. Already, it contained twenty-five people, but compared to a bunker, it was very comfortable. As time passed, however, the number of "residents" increased, for the bombing and the artillery grew more intense from day to day.

I telephoned Sigmund Turkov's young wife and told her to come to the Café Esplanade because it seemed more secure. The next morning she came, as did our men. Following a radio order, Mel and Sigmund had gone to the outskirts of Warsaw and then returned after a second order. Mel reported that he had been part of a stream of thousands and thousands of men who had marched forty miles—a perfect target for the German planes. They slept in a field and were machine-gunned by the planes the next day. They hid in a forest for one day, but because of the Germans' nonstop bombing they left the forest at night and discovered that an order had come to return. They walked all night long to Warsaw, dragging their feet, tired, exhausted, barely alive. Once Sigmund found out where we were, he came to us. Sigmund's brother, Jonas, and the others went to their homes.

During the first few days one of the owners of the elegant restaurant across the street, The Silver Rose (owned by two Jews, Roher and Zeidel), invited the "residents" of the bunker to come and have a good soup known as a one-pot dinner. However, soon this was no longer possible because, first of all, about two hundred people gathered in front of the restaurant and the food supply gradually was depleted. Second, it was dangerous even to cross the street because of the bullets flying overhead.

In our cellar at the Café Esplanade, Hochman, the Jewish owner, consoled the people the first few days. However, when the crowds became thick because of a continual influx, he would shout, "What's going on here, folks? This isn't a real bunker. As soon as the first bomb hits, you'll all be buried." No one heeded him because there was no place else to run. The Polish government had not prepared any air-raid shelters, and the people had confidence in such a large house. (During the Warsaw Ghetto uprising in 1944, it was completely burned down.)

Several Jews and Poles in the bunker agreed that a twenty-four-hour guard should be placed outside. A committee was formed, and Mel was chosen one of the commanders of the bunker and the house. He also had to watch for bombs hitting the roof and for outbreaks of fire. Mel is a very restless person, although outwardly quite calm. An active man, if he has nothing to do, he cannot find a place for himself. In the bunker he kept the guard duty roster for every able-bodied man. Mel was also in charge of seeing that committee decisions were carried out. Twice a day he would be on the roof of the house, as well as on guard duty by the gate. He walked about in the overcrowded bunker to see if anyone needed help, even though there was little he could do.

One time a man who was scheduled to be on guard duty at the gate fell ill. Mel immediately substituted for him. Just then two Polish soldiers came to inquire about some people. When my husband went down to the bunker to seek out the men, shrapnel hit the gate of the house at the very place where Mel had been standing, and the two young soldiers were killed.

Because of my husband's activity, most of the time I sat alone in the bunker, while other men sat with their wives.

My daughter sat with Rosner, who tried to make conditions as comfortable as possible for her; for instance, he placed cotton in her ears to shut out the loud noise of the shelling. All this while, my husband was a "commander." Yet those who know Mel realize that he never neglected me but did what he had to do.

The hot September days of 1939 passed by slowly until we came to Yom Kippur. (I think it was September 23.) That day was the culmination of the barbaric strafing and bombarding of Warsaw. During the continuous firing and exploding of bombs, Jews gathered in a corner of the bunker for "Kol Nidre." Many of them had long not prayed on Yom Kippur or gone to the synagogue at all. Several Jews had prayer shawls, which shone strangely in the dim candlelight (there was no longer any electricity, and the owner of the house lit two candles). It created the atmosphere of a prayer service conducted by the Marranos in the cellars of Spain. People did not say "Kol Nidre," they merely wept. There was no prayer leader. My daughter and other women looked on and wiped their eyes. I could not cry. I was captivated by the picture that had never been painted. From childhood on, I had been used to the theater, but I knew that this was no theater. This was real life. Somehow I couldn't accept the fact that we were experiencing this. As usual in awful moments during my life, I suddenly became an observer.

Some Poles who looked on, too, asked respectfully, "Pray to God for us also."

The following day, Yom Kippur, was pure hell. The German planes flew overhead ceaselessly, right over our roofs, casting bombs and spewing machine-gun bullets to the accompaniment of artillery. No longer was there any light in the bunker, and no water or food either.

A day or two later David Helfman left the bunker one evening to find out how his relatives were doing. After returning he said, "Madame Kaminska, you no longer have a theater or a home. Even my apartment where you kept some of your things is gone. Everything is burned down. The foundations are still smoldering."

I didn't reply. I looked at Ruth, at Mel, at Ruth's father, Sigmund, and at a few other friends, and remained silent, perfectly calm. I didn't feel a thing that should have agitated me. It was no longer the same life. It was no longer the same world, so why should I have been surprised!

The following night the shooting stopped and it suddenly became quiet. Exhausted people fell asleep in the quiet bunker. I lay on the floor like everyone else and suddenly remembered that my archives, covering twenty-five years of my work, had been destroyed. All the pictures from the theater and of my close relatives. No trace of my creative work remained. And then I began to cry.

As mentioned, there was no longer any food; however, I felt no hunger. In general, women had an easier time of it, but some men fell ill from lack of food. One late September day several of the desperate people went out to the street to see if they could find something to eat. Suddenly they returned and joyfully announced that the nearby Philharmonic concert hall had been destroyed and that in the ruins, in the cellars, there was an endless supply of crates of sugar that had been prepared for the military. "Everyone, take as much as you want," they said, and urged the men to go.

Some of the men went, Mel among them, and they returned carrying heavy creates. When the crates were opened, we found extremely hard sugar which even the strongest sets of teeth could not crunch. There was no water. Nevertheless, people broke off pieces and held them in their mouths until their hunger seemed to be stilled.

In the bunker there was a deaf man who could not hear the shelling. Several times a day he would run into the street to get something to eat. His deafness bolstered his daring. He would knock on doors of stores and apartments. Amazed at his courage, people always gave him something to eat. Because of this, his wife never lacked for food. He would even sell some of it, and since he admired and respected me, he always had something for me to buy.

The last day before the cease-fire we still felt the maddening bombardment. Our house shook. In the courtyard incendiary bombs were found that our home guard defused, and with all this—we don't know from where—rumor spread that the Soviets were coming to help. Not far from Warsaw, so the story went, Russian tanks were standing. Planes with the red star had been seen. Unfortunately, wishful thinking had brought on the fantasy. The next morning came the sobering facts. Along the peripheries of the city, German tanks rolled in, and no one any longer had any illusions about coming help.

15

Under German Occupation

SHOOTING ceased on September 29, 1939. The Polish army could no longer resist, and the Germans already saw the signs of the coming capitulation.

We went out into the streets and brought back confirmed reports that Poland was surrendering. Warsaw no longer had a radio station. One of the last reports on the radio was on September 18: the Soviets had occupied all of eastern Poland. This was a sign that the heroic defense of Warsaw had been in vain. My husband's "prophecies" were realized. Sad and broken-hearted, we accepted the news that the city was surrendering. Yet the people breathed more freely, for now we no longer heard the wild firing. And if everything was lost anyway, why then the battle in vain?

Warsaw, too, had to suffer death throes.

Ruth and several other people went out into the street. There they first saw the horror of the siege: houses in ruins, dead bodies that had not yet been removed from the places where they had fallen. Shot horses were surrounded by people who were cutting pieces of flesh. They were even fighting over "better cuts."

I, too, went out. I couldn't believe what I saw. Suddenly a newspaperman I knew came up to me. He didn't recognize me. Only after I had begun speaking to him did he slap his forehead and say, "Ida! What you look like!" He said that the Germans were waiting only to have the streets cleaned up for them, then they would march in jubilantly.

"And the Russians?"

"A foolish dream," he replied. "They divided the Polish earth with the Germans."

Suddenly airplanes appeared. German ones, of course. At first we were frightened, but we soon saw that they flew so low that we could almost see the pilots. They were inspecting the streets. My daughter called out humorously, *"They're running now instead of the trolley cars."*

A man who had a battery-operated radio called to me: "Come into my house. After all, you understand Russian." I entered and what I heard confused me thoroughly. A radio station in Lemberg informed us that life proceeded normally in the liberated city, just as in all other cities that had been finally "liberated" from the Polish yoke.

Warsaw was in ruins. My apartment and the theater had been destroyed. The only thing I had left were my relatives. I asked Mel, "Is there a chance of our going to Lemberg to your family?"

"There is a way to leave Warsaw," my husband said, "but only by foot." Ruth was too exhausted to begin the trip immediately, so in the meantime we left the bunker with the few belongings we had. David's former wife suggested that we stay at her house until we found another place. We agreed. As we made our way through the destroyed streets, Ruth asked if Addy could join us. "Of course," I said.

We heard screams from all sides. The smoke from burning buildings was suffocating. We had to climb over stones and bricks. It seemed that all this was a movie in which I was performing. Frankly, I couldn't believe it was real. Through the noise my daughter cried out, "Mama! We're living through this!"

"No!" I shouted back. "Acting in a movie!"

Passing a well-known cinema that had been bullet-riddled, we noticed a poster for the film *Life Is Grand*. Ruth commented, "Perhaps it isn't so grand."

On the way I visited my two cousins (both named Lena)

in whose bunker we first stayed. Their house and apartment were unharmed, and they were glad quiet finally reigned. (Later they died at the hands of the Germans.) One cousin, Lena, was married to the distinguished physician, Dr. Bielinky, who had been in the hospital during the time of the bombing. (The whole family perished in 1943.) Lena offered me money, for she knew that everything I possessed had been burned. I told her I didn't need any. She began crying and put the money into my pocketbook. We went into a house on Mirovska Street which we had left during the first bombardment, and the owner gave us an apartment. As a result of the bombardment, there were no windows, the stairs were broken, all three beds were legless, and there was no light or water. On top of that, it was cold, for we were already into October.

Ruth and I slept in one bed, and Mel and Addy Rosner in the other two. The next morning Addy asked me if he could marry Ruth and move in with some friends who had a warm apartment with running water.

I agreed. I couldn't even provide basic things for Ruth. I gave her a ring with diamonds, my last extra pair of silk underwear, and two cans of sardines that some people had saved from a burning cellar. That was the dowry I provided my only daughter, from whom I had never been separated since her birth (except for the tours, which were of short duration).

When Ruth and Addy left, I sat down and imagined my daughter's wedding under normal circumstances.

Knowing that we were among strangers and under bad conditions, the Lipman family invited us to come to them, even though their two and a half rooms were already occupied by Lipman and his wife, their elder daughter, Anya, and her husband, Isaac Turkov, their younger daughter, and Lipman's parents. The latter had their own apartment, but Lipman wanted the entire family to be together at such a time.

We accepted their offer—just so that we wouldn't be alone.

The next day the Germans were already in Warsaw. We

didn't dare set foot outside; nevertheless, we had to look for a piece of bread, a potato, and water. When I saw a German for the first time, my heart began pounding. The first few days they still were relatively proper. They still didn't know that they could take whatever they wanted from the Jews. My husband walked one and a half miles to the Wisla River for water. A day later, he and our friend Djidek Brandes went with a wheelbarrow to get coal from the railway station.

Anya and I went out to buy food. We met a German who naïvely asked where he could buy a good radio. He didn't know that he could enter any Jew's house and take away his radio and other things as well. The streets were full. Village peasants mingled with city shoppers, and Jews were among them. Some of the Jews carried merchandise draped over their backs, like Hotsmakh in Goldfaden's *Sorceress*.

Suddenly a peasant woman pointed out such a peddler to a German policeman, saying, "German, the Jew has money. The Jew has a lot of money." The policeman struck the Jew on the head several times with his nightstick. I screamed. Anya dragged me away. My knees trembled. I wanted to get home quickly, but Anya still wanted to purchase something.

The Jews shouted to the beaten peddler, "Run with your merchandise! The policeman is coming!"

The peddler answered, "Let him go to hell!"

"He's beating people," cried the other Jews.

"Let him go to hell head first!"

"But he'll take all your goods away!" the other shouted.

"Then let him fry in hell and remain there," the peddler replied with stoic calm. "Tomorrow I'll come back with a new batch of goods."

Farther on we met a policeman examining the license of a Polish peddler. Since the German policeman didn't know Polish, he stopped me and asked me if the license indicated whether the man was a Jew. Even though I saw that he was a Pole, I told the German, "No, it doesn't say anything here about his nationality or religion."

Two days later I met two Jewish women who told me

that they had already been on the other side—that is, on the Soviet side—and that they had returned to take their parents. "Don't you dare remain here. They're waiting for you over there."

In any case, we had already decided to leave Warsaw. My husband and Djidek Brandes began to look for a means of transportation out of Warsaw. I went to visit Ruth, who had caught cold in the chilly apartment we'd lived in. I told her to be ready to leave town as soon as the opportunity presented itself. However, it was difficult to find an opportunity because the prices of private cars and taxis rose from day to day.

During these nights we couldn't sleep at all. Once I heard shouts in German: "Open up!" The woman porter opened the doors. The Germans ran into the courtyard with drunken shouts. Everyone was asleep. I heard the Germans approaching our floor. In the first apartment slept Lipman's parents. His father had an obviously Jewish beard. Here no one could deny that they were Jews. I listened and trembled. A little later we heard a Jew's outcry, accompanied by a German's laughter. I clapped my hands over my ears and restrained myself from waking anyone. When I removed my hands, I heard the Germans departing with the same drunken laughter and the porter shutting the gate after them.

In the morning I discovered that Mrs. Lipman and her youngest daughter had heard everything, too. The woman porter came and told us that the Germans had asked her where Jews were. "Since I wanted to protect you," she said, "I brought them up to a poor Jew, and there the Germans cut away half his beard and took away his watch and several other items."

Later we saw this man with a bandage over half his face and a portable store of merchandise on his back. The porter, of course, asked for a few zlotys as compensation for protecting us. Thus, even during the first days of the German occupation, began the business transactions for human lives.

Again we sought an opportunity to leave Warsaw. Anya

Lipman (her stage name was Litan) and Isaac Turkov were supposed to go, too. Anya's father regretted the fact that some of us were leaving the apartment. In those days one was happier with more people around. Lipman, feeling gloomy, had a talk with me. "Ida, why do you want to leave, and why are you afraid? Don't you know that there are more than half a million Jews here in Warsaw? [Before the war there were 350,000; during the war people came here from smaller towns.] Can you imagine them killing half a million Jews?" he asked me.

"I don't know how they will do it," I replied. "But they will find ways. First they will humiliate us and then kill us." I must admit that when saying this I felt I was exaggerating, but my intuition suggested horrible scenes.

"You're a child!" Lipman said, ending the conversation, and his voice sounded frozen. Soon, he also departed from Warsaw, leaving only his mother and father. Like all others, the old couple perished, too.

One day we learned that two cars had been hired. Ten people would travel together: Mel and I, Ruth and Addy Rosner, Isaac Turkov and Anya, Edushna (Edja) and Djidek Brandes, Rosner's cousin Lothar Lampel, who was a singer in Addy's orchestra, and Moshe Perenson, a teacher who helped in hiring the two cars. The decision was to leave on October 17, 1939, at 5 A.M. The days were short, for after six it was forbidden to appear on the street. The condition of the Jews grew worse from day to day.

I went to say good-bye to all my relatives. The first was my cousin Abraham Halpern, the impresario. He said he was happy that I was leaving. And what about him, I asked. Too late, he said, I'm too old, and he began crying. Then I went to see my former father-in-law, Naphtali Turkov. He wasn't at home, but I saw his twin daughters, as well as Jonas Turkov's wife, Diana Blumenfeld, and her child. I said farewell, sent regards to their father, and left a house full of people who liked me and for whom I had affection.

On the way I met Dr. Mikhael Wichert, a cultural activist and director of the Young Theater.

"What?" he wondered. "Are you leaving now, when there
will be a great opportunity for your work? Now there will
surely be a ghetto here. A Jewish cultural organization. Now
all the assimilated Jews will come to the theater. Stay here!"
I couldn't understand such a view.

The last person to whom I bade farewell was my former
husband, Sigmund Turkov. I attempted to convince him
to leave, too. He replied, "I won't move without my baggage,
plays, and archives. Moreover, whatever happens to the rest
of the Jews will happen to me too." Curiously, all his belongings remained undisturbed in the hotel where he resided
until after the war. In 1942, with the help of David Helfman,
who himself perished, Sigmund managed to escape to Italy.

On the morning of October 16 we suddenly decided to
pick up Mel's fur coat, as well as mine, an expensive broadtail. Luckily, the storehouse remained unscathed. From there
we went by carriage to Ruth's house. I felt strange traveling
through the Warsaw ruins. Suddenly a German stopped us
and took Mel to work at debris removal. I remained alone,
depressed. At Ruth's apartment house I discovered that she
had already moved. The owner did not know her address.

My depression knew no bounds. My husband had been
taken away, I didn't know where my daughter and her
husband were, and tomorrow at dawn we were to depart.
I passed the place where Mel had been taken; I looked about
but couldn't see him. I still had a slight hope that I would
find Mel at home. Soon it would be curfew. I ran up to the
front gate and met my old friend Grisha Rotshein. He was
the son of an actor who had performed with my parents and
later with me in operettas. Seeing me in such a distressed
state, he promised to find out where Ruth and Mel were.

I didn't find Mel at home; then suddenly he appeared. They
had wanted to keep him another day, but Mel told them that
he was a Ukrainian and wanted to go home. A German who

knew some Ukrainian tested him to see if he knew Galicia and the Ukrainian language. Since my husband knew it excellently, they let him go. Soon after, my children came and I calmed down.

That evening our dear friend David Helfman came to say good-bye. We had been so close over the years, sharing the good and the bad. Now he didn't want to come along. His excuse was that he didn't want to leave his mother, but behind this excuse lay another: his great love for Edja, who was going to leave with her present husband, Djidek Brandes.

While David was visiting us, we heard a knock on the door. I was astounded to see Mrs. Slapak, an editor of *Nashe Slovo*. Such a late visit! She called me to the corridor and whispered, "Leave immediately."

"I'm leaving at dawn," I said.

"Leave earlier," she urged, "because this night can be a dangerous one." She knew that the Germans had compiled a list of the people who were to be arrested first, and she was telling me confidentially that my name was on that list, among the directors who had produced anti-Hitler plays.

I was touched by the visit of this Polish woman who had dared to come visit me so late. I thanked her heartily and sent her home so that she would arrive before the dangerous hour. Indeed, she arrived home safely, but two years later she was killed along with several other Polish intellectuals.

That night I couldn't fall asleep. It was quiet, but every sound in the street made me nervous. Were they coming after me? Would they stop us the next morning as we were leaving? Moreover, we were told that the road we had chosen was patrolled, and those suspected of escaping the Germans were tortured. Patrols and searches didn't scare me at all, but torture did.

16

Fleeing

AT dawn we took our two valises with our belongings. I wore my fur coat and over it a raincoat. Mel left his fur coat behind to reduce his burden. Precisely at 5 A.M. we all met at the gate. My cousin Lena Brodaty came to say good-bye to us, accompanied by one of her sons. The other had already gone over to the "other side." I never saw either of them again.

It was October 17, 1939, a beautiful sunny day. With hearts pounding, we entered the cars.

We began to journey, our faces masked with happy expressions in our attempt to cheer one another up. Sad faces are a sign of Jewishness. On the way we encountered large groups of people who were working on the streets, guarded by Germans. We feared they might remove the men from our car, but the first two dozen miles passed without incident. Near the village of Yadoveh the Germans had blocked the road. "Halt! All Jews out at once!"

I just had time to quickly tell my fellow passengers, "No fear and no tears."

"Who are you?" the Germans asked.

"Actors."

"All Jews are actors," one of the Germans called out. I thought to myself, perhaps he's right.

We were ordered to display all our belongings. Addy Rosner and his cousin spoke better German than the man who stood before us. Rosner showed his trumpet, his pictures and posters in German. There was also a bottle of cognac among the packages. Rosner had received this in Warsaw from Germans who had commissioned him to play for them several days hence. Later we learned that when they came—after his departure—and did not find him home, they demolished his apartment.

Addy gave them the bottle of cognac, which they could have taken in any case. He talked nonstop until they finally told us to repack and continue on our way. The Polish chauffeurs couldn't get over it. It was the first time, they said, that Jews were not beaten or robbed. Our only discomfort, then, had been a fright. Addy felt quite self-confident and said, "The Germans I can handle. It's the Russians I'm afraid of. I don't know if they'll let us in." I was not afraid. I knew Russian very well and hoped we would be able to cross to Bialystok.

The chauffeurs led us to a place called Malkin and said that they couldn't go any farther. About two miles from that point was the demarcation line between the German and Soviet zones. I asked them to drive closer, but they refused. They said that the other day the Germans had shot a chauffeur at that very spot. We drove into the village square with the two limousines as though we were going to a wedding. Peasants stood in front of their small houses. Most of them were women, for the men were busily engaged in taking Jews across the border. This was good business for them. A woman ran over to us and invited us to her house. Her husband, she said, would take us over to the other side. It so happened that today the Soviets were permitting entry.

We entered the woman's house, which had two small rooms. She prepared tea and a light meal. In one room lay a wounded Polish soldier whom the villagers had taken in.

All of us had come into the hut except Rosner and Lothar, who stayed outside to look around. I left the house for a while. There stood a Pole who told me softly, "Don't stay here. There's a train station close by where the Germans are doing horrible things to the Jews. This woman just wants to earn some money from you. She could be the cause of your undoing."

"What should we do?" I asked.

"Take your belongings and go through the forest here. The border is near, and it's open."

I returned to the hut and told this to my friends. Addy and Lothar were not there. Somewhat carelessly I asked the lady of the house, "What's happening at the railway station?"

"Nothing," she said. "There's some work going on over there, but the Germans won't come here."

Just then, ironically enough, two Germans entered, followed by Addy and Lothar, both of whom were pale. "Oh, here they are!" called out a short, fat, bespectacled German. "Come! Come with us! All of you! We need people for work."

"Women, too?" someone asked.

"Everyone," the German answered and then, pointing to me, Ruth, and Djidek Brandes, added, "Except you. After all, you are ethnic Germans, so you can remain."

At this point my untimely sense of honor rose to the fore, and I added, "No, we, too, are Jews."

"Then all of you take your bundles and move on."

Rosner then whispered in French, "Leave your money and valuables here." I pushed my pocketbook, which hardly had any money, into the bed. My husband took one bundle on his shoulders, and we left. Then the German pointed to our two suitcases. The lady of the house said sweetly to him, "They're mine; they're mine."

We went out into the beautiful sunny day to the train station, thinking dark thoughts. The blond German walked alongside me and asked, "Where did you learn such good German?" His use of the personal "thou" form of address shocked me, but remembering that we were almost at the threshold of the frontier, I restrained myself and answered, "I know several languages."

Silently we crossed the tracks and immediately found ourselves at the damaged railway station. Even from afar we heard the noise of a crowd: many Polish men and women mingling with about twenty Germans. One of the men accompanying us called out, "We are leading the chosen people." The reply was a derisive burst of laughter and hoots from the mass of people.

Then a tall, horrible-looking man with a rectangular, horselike face emerged from the group of Germans. In his long paw he held a revolver. With his other hand he pointed at my husband, spinning the revolver on his trigger finger. "Give me all your money," he shouted. "Later I'm going to make an inspection. If I find one zloty on you, I'm going to put a bullet in your brain."

We all stood petrified. My daughter emitted a cry, "Mama!" We all began looking in our pockets, giving everything away, up to the last zloty. My husband attempted to engage the monstrous German in conversation.

"The Führer has given permission to each individual who leaves the German zone to take up to twenty zlotys with him."

The monster's reply was a wild shout. "Shut up, Jew! Don't you dare mention the Führer's name. Hand over all your money. Every penny is going to help our people through the winter campaign."

Mel diligently searched through all his pockets and gave every zloty away. How great was our surprise when, on the other side, he discovered in a pajama pocket twenty zlotys of which he did not know. Had the ugly German discovered this, who knows what he would have done to Mel.

This was not the end. The Germans asked us to open up our valises. They fell onto our belongings and viciously pulled out silk shirts, slippers, socks, even playing cards.

"Is this also to help you through your winter campaign?" I asked. The short fat German who had brought us here smiled and slipped the cards into his pocket. Then the Germans threw the lingerie and women's things to the waiting Poles, who fought one another for every little item. The Germans looked on with great pleasure as the Poles, recently so tragically defeated, beat one another for things the Germans threw to them.

Then came an order for the women to sit down on the wet bare ground.

"The men will go wash down the cars till they shine." We then saw them through the windows they were washing. They ran with pails to a water pump eighty yards away. They did all this speedily in order to finish sooner.

Meanwhile, the short fat German returned to us. "You haven't hungered enough," he told Edja. "Too fat. What do you have down there?" Over her fur coat she had sewn a raincoat. He touched her coat and screamed, "Take it off!" practically tearing off both coats from her. He took the fur coat away and returned the raincoat.

This incensed me and I said, "I also have one," and I showed him my broadtail fur.

"Oh," the German said to me, "you're thin. I'll let you keep yours." Then, pointing to Edja, he said, "She'll be warm anyway without hers. I've got an ethnic German woman here who has a fever," he justified himself.

Whenever our women began to cry, I would say, "Don't cry." We sat on the ground next to a wall, while the men worked. The two Germans who had removed us from the peasant's hut would occasionally approach and look bemusedly at us. I asked them why we were sitting here so long. One of them said that when the men finished working, the women would begin.

Suddenly a young German with a skull patch on his sleeve came to us. He was accompanied by a young blond Polish woman. With bestial anger, he screamed, "Take off that fur!" and grabbed my hand.

I tore my hand out of his and said, "I will take the coat off myself."

This didn't satisfy the wild German. Seeing our scattered things, which had already been searched once, he shouted, "Whose things are these?"

"Ours," I replied. "They've already been inspected once."

"Inspected?" he shouted again. "Take everything away. All these valises and bags." Those who stood about dived into the items and, of course, took them away.

Once again I appealed to the women, "Just no tears."

As I write these memoirs and consider what happened to us then, I realize it was nothing compared to the cruelties that millions of Jews experienced later under the German occupation. Nevertheless, at the time, our encounter with the Germans was a shock.

Standing thus, already robbed, we suddenly heard to our left a voice saying in Polish, "Poor people, what have you fallen into? Since Sunday this place has been a hell." From the man's dress, it was apparent that he was formerly a railway employee. He looked to the side as he spoke, to make it seem he was not talking to us.

I replied in the same fashion. "What will they do to us?"

"I don't think that any harm will befall you," he said. "Somehow you look different. After the men finish their work, a train will come and then they'll let you go."

Then the short fat German approached us again, along with two others. I complained that he let me keep my fur coat and that the other man took it from me. My daughter interrupted me, saying in Polish, "Mama, who are you talking to?" The German understood the word "Mama." He laughed. "Mama! Looks like your sister!" He then pointed to Ruth and said, "She is pretty. Beautiful!"

My heart began to pound. In Warsaw, I remembered, people said that at the Malkin station the Germans took girls into the wagons and raped them. Perhaps we women should flee, I thought. The Germans still stood there. The shorter one tried to justify himself. "I'll tell you why we are doing this. Because the Jews are responsible for the war. They wanted it. Jews are ninety percent responsible for it."

"Who are the other ten percent?" I asked. The German thought for a while and mumbled, "The Poles."

"Then why did you take one hundred percent of our belongings and give them away?" I asked. "At least give us back ten percent."

The German looked at me, smiled, and departed with his colleagues. Anya Lipman said they would surely bring back some of our things. I talked about fleeing as soon as possible, for I still kept thinking of my daughter, but the other women maintained that we dare not leave our men alone.

Turning around, I noticed another German standing and gazing at us. On his face there was a different expression. His uniform was apparently of a higher rank. "I'm going to talk to him," I told the women.

"No, Mama!" Ruth held me back. "You see that they're not human beings."

My reply was "But this man has human eyes." I approached him. The women followed me. He was a blond-haired German, wearing glasses, beneath which I noticed eyes full of tears.

"Don't think that all Germans are heartless," he said, his voice trembling. "My heart is breaking."

From everyone's eyes the hitherto restrained tears suddenly gushed forth. Now I no longer said, "Don't cry." I turned to him. "*Mensch*, help us."

"What can I do alone?" he replied. I asked him to help us secure our release from here. Then he crossed the tracks and from afar motioned to us to follow him. I was afraid that all of us crossing the tracks would be noticed by the Germans and the Poles, who were standing farther off. Nearby there was a gate at which a German with a rifle stood guard. I walked up to him determinedly and told him that everything had been taken from us and that we would like to leave. The German shrugged his shoulders as though to say, well, go if you want to. I motioned to my women, and we all went through the gate. The German guard played dumb. Farther on, another German stopped us and asked, "Where to?" I actually screamed that we'd been given permission, and we left.

I don't know how we managed to reach the hut from which we had been taken. The two cars were still there—the cause of our falling into the Germans' hands. These limousines had made the Poles wide-eyed, and they informed on us. There were various types of Poles, including those with compassion and those who wanted to profit from somebody else's misfortune. As we had just seen, there were people with considerate hearts, but they were very few.

In the hut everybody looked for their belongings. I asked about my two little valises and the house mistress told me she had hidden both beneath a bed in another room. She told us that her husband had come back from his first tour and that as soon as our men returned he would immediately go with us to the border. The period of waiting lasted only twenty minutes, but it seemed like hours to us.

As soon as the men returned, they said, "Quick. Run. Let's go. Is there someone to take us?"

"Yes," we said.

"Then let's move."

We immediately made ready to leave. (The men told us that when they had finished their work, the Germans ordered them to wash their hands and go.) The women climbed up on the wagon with their few remaining belongings, and the men followed on foot. The peasant driving us instructed: "If you look cheerful and laugh, they won't bother you." Despite our feelings, we play-acted, pretending we were happy.

My husband told Djidek, "Of course we can be happy now. We don't have any luggage to worry about." Then I reminded Mel that we still had two suitcases, which was still something. Whereupon Mel called out, "What? Where?" It turned out that in our haste we had forgotten the two little suitcases in the other room of the hut. Mel wanted to turn back and get them, but at this point everyone raised a tumultuous protest. They would not permit it. The peasant assured us he would bring the suitcases to the border point later.

"We'll soon be at the border," he said.

Suddenly we heard a shout from the distance. "Halt!"

"What do we do now?" the peasant asked.

"Drive on!" we shouted. "Quickly!"

The wagon proceeded and the men ran behind it. Just behind we saw a sign in Russian and German: Demarcation Line.

"No more Germans here," the peasant said.

Now we no longer needed orders to be happy. We all embraced and began to kiss one another.

The peasant pointed to two Soviet soldiers approaching in the distance. We jumped off the wagon and ran to them. Seeing the five-pointed stars on their caps, tears of joy began flowing from our eyes. We were liberated people who had just escaped the greatest peril and were now standing on safe ground.

The soldiers asked us why we were crying and where we wanted to go.

"To you," we replied.

"By all means," the Red soldiers said.

Djidek Brandes, Rosner, and his cousin did not understand Russian. Full of curiosity, they asked what the soldiers had said, and we explained. Now, no longer able to restrain themselves, they fell upon the necks of the Soviet soldiers and asked them where we were to go now. They pointed to a nearby place.

We paid the peasant for his service and told him that if he would bring us the two forgotten suitcases, he would get further payment.

We removed everything from the wagon and hurriedly ran through a wide gate. At a table, in the middle of a field, a soldier wrote down the names of everyone who had crossed the frontier. Other soldiers stood there, as well as Jews who, like us, had escaped hell. Some of them were bloodied but with happy faces. Along with other questions, the soldier asked if anyone had belonged to the Communist party. Among the Jews, one of them boasted that he was indeed in the party.

The soldier asked him, "What is your name?"

"Greenberg," the Jew replied.

"Greenberg? Greenberg? I've never heard of such a man. I've heard of Marx, Dimitrov, but not of Greenberg," the soldier said quite seriously.

Soon Addy Rosner began to play the trumpet that he had brought safely through the German side. His triumphant tones attracted the interest not only of those who stood by the side of the gate but also of the Germans who stood on the other side. At first I did not notice the Germans, but then when I saw them talking to the Soviet soldiers (I don't know what language they used, perhaps the international tongue of commerce), all my joy vanished. I mentioned this to my women, who sat next to me on a bench. Ruth suggested that we explain to the Soviet soldiers that the German soldiers were the enemies not only of the Jews but also of the Russians.

"Don't worry, they know this, too," said Edja.

At this point Anya Lipman laughed and said, "Don't be silly! This is no flirtation. The Germans want to get some military secret from them, and the Russians simply want to buy something: a bit of clothing, a shirt, a watch. Just look at them. Look at the Germans' appearance and look at theirs. Didn't you see through the Soviet soldier's dry welcome: 'By all means!' when we told him we were coming to the Russians? It's as though he said, 'Yes, some bargain.' The Soviet soldiers are talking to the Germans to see if there's a chance of crossing over into their territory."

These cynical words agitated us, especially at a time when we had just been saved from the Germans' murderous hands.

One could not be angry too long at Anya, however, for she was an unending source of blitheness and humor.

Immediately after registration, we were permitted to go to the railroad station and travel to Bialystok. We all decided to wait for our bit of baggage, which the peasant promised to bring us. We thought it would be worth waiting until evening and perhaps even until the next morning. So we sat down on the grass and only then learned from the men what they had done in the wagons.

The Germans had sent Jewish men to clean up the cars because typhus patients had previously lain there. The Germans didn't give our men any utensils to clean the cars with. They had to do everything, even clean the toilets, with their own hands. When Rosner nicked his finger and asked for a bandage, he was told, "It makes no difference. It's only impure Jewish blood." Nevertheless, when they finished their work and their guard was pleased, he ordered them to wash their hands. He feared that if someone remained with the Germans, he might pass the disease on to one of them. The men had also seen our fur coats and other belongings taken from us. Then we found out that five hundred dollars —a fortune at the time—had been sewn into Perenson's knapsack, which had also been taken away. We learned, too, that the Germans had sought us out in the hut because Addy Rosner and his cousin had walked through town speaking German. By meeting them, then, the Germans had discovered our presence.

We no longer expected the peasant to return. Indeed, he did not come back, and so we were left without belongings and without money, which also remained in the peasant's hut. My son-in-law, Addy, said, "The main thing is that I've still got my trumpet and my mouthpiece."

In the evening we found a peasant hut where we spent the night, some in beds, some on the floor. Only in the morning did we first see in what sort of filth we had slept, so we quickly left the hut for the hired wagon and went to the train station.

The name of the village was Zavisty Dzikie. It was a beautiful autumn day. We rode to the train station loudly singing Yiddish songs. The train was packed. We barely made it into the wagon and stood in the corridor, but what did we care, if we were able to leave Hitler's hell. The train moved very slowly. We told jokes and, in our hunger for laughter, laughed hysterically.

We finally arrived in Bialystok at night. The streets were dark. The city teemed with people, most of them Russian soldiers. Bialystok was unrecognizable. Every place was overcrowded, but finally we found a spot in a small café, thanks to the fact that we had been recognized. We kept meeting people we knew from Warsaw and other cities. We met my old friend Aaron Irlicht. He was without his wife, who had remained in Warsaw.

When my husband and I tried to find a room in the beautiful Hotel Ritz, where for years we had been steady clients, the manager told us regretfully, "Don't you understand? Now it's no longer what it used to be. Now there are ten to twelve soldiers in a room. Everything is broken, filthy. I don't even have a room for myself, but I still have to stay here."

Our entire family then went to Helfman's relatives. They received us cordially, but there was no use in thinking about normal sleep or bedding. The apartment was in a terrible state, and to top it off, there were also dogs, cats, and cockroaches. Just like the city itself, apartments had turned into hovels.

At six in the morning I phoned the manager of the Ritz Hotel to arrange baths for all of us. "Not easy," he replied, "but for you I'll do my best." In the Ritz we took turns using the tub. It was already cold outside, and we had to put on our old, nearly wet clothes. We thanked the manager and then once more went to the café. Here again we met friends and actors, and through them we were able to rent a clean private room. (In Warsaw, I was told, a rumor spread that at the border I had been stripped naked and sent to

Germany. They had heard something, and the fantasy, supported by the well-known German cruelty, added the rest.)

Meanwhile, the news of my presence in Bialystok had been broadcast over the radio, and everyone knew of it in town. I was invited to the city's Cultural Affairs Department, where I was asked to organize a theater. At first a collective base was planned, but soon thereafter, I was promised, it would have governmental support.

I neither refused nor accepted, wanting to delay my decision until Addy Rosner could go to Lemberg (Lvov), where he was very popular. Incidentally, my husband was also drawn to Lemberg, where his brothers lived (one was serving in the Polish army), and to the nearby town of Zholkiev, where his father lived. My name, too, was known in Lemberg, and in any case, Lemberg was a much bigger city than Bialystok.

We were all given documents, on the basis of which we were able to vote for the town council. On the third day of our stay in Bialystok, Edja's husband, Djidek Brandes, fell ill. He developed a high fever—typhus. He had caught it by cleaning the typhus-infected cars.

Meanwhile, the peasant who had driven us to the border sent us our documents, the only things that had remained from our baggage. "The Germans took everything else away from me," he informed us.

Ruth, Addy, and Lothar went to Lemberg to see what they could discover there. Mel, too, went for four days. At this point, Bialystok Jewish merchants, having learned that we had been robbed, told me that I could take what I wanted free of charge. They knew that in any case everything would be taken away—nationalized. I took only a coat for Anya, who was wearing mine, and one for Edja, who had none. I didn't take more because I considered this a donation, one of my conventional prewar complexes.

Other people came to me with the suggestion that we travel farther. My family and I were promised everything we wanted until our arrival "somewhere" on the other side of the ocean, but I declined. It seemed absurd to me. Why should I leave? I had finally arrived in a land where everyone was equal, where Jews were treated equitably, where I was offered a proposal to lead a Yiddish state theater that had hitherto been only a dream. Should I leave all this and seek a place where I could become rich? That never had impressed me.

Djidek Brandes's condition continually worsened. Edja became despondent. We had seen much misfortune all about us, but when it came to personal tragedy, it was hard to justify it with the expression "Everyone's sorrow is half a consolation."

Mel returned and we decided to go to Lemberg. "That city too is not what it used to be," he said, "but it's no comparison to Bialystok." Moreover, I had been invited to direct a theater there. I didn't have to think this over too long, especially since my daughter was there and Addy was already performing in the Café Bagatelle and had achieved a great success with the Soviet audience.

Saying good-bye to those who remained behind was heartbreaking. Edja sat by her dying husband, and I came in to bid him farewell. Isaac Turkov and Anya had to remain behind, too, because they were waiting for Anya's parents, the Lipmans, who were expected from Warsaw.

My veteran stage manager, Chaim Goldzader, had just arrived in Bialystok, and he would accompany us for several years. Good actors and friends of my theater also arrived: Adam Domb and his wife, Sonia Altboim, as well as Leon Herbst. A large group of people from my theater had gathered, and after my arrival in Lemberg, I invited them to come there, too.

From the one-time pleasant Jewish city of Bialystok, now so radically altered, we moved to Lemberg. The trip was an awful one, perhaps because we rode the train without payment. The wagons were overcrowded. The train stopped for hours at certain stations. We had to change trains twice and sleep in a small town. It was difficult to secure food or coffee along the way. When we entered a café to have a glass of tea or a cup of coffee for breakfast, Russian soldiers and officers were already drinking bowls of soup and having several glasses of beer. The Russian women we continually met always stopped me. They touched my coat, dress, pocketbook, hat, and constantly asked the same question: "Do you want to sell?" All this was very strange to me. The clothes on my back were the only things I owned, dating back to the first weeks of the war. And they, who did not experience war, had none of these items. How could it be? This was the first of my naïve surprises. Finally, after two long days, we arrived in Lemberg.

We went to Mel's older brother, Mark Melman, and were admitted by his Polish housekeeper. She told us that Mark was visiting his father and his other brothers who lived in Zholkiev, thirty kilometers from Lemberg. Mark's wife, Basha, a physician, was working at the hospital. What a joy it was to come into the apartment! At long last, a beautiful, clean home! First we phoned Basha, and then we ran to see Ruth and Addy, who lived at the Hotel Bristol. It was very difficult in those times to get a hotel room, but for Addy Rosner many things were easier than for other citizens. The clean city of Lemberg, too, had changed; nevertheless, it was cleaner than Bialystok. As in Bialystok, the radio loudspeakers on the Lemberg streets continually thundered into one's ears. On these streets we, especially Mel, met many friends.

My daughter was not feeling well at the time, but it was a joy for all of us to see one another. Addy was earning good money performing at the Café Bagatelle, which had not yet been nationalized. Many Russians visited the club, especially groups of high-ranking government officials, and many made offers to Addy to found a state jazz orchestra under his direction.

We visited the Arts Department, a section of the Ukrainian Ministry of Arts, and were very warmly received. The department head told me that the Yiddish theater, like all others, would soon be supported by the regime. Meanwhile, I was appointed the director of the existing theater and was also offered some money, which I sorely needed. I requested that they inform the Bialystok Cultural Affairs Department that I would not be able to return there. The department head responded that they had word from Bialystok that another director had already been appointed because an order had come from Moscow that I should be the director of the Lemberg theater.

From there we went to the Yiddish theater in order to meet the actors. When we arrived, they were rehearsing *Uncle Tom*, directed by a well-known Polish director, Bronislaw Dombrovsky. I wanted to wait for a break in the rehearsal, but the actors spontaneously stopped and rushed to gather around me.

Dombrovsky turned to me and said, "I beg you to come help me here. We have talented actors, but there are also some who like to insert little songs, bits of scenes, and jokes into the plays. I don't want to fight with them, but I cannot permit this."

After the rehearsal I spoke at length with the actors, among whom were several excellent performers including Simcha Natan, his wife, daughter, and son-in-law, as well as several others who had performed with me until the outbreak of the war. I tried as delicately as possible to have them understand what Dombrovsky requested of me but I sensed that my words were not enthusiastically accepted. When I later showed them the letter of appointment as director of the theater, a few of them received this with sincere joy. Later, however, I discovered that after my departure part of the troupe cast fire and brimstone at me. They asserted that I was "a capitalistic director who exploited actors," that I had my own theater building in Warsaw, and that they would go to the proper authorities and do what was necessary, even create a separate state theater.

I couldn't understand this at all. Perhaps this happened

because I was a stranger. Most of the people in the theater were Galician Jews and feared I might do an injustice to the local actors by favoring those who had played for me in Poland. Objectively speaking, the latter were indeed of a higher intellectual and artistic rank but I was far from doing anyone an injustice.

A few days later everyone was very "sweet" to me.

In Lemberg stores, too, I was offered various merchandise, and people wanted to sell me items on credit—precious things, even furs. This pleased me, but again I declined.

We lived at Mark and Basha Melman's apartment. Mark, who managed a factory in Zholkiev at that time, often told with humor and satire how he got along with the Russians. As a one-time factory owner, he didn't find it easy. Nevertheless, the Russians liked and admired him for his diligence, organizational ability, and captivating humor. He would often paraphrase popular proverbs and attribute them to Lenin and Stalin. The Russians would accept these as authentic statements of the two Soviet authorities. For all his quotes, they would say, "Correct. That's just what he said."

17

The First Yiddish State Theater

MY husband and I would sit for hours on end at the state Cultural Affairs Department in order to learn the method of organizing a state theater, which in 1940 was something new for us. I included in the ensemble the good actors who had fled from Warsaw. This was a gain for the theater, but the "Lembergers" could not forgive me for this. Their fear of strong artistic competition superseded their natural feelings of compassion for colleagues who had left their homes, some of them their wives and children, in their desire not to remain under Hitler's rule. I wanted to bring Edja from Bialystok; she had all the qualifications of being a good administrator, but she didn't want to leave the grave of her recently deceased husband, Djidek.

Along with the administrator of the Lemberg theater, Gershon Roth, we decided upon the categories of salaries for the actors. We were requested to do this by the Cultural Affairs Department. Once again a storm rose among the Lemberg actors, who argued that I didn't know their worth well enough to decide their salaries.

I knew that this could cause some anguish, so at the first meeting I declared, "If we see that errors have been made they will be quickly corrected." Although I explained again that because of the war I intended to have all the actors residing in Lemberg employed in their profession, a net of enmity toward me was spun by some of the actors. The reason was narrow egoism and a provincial prejudice against those who came from the capital city. This reminded me somewhat of 1919 in Russia.

I wanted to begin my artistic activity with a new play. I found out that the theater of the Red Army had staged *My Son*, by a Hungarian dramatist, Sandor Gergely, an immigrant to the Soviet Union. As soon as I received the play in Russian from the theater, I immediately translated it and began rehearsals. The male lead, a very dramatic role, was assigned to Simcha Natan, who was a very popular and excellent comic character actor, but he grew frightened and suspected me of desiring his downfall. At that time I had no one else for the role, so I assured Natan that we would both work together and the result would be a good one. This indeed was the case. Natan surprised everyone with his interpretation.

Since we were not presenting plays during that period, we had time for afternoon and evening rehearsals, and since the actors worked diligently and learned the roles quickly, we were ready to start performances after two weeks. I notified the Cultural Affairs Department and invited them to the general dress rehearsal.

"What? Already the premiere? What kind of potboiler are you putting on?" asked Lehyin, the head of the theater section.

I felt very insulted and, in the presence of several officials, answered, "How dare you speak to me like this? It's your duty to come here, and you have the right to prohibit the performance if you really will judge it to be a potboiler, but you have no right to prejudge it. Young man, you know the theater of one land, and I know the theater of all of Europe. When I began to direct plays, you didn't even know what theater is."

In retrospect, these words were perhaps a bit too sharp, both in form and in content. My answer, however, in front of eyewitnesses, quickly spread among Polish actors, and they quietly expressed their amazement at my daring. Lehyin attended the general dress rehearsal and later came backstage. He apologized profusely and expressed his astonishment at my directing and acting. He congratulated all the participants, especially Natan and my husband, Meir (Mel) Melman, who was a great success in the role of the son. Lehyin declared that he would send all the Russian critics and actors to see the performance. This was my first satisfaction, for both Mel and my sister-in-law, Basha, were certain that after the fuss I had raised with the Soviet power I would either be arrested or, as was the custom at the time, be sent to exile.

At that time the Soviet leaders filled responsible positions with people they trusted who also happened to be looking for good jobs. So the administrative managers in our theater were changed several times, which pleased me, for I had rid myself of this burden. Mel, who was my formal representative, was pleased, too.

My energies were devoted mostly to the artistic aspect, and I had several successful productions. Among them was *The Sheep Well*, by Lope de Vega. In Warsaw this play had been presented more elaborately and on a larger stage, but nevertheless it was a very great spectacle.

A short while later the Soviet administrative director called me and said that according to Soviet law one person could not receive wages for two positions; I had to decide whether I wanted to be artistic director or an actress. My reply was that I would prefer to remain the director.

"No, this can't be," he interrupted me. "In no case will we agree to your resignation as an actress in this theater."

"Well, then, you've decided for me yourself."

At this point the administrative director declared that the Cultural Affairs Department also wanted me to continue staging plays. For each play I directed, they would pay a separate honorarium. Then he related the real reason for our conversation: the artistic director of the theater had to be a man from "the other side." Besides, the Yiddish theater in Dnepropetrovsk (formerly Yekaterinoslav) had been dissolved, and several actors plus a director were being sent to Lemberg. Therefore, some actors would have to be dismissed from the current ensemble. At this point I became angry. "What? Are you going to fire people who live here and who have performed here for years? Is this just?"

"What can we do?" the administrative director interrupted me good-naturedly. "If you saw wood, you get sawdust. You'll have to admit that these are not ordinary times."

"Indeed the times are not ordinary," I replied. With these words I ended the conversation and left the room. However, at the same time I was pleased that I was no longer the director and bore no responsibility for this.

The directors changed continuously. First there was a Russian, then a Jew, then a Ukrainian, and then once again a Jew, Isaac Zaiken, who remained until the end, that is, until the outbreak of hostilities with the Germans. Zaiken was an intelligent, good-humored person, but a man of limited ability in the theater.

My husband was chosen as vice-president of the professional organization of theater artists in Western Ukraine, a paid position. Therefore, he only performed occasionally in the theater, receiving an honorarium for each performance.

There were three directors: one permanent and two freelance. One was the well-known Soviet director Boris Litvinov, who staged for us *The Banquet*, which, however, was not a first-rate play. Its author, the beloved Peretz Markish, was a far better poet than dramatist.

The group from Dnepropetrovsk was generally good, but it contained few talented performers. Their acting style was in sharp contrast to ours. When they had become "citizens," they called meetings in order to elect a new committee—a professional organization of all the workers and employees in an enterprise, without exception. Decisions of the committee carried great weight concerning working conditions. The plan of the theater had to have the committee's approval, and they were not only representatives but also comanagers.

To my great amazement, I was almost unanimously chosen as the chairman of this committee, even though I was not a party member. I couldn't understand this. I knew that there were people who were agitating against me, even among the Dnepropetrovsk people, and suddenly there came such a surprise. I attempted to decline, but I was informed that this would be considered sabotage, a word that chilled one with fear. Well, what could I do? I remained the chairman. I opened all the meetings and performances and held speeches, which pleased the Dniepropietrovsk group. However, they called my attention to the fact that I never mentioned the "father of peoples—Stalin," that I did not speak of our fatherland, the Soviet Union, and, in general, that I shouted no praises and "Long live!"

I refrained from doing this not because I was in opposition. On the contrary, at that time I had much faith in and trust in the new regime. I just simply couldn't bear any of these remarks and couldn't stand listening to them from anyone else.

In 1940 and 1941 many artists and writers came to Lemberg from Moscow and Leningrad. Others, from theaters in various towns in the Soviet Union, made guest appearances. Among the writers was my old friend Peretz Markish, a man beautiful both in appearance and in poetic talent.

Events in the world interested us very much. We knew that news in the Soviet press was one-sided, molded to propaganda needs, and we listened almost nightly to my brother-in-law's radio and tuned in the BBC in German. We also listened to Radio Germany. On rare occasions we were able to catch Radio Jerusalem. For me this was a very emotional experience because my only brother, Yosef, was in Palestine, and I had been unable to correspond with him since the beginning of the war. Of course, we also tuned in Radio Moscow in Russian.

Writing down the news of the various countries, all of which was broadcast at the same time, would have been grotesque and a lesson in perfidy as well. It would have mirrored lies and unconscionable licentiousness. The BBC would inform us about the persecution of the Jews (incidentally, only at the beginning of the war). From Germany we would hear about the Thousand-Year Reich and its great leader. And Radio Moscow in 1940 would praise "the understanding between Soviet Russia and Germany as a foundation for peace in eastern Europe." As proof of the decline of capitalism, they would point to the defeats of France and England.

Late one night I heard a violin concerto. I told my sister-in-law, Basha, "I accompanied my brother once for this piece. The violin sounds like my brother's playing." I couldn't tear myself away from the radio. At the end of the concert I heard in English, to my great joy: "You've just heard Grieg's Violin Concerto performed by Yosef Kaminsky."

I had a similar experience when one day I received a letter from Addy Rosner in Bialystok telling me the date and time his orchestra and singers would perform on the radio. We all tuned in and heard a woman singing in Russian but with an accent. At the end of the song the announcer stated that the singer had been Ruth Kaminska. This surprised me, for I hadn't known that Ruth was singing with Rosner's ensemble.

18

Understanding Less and Less

AMONG the visitors to Lemberg two months earlier were the noted film directors Sergei Gerasimov and Friedrich Ermler. They showed their finest films for actors, delivered introductory remarks, and then asked the audience for questions. Many asked questions in Polish, which were translated, and Ermler wrote them down. He was a lovely, intelligent person with European manners. He showed his famous film about Sergei Kirov, a well-known Bolshevik leader, the boss of the Leningrad party, who was assassinated by another Bolshevik. This scene appears at the end of the film, but no one knows the identity of the murderer, except the audience. When people bid good-bye to the coffin of the slain Kirov, his assassins pass by with mournful faces.

I asked one of my naïve questions. "The acting is very good, and the film is well-directed, but the scenario isn't clear. We see the enemies of the regime, but the film doesn't explain *why* they are the enemies. After all, they, too, are plain workers, proletarians, so why are they destructive elements?"

The discussion had to be adjourned just then, for the stage was needed for a show and I also had to leave for my own performance, and it was decided to meet later that evening in the same theater. When I returned after my performance, the audience had already gathered in the huge, fully packed room. Ermler was just beginning to answer the previously

asked questions. Every question was answered except mine.
I reminded him of this.

"Oh, yes." He thought a while and then replied curtly,
"Why don't you read the short course of the party's history?"
The short course—Stalin himself was one of the authors—
was the political bible of that time, which no one dared
doubt.

Indeed I did read that history, and I was astounded. How
could history be perverted in such fashion? How could the
name of Trotsky be eradicated from the history of the rev-
olutionary period? How could events be falsified that I—and
not only I but the entire Russian people—was eyewitness to?
The short course not only explained nothing to me, but it
confounded me as well.

Subsequently, I began to see other incomprehensible things.
People would come from deep inside the Soviet Union and
tell about the dire need there, the apathy of the masses, and
the spreading hatred against the Jews. They also told horrible things about the trials of 1937-38, the inquisitorial meth-
ods of investigation, and other like incidents.

The clean city of Lemberg became dirtier and dirtier, and
the lines in front of the stores ever longer and longer. One
day, while sitting in a formerly elegant restaurant that was
now very neglected, we noticed a young Red Army soldier.
Several bottles of beer stood before him on the table, as
though he feared an impending shortage. The soldier asked
Mel and me to join him at the table.

"Poles?" he asked.

"No," we answered in Russian. "Jews."

"Well," he said, "we protect Jews, too."

"What does he mean?" I asked Mel. "Why does he say
'Jews too'?"

Then came the era of "exile." At first, supposedly only
former Polish military personnel were sent away, but later
their families were exiled, too. Next came the turn of peo-

ple who came from Hitler-occupied Poland—those who did not want Soviet passports but were waiting for the end of the war to return home. Under the pretext that they might be dangerous to the Soviet regime, tens of thousands were exiled for hard labor to the Arctic regions. Were it not for the German-Russian war, which started one year later, these people would have remained in exile forever. Poles as well as Jews, even rabbis, were exiled. Many Jews, fearing this exile, returned home to Nazi Poland, where they found death.

The time came to elect a new committee for the theater. I declared that I was not offering my candidacy, and as though in spite, they unanimously re-elected me. I then declared that I would not come to any of the meetings. Several days later I was summoned to a party meeting, even though I was not a party member. I was informed that I was committing sabotage and that repressive measures could be taken against me.

My reply was a question: "What right do you have to carry out a judgment without even asking me the cause of this so-called sabotage?" When they asked, I responded that there was much I didn't understand and disagreed with. How, then, could I be a representative of such an important group? The director, Zaiken, realized that the discussion should come to an end. I must admit that I was somewhat frightened. As it turned out, my forthright stance made a strong impression.

19

My Political "Career"

A few days after my last conversation with Zaiken, I
met him along with several representatives of the party
committee. Zaiken asked me why I had made that remark.

"Because I'm confused," I replied. "You may be right,
but there are quite a number of things I don't understand
and don't agree with. So how can I give political directives if
I don't understand them? That's why I am requesting to be
freed of this responsibility. I'll do everything necessary. I
will direct, I will act, and I will help out, but I will no longer
serve as the political director."

A long silence followed, and they replied that they would
give me an answer. However, they did not. They no longer
asked me to come, and I stopped going to the meetings. I
worked, I fulfilled my duties. I adapted plays. I completely re-
vised Abraham Goldfaden's *The Tenth Commandment* for
a new production. Not the way it had once been reworked
for the Warsaw production of 1926 but in an entirely new
fashion. I thought it was a very successful adaptation.

In 1940 elections were held for the city council. One day
I received an invitation to come to one of the borough offices. My heart foretold me ill, but I wasn't as frightened as
my sister-in-law, at whose house I lived. I had the opposite
feeling. Perhaps they were going to elect me! Just as I pre-
dicted, they offered me the post of deputy in the City Council.

I began by saying that perhaps my having many relatives

outside the country could be a drawback and that they should know of this in advance. I sought all sorts of excuses, but nothing helped. Once again I was naïve. Everything was determined from above. All my disclaimers notwithstanding, I was informed that they hoped I would accept the great honor given to me and the great confidence expressed in me and that I would appear when summoned.

The day they were supposed to call for me and have me appear before my electors, I feigned illness and lay in bed. Two young commanders came to me, one of them a Jew, the other a gentile. They told me, "You must go. They are waiting for you. Nothing will happen to you. We shall bring you there and back. Please understand that the voters must see you and speak to you."

Who were the voters? A tank regiment of the NKVD (military men from the Ministry of Internal Affairs). They already knew that they would have to elect me as a deputy in the City Council.

The ride was a long one, and I didn't know where I was being taken. When I arrived, I saw a huge red banner hanging in the distance, visible even from afar. I also saw an enormous life-size picture of myself, underneath which was written who I was and why they had to vote for me.

At first I was brought to the commander of the regiment and then to an outdoor square. The ground was snow-covered, and it was a sunny, brilliant, frosty day. All about us stood the tankmen; there were almost no Jews. Off to a side was the regimental band. All this made an extraordinary impression on me; the scene was somewhat grotesque, for they all were standing. At the edge of the square stood a table with two chairs. I sat down on one, and the regimental commander on the other. He spoke about me, and then came my turn to speak.

I have a natural talent for speech-making, but here I didn't know what to say. I wanted to make do with few words. I expressed my gratitude for the honor and said that

I would work to the best of my ability, and then I wanted to conclude. There was silence all about me. They understood that I would continue. I stretched the words as artfully as I could, said that this region needed people who knew the current conditions, and I concluded again. Once more silence reigned. They still wanted me to continue. I realized that unless I ended with the words "Long live Stalin, long live the Soviet Union," I would not be able to end. As I have previously mentioned, I had never uttered these words. Nevertheless, I had to end. So I said a few more words, and that finished it.

Again silence. I expressly declared that I had no more to say. Then the commander of the regiment stood and concluded for me. He remarked how bad the situation had been until now. (It didn't even dawn on me that I had to say this.) He also stated that beforehand I had had no place to live and that I'd had nothing to wear and only now had my true worth been fully appreciated. Now I was being given everything I needed. When he concluded with the words "Comrade Stalin," everyone knew that the band had to begin playing. I looked at the people who stood all around me. I saw the apathetic faces of people who cared about nothing and certainly not about what I had said. They just knew that they had to stand there, that the band had to play, and that they had to applaud.

In a word, I was elected unanimously.

Several days later I was called to the presidium of the City Council to collect my deputy book. When they saw who my electors had been, they stood in awe of me. I took the booklet and departed, smiling. I attended the opening session of the City Council, which took place at the great opera hall. It was packed with people, but none of the deputies actually participated. At the time of the second meeting it rained and I didn't want to attend. My husband and sister-in-law reprimanded me for not going, asserting it might cause me harm and so forth. I didn't attend, but the next morning all the newspapers reported that I had been there. I ceased attending. I saw that everything was accepted unanimously and organized in advance. The council had only formally to agree. This made me conclude that my presence was completely superfluous. The deputy book that I held on to gave me the privilege of riding in the front of a bus and entering a store first without standing in the endless lines. (It grew increasingly more difficult to get into stores because of the huge lines.) That was the sort of deputy I was.

I recall an evening that took place in the great opera hall in memory of the greatest Polish poet, Adam Mickiewicz (1798-1855). The occasion was the eighty-fifth anniversary of his death, in 1940. By this gesture the Soviet Union wanted to demonstrate to the Lemberg Poles (the city had a substantial Polish majority) that from the point of view of culture they were "internationalist."

During that evening I also performed. I read in Yiddish a fragment of Mickiewicz's finest work, *Pan Tadeush*, translated by David Koeningsberg (murdered by the Germans). Afterward the famous Polish writer and essayist Tadeush Bey-Zhelensky, then professor at the Lemberg University, congratulated me on my reading and said, "I have never before heard Mickiewicz in Yiddish, but I understand everything because of the excellent reading. It sounded beautiful."

This was my first conversation with Bey-Zhelensky, and it pleased me very much because I was one of his admirers. He, too, was later murdered by the Germans.

In the summer of 1940 we decided to spend our vacation visiting my daughter in Leningrad. Addy Rosner and his orchestra at that time were performing in a summer theater, and they enjoyed extraordinary success. This was the first time that my husband and I went deep into the Soviet Union. We were advised to visit Kiev, where there was a Yiddish theater. Our friends in Kiev promised to provide us with train tickets from there to Moscow, and thus we would also be able to visit the Ukrainian capital. In the Kiev Yiddish State Theater were the old actors from my mother's time: among

others, Yaakov Liebert and Gershon Weissman, who had
briefly been married to my sister, Regina.

After one night in the sleeping car—actually it was a
regular car with added bedding—we arrived in Kiev, where
a large group of actors awaited us, friends and strangers.
Since we intended to remain overnight, we asked our Kiev
colleagues to find us a hotel room. "Impossible," our friends
declared. "Rooms have to be ordered weeks in advance." So
they decided that we would sleep in the Actors House. When
I saw the place, I was appalled. Boards covered puddles of
water. I was told they were rebuilding. In the hallway I saw
a convention of cats. I'd never seen so many cats gathered in
one place. "Too late," I thought. "I hate cats. I'm afraid of
them." I was brought into the room of one of the actors, a man
I didn't know. He very amicably told me that he would give
up his room for me, that he and his wife would go to sleep
at a friend's house. Meanwhile, I went to visit Weissman, at
that time considered a well-to-do actor, and found him in
two tiny rooms. Eight families shared one kitchen and one
toilet.

All this was incredible for a state theater. Was this the
way well-to-do actors lived?

I was then taken up to Liebert's room. He and his wife
lived in somewhat better circumstances. He told me confidentially how his son, a colonel, had been arrested and tortured in 1938. Even Liebert himself had been arrested. Why?
Because an old sister from Warsaw had visited him. We all
knew her. The old woman earned a living by repairing bedding and sewing in other people's homes. She was a dear old
lady, and when she returned to Warsaw, the NKVD insinu-
ated that she had been engaged in espionage. For this, Liebert was incarcerated; so was his son, who was then of high
military rank. Finally, however, he was released, as was his
son, who returned to the army. Liebert showed me marks
on his head, his "souvenirs" from the investigation.

I wanted to go out to see Kiev. I remembered it from long
ago as a beautiful city, and in this gloomy mood I wanted to

be out on the street and sit down at the Café Continental. My friends took me to the Continental Hotel, which had a beautiful garden restaurant, but it was impossible to get in. For hours on end a long row of people had been waiting. This was no surprise, for it was the only place at that time where one could spend a civilized half hour. However, waiting was not for me, so we went to a small restaurant. It was beyond my strength to remain there. Flies were buzzing all about, millions of flies that squatted down on every bit of food and on every drink. We left and went to visit Kalmanovitch, an actor who knew me from childhood. Kalmanovitch was ill and wanted to see me.

"Now you'll see a beautiful apartment!" my friends stated. It turned out to be—according to our Warsaw standards—like the small apartment of an average Polish worker. Once again I was disappointed.

In the Actors House we slept in the room of the actor who had gone to a friend's house. The next morning a bowl of water was brought in for washing. If I preferred, I could wash in the kitchen, where every minute another person entered. When I went into the bathroom, I was given a separate wooden board, for each resident had his own.

During my previous night's walk I noticed a sign: "Café Chocolat." I wanted to go there for breakfast, but all they offered in the morning was borsht. Nothing else. There was nothing to be had in the stores. This was 1940, when war had not yet reached that region. Lunch was prepared for me in the Actors House—a chicken that had been purchased at the *kolkhoz* market.

From Kiev we went to Moscow and were met by my childhood friend Grisha Rotshein, a member of the Djigan and Schumacher troupe. Grisha brought us to the apartment of the director of Rosner's orchestra (both of them were in Leningrad), which was to be our residence for the day. It wasn't a bad place, but it was so full of things that one could hardly move about.

We ate breakfast at the Hotel Europa. There the waiter

asked us, "What would you like to have?"

"A regular breakfast," I replied. "Rolls, butter, a piece of herring."

"Unfortunately, we don't have these items," replied the waiter.

I then asked, "Then how do you live?"

Mel pulled my sleeve and whispered, "Why are you asking such questions? They've been living this way for twenty years, and you're asking them how they live!"

The waiter heard us talking in Polish. He probably assumed we were foreigners, for soon he brought us butter and herring.

Strolling along the street, I saw wonderful items in the show windows. "Quite nice," I said, but Grisha laughed at me.

"All of it is fake, painted," he said. "None of these are real. Getting anything is very difficult. Only the chosen few get to make purchases in a store. Things are to be had only at the bazaar."

In the evening we went to Djigan and Schumacher's garden theater, and the next morning had a visit from a relative of Sigmund Turkov, whom I knew from Kharkov and who had come especially to see me. From him I heard something that distressed me. "Run away as soon as you can," he told me. "Flee! Go back! This place was never good for Jews and it never will be."

None of this made sense to me. What did he mean by Jews? Wasn't this the land where everybody was equal?

The next morning we went to Leningrad where Ruth and Addy met me. They took me to a hotel where I had such a roomy suite I was astonished. There were three large, wonderful rooms, and even a credenza with a silver tray and crystal glassware. The large bathtub was luxurious, but the bedding was torn and mended.

The next morning I stood at the window and saw a long line of people stretching over half the block. I did not know why they were standing there. Meanwhile, my son-in-law ordered breakfast. Although he and Ruth had a luxurious apartment, they came in to eat breakfast with us, for our dining room was larger. An old waiter dressed in a frock coat entered and brought in a magnificent breakfast. What didn't he have! Caviar and lox, all sorts of baked goods, and cream. Here was everything one wanted, and on the opposite side of the street, as I later discovered, a long line of people was waiting for—bread!

In the evening we went to the park of a summer theater for a performance by Addy Rosner and his orchestra. He was a beloved star in Leningrad and had a fine orchestra. The house was full, and the audience was variegated. For the first time I heard my daughter singing onstage, accompanied by a large orchestra. Ruth sang the same song I had heard on the radio. She was heartily applauded but regretfully could not offer an encore, for she had just barely managed to learn that song in Russian, which then was still a foreign tongue for her.

I had been in Leningrad (then called St. Petersburg) during my childhood, but I could remember nothing from that visit. During the day we toured the city, which has many interesting sites, including the famed Hermitage Museum. Leningrad made a better impression on us than did Moscow. Of course one cannot judge from only one day.

In the evening we gladly would have gone to the theater, but during the height of the summer almost all the theaters were closed.

Our short vacation ended quickly and we had to return to Lemberg, traveling again through Moscow and Kiev. My farewell with Ruth, who was always my closest friend and my only daughter, moved me deeply. I also said good-bye to Rosner and members of his orchestra whom we had met previously. We hoped soon to see one another again, for their home base was Bialystok (formerly in Poland), which was not too far from Lemberg.

The Moscow Yiddish Art Theater, headed by Shlomo Mikhoels and Benjamin Suskin, was on tour in Kiev. In the afternoon Mikhoels invited me to his hotel for lunch, and in the evening Mel and I were at the performance. They played *King Lear*, directed by the famous S. E. Radlow, Yiddish theater staging Shakespeare! And this performance already had a general European recognition. Mikhoels was a fascinating man, and this quality emerged onstage in his interpretation of King Lear. I couldn't judge him too well as an actor, but he drew one's attention. Everyone liked Suskin in the role of the Fool. Many people said he was better than Mikhoels; however, I could not say that. Suskin was very good—he was impressive—but in Mikhoels one could sense quite strongly the intellectual man. Possibly Suskin was more thespian, more commanding, and had more dramatic technique. After all, my opinion is not beyond question, for I saw neither of them in any other performance. The role of one of Lear's daughters was played by Sarah Rotbaum, whom I knew from Warsaw from many years earlier. She was the sister of the director Yaakov Rotbaum, who worked with us after the war, and of Leah Rotbaum, who after her return to Poland in the fifties was a well-known director in the Polish opera.

We were very happy to see old friends. After the performance we went backstage. Mikhoels sat in his dressing room like an emperor, surrounded by young actresses. One of them fanned him, another served him coffee, a third asked him what he wanted. Everyone fawned over him. I don't recall anyone dancing around a prima donna the way they crowded around Mikhoels. It was an unforgettable experience.

My general view of Kiev did not change with this return visit. I felt hardship and want, which I had not even sensed in 1919, when during the civil war I gave birth here to my daughter.

20

In Lemberg and Rovno

WE arrived in Lemberg somewhat breathless, although the city still did not have its pre-1939 atmosphere. Here, too, one already saw long lines for food, yet another mood reigned, more light-hearted in character. For example, when we arrived, my sister-in-law was in the hospital and the maid was not at home. So we telephoned Dr. Melman and waited at a café till the keys were brought to us. How pleasant it was to sit in a Lemberg café after our travels from Kiev and Moscow.

The atmosphere was pleasant, somewhat Viennese. They served us whatever we wanted for breakfast. We breathed easier. Moreover, our apartment was similar in comforts to the one we had in Warsaw. Actually we used only one room, although we had the entire apartment at our disposal. How different this was from the private residences we had seen in the three Russian cities. Now we first realized how high was our standard of living before the war. It couldn't be compared to that of people who were on the same social level in the Soviet Union. Perhaps there were luxurious apartments in Moscow and Leningrad, but only for the very select few.

In Lemberg we once again began our normal routine of work, but by the end of 1940 we already sensed a certain unrest. We heard foreign newscasts from which we gathered that the West was warning the Soviet Union of the German danger. However, the Soviet citizens in Lemberg and in all of Russia considered this British provocation; after all, they had a nonaggression pact with Germany. At that time France was already on its knees and England was being bombed continuously, but the Soviet people believed only their official propaganda.

Our director, Zaiken, who was an official lecturer in international politics and was indeed interested in world affairs, laughed at all the reports that Germany was preparing to attack the Soviet Union. "What are you talking about?" he said. "We have a pact with Germany, and moreover, the Germans are afraid of us. We showed what we could do in the war against Finland."

We assumed that this was either naïveté or the result of heads stuffed with propaganda. We certainly did know what the German military machine was capable of. Now we had further evidence, not only in the Polish collapse but in the greater one of France. We also were witness to the difficulties the Russians had on the battlefront with the tiny Finnish nation and to the hardships in the Soviet Union itself. The Soviet regime continually informed us in Kiev and Moscow that all the shortages were a result of the Finland campaign.

When we worked out plans for 1941, I asked the director, "What happens if there's a war?"

Zaiken replied, "Our army will take Berlin and we'll continue playing here as usual."

"Well, fine," I thought. "Blessed are those who believe."

We were into 1941. Suddenly an event occurred in my life that caused me much concern and insecurity. I thought that I was pregnant and went to a gynecologist for an examination: All signs pointed to it, but the doctor assured me I was not pregnant. Just then I received a phone call from Ruth in Bialystok that *she* was pregnant. Could it be that we were both in the same circumstances? I played young roles, looked very young, and felt fine.

On May Day, as a deputy, I was invited to sit on the platform during the rally. I didn't want to be there, but my curiosity to see what was happening overwhelmed me. A group of German officers who had been invited from the other side of the border repelled me. Here were Hitler's officers observing a parade of Russian soldiers, tanks, and artillery. Just a few days earlier I had heard the warnings of the BBC and here were the future aggressors, apparently laughing amicably and for all intents and purposes on very good terms with the Russians.

I suddenly felt very ill, left the platform, entered a store for a drink of water, and went home. The next morning I went again to the same gynecologist, who now told me I was in my sixth week of pregnancy. I was in despair. I felt that dark clouds were hovering overhead. Perhaps the Germans would attack. I was working, but I didn't know what would be, and my daughter was pregnant, too. Perhaps we would have to run, flee. I wouldn't remain with the Germans.

At that time I was working diligently, performing frequently. When I was scheduled to have one day off, I asked the director for three. I had decided to terminate my pregnancy, and for that I needed three days in the hospital.

Abortions in those days were strictly forbidden, and one had to do various things to enter a hospital for this purpose. I spoke to the gynecologist and also, of course, with my sister-in-law, who was a physician in the hospital. I kept it secret, but in the theater—I don't know how—everyone soon knew what was happening.

On the appointed day I telephoned the doctor. He told me I needed a special form from the city health department to enter the hospital. This was not hard for me to obtain, but again it took some time. Analyses, bureaucracy, papers. In short, when everything was finished, I phoned the doctor. An assistant informed me that the military that morning had taken the doctor to one of the suburbs for a consultation. He would return in the evening. That evening I spoke to the doctor and made arrangements with him for the following morning even though I had only two days left.

The next morning the doctor phoned me that he had to leave again for half a day but would perform the surgery that afternoon. This left me one and a half days. One day later I had a very important performance. I told the doctor that we must postpone the operation for several days.

At that time I began an intensive tour of work. As I have previously mentioned, I reworked Goldfaden's *The Tenth Commandment*, which the ensemble liked very much. People familiar with the first adaptation of 1926 considered mine superior. Those who didn't know it were amazed. We began rehearsing, and I literally could not tear myself away. I was busy with the scene designer, Fritz Kleinman, with the composers, and with everything else connected with the premiere.

The premiere of *The Tenth Commandment* was festive, and the production grand. Up to that point I could think of nothing but the coming musical play, and during the evenings I performed again. Weeks passed. Soon it might be too late to do anything about my pregnancy. Once, on short notice, we had to travel to Rovno, one of the great towns in Volin (formerly Poland), where I performed Sandor Gergely's *My Son*, and then returned to Lemberg.

Days flew by and once again I had to go to Rovno. By now we were into the latter half of June 1941. I was scheduled to leave on Sunday. During the day I planned to see *The Tenth Commandment* and in the evening perform in *Mirele Efros*. My husband, as I stated previously, worked only sporadically in the theater and did not plan to go with me. Then, about an hour before my departure, Mel phoned and said he was being sent on an urgent mission to Rovno and would join me. When Mel saw me, he wondered why I was taking so much luggage. "You are only going for two days! But do as you see fit." He meant that in Rovno they knew me from before the war, and I had to dress no worse than I did in those days.

We arrived at Rovno before dawn and went to a private dwelling, where the owners awaited us. While drinking tea, we heard David Oistrakh performing a violin concerto, broadcast on the outside loudspeaker. It was a quiet, beautiful summer morning, June 22, about 3:30 A.M. We washed and went to sleep. Later, we were awakened by shooting and bombardment. Mel jumped out of bed and ran to the window. Looking up at the sky, he said, "Get dressed!" then added, "They've played us for the fool."

I dressed quickly, my heart pounding. Once again I saw horror before my eyes, visualizing what I had seen in Warsaw. We went outside, saw the police.

"What happened?" we asked.

"We don't know," they replied, "We don't know. Perhaps these are tests. Go back to your homes." They were totally confused.

"We have to go to the theater for a rehearsal," we said. Actually, it was too early for that. "For a performance tonight."

The police smiled ironically but let us pass.

In the theater we met many other frightened actors, especially those who were to perform in the matinee. We who had lived through the First World War and the bombing in Warsaw recalled what had happened. Theater colleagues who had come to us from the Soviet Union were shivering with fright but consoled themselves optimistically by saying, "We'll teach them a lesson."

Meanwhile, we witnessed an event we had not seen in Warsaw during the first day. The evacuation of Rovno had already begun. This directly contradicted the song the Soviets had been singing for months on end: "If war breaks out tomorrow, we'll march on and annihilate them."

Even during the first few hours we saw automobiles and then trucks, horses, and wagons. They were fully packed with everything imaginable, including furniture, and all were heading in one direction: eastward. Both Russians and Russian Jews, the ones who had recently emigrated. Fear overtook the entire city.

When the time came for the matinee performance, director Zaiken ordered, "We will perform."

"How can we?" we asked. "Planes are continually flying overhead. They're shooting."

"I have no orders to cancel the performance," Zaiken announced.

A nightmarish performance ensued. The only ones in the audience were my husband and I, Zaiken, and one other actor. We sat in the theater with a few children from the street who had requested permission to enter. There was no one else. Goldfaden's great play, *The Tenth Commandment*, was performed with absolute earnestness. Suddenly there was an outbreak of shooting. The children began crying and fled from the theater. The city was being bombed. Zaiken wanted to calm the actors.

"It's nothing. . . . Don't worry. . . . The bombs are falling far away."

We, however, with the experience of Warsaw behind us, knew that the bombs were falling in Rovno. I again turned to Zaiken.

"What sense is there in having the actors perform for us at such a time?"

Once more I heard the strange reply, "I have no orders to stop the performance."

The performance continued to the final curtain. The end of the play is very expressive and symbolic. The lead actor comes onstage (in our production it was Simcha Natan); he turns to the audience, then to his fellow actors, and says, "Farewell. Let's hope we'll see one another again in good health."

Unfortunately, for many in our ensemble, in the orchestra, and among the stagehands, this was a last farewell before death. They became victims of the war's spreading destruction. I don't even know where they are buried, or what became of the great orchestra, chorus, and ballet who accompanied us in this last macabre performance.

That night the theater closed. We no longer waited for

the order for which the disciplined and frightened director, Zaiken—poor soul—waited.*

There *were* orders, but of a different kind—not to go out on the street, to go down to the cellars during the artillery barrage, not to kindle any lights at home—in brief, orders for the population behind the front lines.

Since all of us were not actually in our own homes, but were guest performers on tour, most of us remained in the theater to be together and to hear newscasts, which hardly described the true situation. Since there were no windows in the foyer of the theater, we gathered by a large table illuminated by a candle. We sat and waited. I lay down on the table and gazed at the nearby phone. Occasionally someone dashed outside to learn what was happening.

During all this time, traffic moved through the city: wagons, autos, carts dragged by people. All of them were loaded with baggage. All had one goal: to flee, to flee.

There were sixty-two of us in the theater. We would get frightened whenever someone ran in with a message. We all waited for a suggestion or an order from the director, but Zaiken said only one thing: "Men are forbidden to leave; they may be needed for military service."

"How about the older ones?" asked some musicians in their fifties.

"Everyone must remain. Perhaps even the older ones will be mobilized," Zaiken answered.

Everyone was afraid to move. Some actresses came over to me. They assumed that I was the calm one. This was only my outer state. In truth, I was very much afraid for my husband and for everyone around me. I also had an intuitive fear of the Germans. Another thought gave me no peace: the fate of my daughter. We heard that Kiev had been heavily bombed. Ruth had been there at the time, and pregnant as well. Suddenly I had the idea of trying the telephone. I

---

* The loyal Isaac Zaiken was later a major in the Russian army. In 1943 the authorities discovered mismanagement in his battalion. All guilt was placed on Zaiken, the Jew, and he was executed by the Soviets.

clicked away at the receiver until, to my surprise, an operator answered. I asked her to connect me with my daughter,
Ruth Rosner, who lived at the Continental Hotel in Kiev.

"Are you crazy? Are you out of your mind?" the operator
replied. "Who are you, and where are you calling from? Are
you the wife of an officer?" the amazed woman kept asking
me.

"I'm calling from the theater; my name is Kaminska."

"Ida?" the operator asked.

"Yes."

"I've seen you perform."

She then attempted to do what she herself said was prohibited, and she succeeded. I placed the call to Addy, since
his name was more well-known. Indeed, it was Rosner who
answered the phone, and in my naïveté I told him, "Go to
the Culture Ministry and tell them that we are now in Rovno
with our entire company. We cannot go back to Lemberg.
Ask them to do something for us and get us out of here.
We don't want to fall into the hands of the Germans. Tell
them to issue an order to remove us from here by train."

Addy promised to run wherever necessary and to call
me back. I knew my request was useless; nevertheless, a little
flame of hope kindled in the hearts of all my colleagues. We
waited. Perhaps, indeed, through me salvation would come to
the sixty-two people in our group.

In the middle of the night an answer came. "It's impossible to do anything. There are many such requests from all
sides and they can do nothing."

This time I spoke with my daughter. I had to pretend I
was making an official call. The telephone operator requested
that it sound like an official conversation, lest she suffer unpleasant consequences. I had to control myself and not cry.
I just asked Ruth how she felt and told her that we would make
attempts to move out of here.

The mood in the foyer was nervous and hysterical. People wept. They walked about and asked, "What should we

do? What should we do? We've left our families in Lemberg. Should we return or flee farther?"

Suddenly in the middle of the night two men entered. Apparently they had been informed that people were gathered here. They said they were from the village of Lutsk, which was on fire, and that the Germans were near. One of them appeared to be a military person. He went to the telephone and talked to someone in a very strange manner, using circumlocutions. It seemed suspicious to me. I whispered my feelings to Zaiken, who made a call, and a few minutes later three Russian officers appeared. When they searched the newcomer, they found a revolver and a party card. It turned out he was a spy, a Russian who had been parachuted into the area. The second man disappeared. The officers didn't waste too much time with the suspicious fellow.

There was no doubt about this man, but many errors were made, especially in Warsaw. I remember that many people were held in suspicion, and surely there were many innocent victims. Later in Kiev, too, everyone who was dressed in the western European fashion was persecuted. Many residents of former Poland wore knickers or trench coats; those with trench coats were especially suspected and were chased on the streets with cries of "Spy! Spy!" as though a spy had to have a certain garb for easy recognition.

21

Fleeing Again

AS soon as day broke, I told my husband we must leave,
Mel was a bit more restrained, saying that we should
eat first. We ate breakfast at the apartment of a woman who
served private meals. Meanwhile, bombs were falling around
the city, and planes flew overhead. One alarm followed another. I told Mel to accompany the director to some place
of authority and ask what we ought to do.

When Mel returned, I asked, "Well?"

My husband replied, "The regional commander said, 'If
I were in your shoes, I would have left long ago.'"

Mel packed several things into a pair of knickers, slung it
like a knapsack over his shoulders, and we left the city.
Along the way we met friends who asked us what to do. I
answered, "I'm not giving any advice. We're leaving. I don't
know what's awaiting us, but we're going." Several people
followed without even thinking further. Along the way we
met Simcha Natan's daughter standing in front of a house.
She had just recently given birth to a beautiful boy. Her
mother, Natalie, also an actress, was with her. "Where are you
going, Ida?" she asked.

"I don't know," I said. I certainly could not have advised
them to take to the road with a two-month-old baby.

That day the heat was unbearable. (The end of June
1941 in the steppes.) I broke a branch from a tree and used
it as a cane. In all, there were seventeen people from our
theater who followed us. We were headed in the direction of

the old Russian border. By afternoon we had gone many kilometers beyond Rovno.

Our group had two "commanders": the actor Leon Kaswiner and my husband. Their responsibility was to choose roads, stops, and lodging. They also saw to it that we rested occasionally by sitting on the grass and drinking water from a field canteen. The temperature was ninety-five degrees. At about 3 P.M. we passed a house where we saw two fine-looking Jewish women who were a mother and daughter. We became acquainted and hoped we could get a warm meal.

"Where are you going?" they asked us. We replied that we were fleeing from Rovno.

"Will we have to run away, too?" they asked. We told them that Rovno was not our home.

"Then we'll have to leave our home, too," they continued quickly. "This is where our parents lived and where we have everything we own."

It was very difficult to give advice. One year later I met both of these women somewhere in central Asia. They, too, had been unable to avoid the Jewish fate of picking up the wanderer's staff.

When night fell, we entered the courtyard of a peasant who let us use his stable. Already many refugees from various places were gathered there. We literally dropped into the straw, exhausted. The men took turns standing guard. Despite my tiredness, my husband called me outside and showed me Rovno burning in the distance. It looked like a sea of fire, and it appeared that nothing would remain of the town.

Even though we had experienced the burning of Warsaw, the blazing city still made an awful impression upon us. We were twenty-two kilometers from Rovno and once again felt that a world had crumbled beneath us. Nearly two years ago we had left Warsaw and now, in 1941, the city of Lemberg.

We continued walking all day. From time to time I was

given a ride on a wagon, for my pregnancy was somewhat noticeable. The following day we resumed our trek.
Since the roads were full of refugees, our group decided that
in case any of us should get separated we would meet in the
border town of Koretz. There we met and spent the night.
The next morning we washed and the men somehow managed to shave. The owner of the house where we slept was a
Ukrainian. That night he was the sentry. He didn't conceal
his eagerness for the Germans' arrival; in fact, he expected
them in a day or two.

Outside we saw an empty truck. Perhaps we could get
a ride on it. When we approached, we saw that the truck
was spattered with blood. Then we heard voices from within the house and went back inside. The Ukrainian sat in
a room with two Russians. They were overjoyed. Well, he
was waiting for his messiah—the Germans—and, who knows,
perhaps the Russians shared his hope.

We asked the Russians where they were going and if
we could get a ride with them.

"Toward Novgorod Volinsk," they said, "a town on the
other side of the border."

Fine, we thought. From there we hoped to get a train
farther east. They agreed to take us with them. For a fee,
of course.

We all entered the truck. The two Russians looked suspicious to us. They appeared to be deserters from the front
lines. Perhaps they had changed into civilian clothes here
at the Ukrainian's place. We were used to seeing soldiers
heading *for* the front. We would meet Jewish soldiers and
officers on their way to battle who expressed sympathy
with our plight. They knew that, as Jews, we had to flee.
They would bid farewell to us as though knowing they
would not return. We were moved by the courage, compassion, and determination of these Jewish soldiers, who
knew the character of the enemy that wanted to destroy us.

When we arrived at the village of Koristin (not far from

the border town of Koretz), we suddenly heard the two
Russians shout, "Soon there's going to be an air raid!"
Everyone was ordered to leave the village, but there was no
air-raid alarm, and we didn't hear the buzzing of planes.

A dreadful panic began in the village. Mel said, "I remember such panicmongers in the outskirts of Warsaw. They
were Hitler's agents dressed in military uniforms. Can these
be the same sort?" Soon thereafter these two—strange keepers
of order—threw us out of the truck.

Before they sped away, twelve of our group managed to
scramble back onto the truck, and we rode to Novgorod
Volinsk. Here everyone was stopped and not admitted into
the town. We were not permitted to approach the railway
terminal. We were told it had been bombed. Later we learned
this was a lie and discovered we could reach the next railway
station by going round the town and making our way
through the villages. One of the Russians who was driving
the truck told us to get off. He said there was a reason why
he could not take us now but he would wait for us on the
other side of the hill, which he pointed out. When we arrived,
there was no trace of the truck. We had lost our opportunity.
Now we would have to proceed on foot.

We came to a Ukrainian village. The people looked at us
as though we were some strange phenomenon. They had
never seen such clothing. We were a curiosity to them. We
asked one of the peasant women if we could get something
to eat. She sent us to the village store, where there was nothing to be had. We returned and told the woman we would
pay her in advance and thus managed to get some sour milk
and bread.

After a brief rest we secured, to our good fortune, a
peasant's wagon and continued our journey. In the next village lived Germans. To our surprise the hunger here was
even greater than in the previous town. The German peasants
looked at us with distrust, fearing we might take their last
piece of bread. We assured them that we wished only to

spend the night in their village and then continue on our way. We were quartered in various huts. My husband and I and two other people were taken into a young teacher's house, which was impoverished but very clean. He lived there with his wife and two little daughters. They heated up some water for us for washing, which was very refreshing for me. Then the woman gave us potatoes and sour milk. We slept on the floor on hay and straw and were given clean coverings.

Suddenly I saw Mel leaving the hut. When he returned, I noticed that a change had come over him. I put my hand on his forehead. It was burning. Mel was delirious and had hallucinations. I grew very frightened, for typhus was raging at that time. The next morning we had to get up early to continue our journey. Our group gathered in front of the house, and my husband was carried to the wagon, where he lay burning with fever. Some of the people rode in the wagon, others followed on foot. Riding along, I felt very depressed, wondering what would happen if Mel's condition did not improve.

By midafternoon we reached another village, this time a Jewish one. Once more we were surprised to find that almost everything was available at the bazaar. Yet in the stores nothing was to be had. Bread was the hardest thing to find.

Two of our group entered a store that sold bread. The manager (for this was a state store) shouted at the crowd in Russian, "There's no more bread! Sold out!" Then, seeing our two friends and recognizing them as refugees, he said in Yiddish, "Wait a minute." When everyone had left the store, he gave bread to our group.

We bedded down in a park in the village square. A Jewish woman suddenly appeared and asked what we were waiting for. We replied, "We're waiting for a train to take us farther on."

"We don't know when there will be a train. Meanwhile, come to our house."

Thus Mel and I were lodged in her house and the rest in

other houses. I placed my husband on a sofa, and he gradually began to feel better. It turned out his illness was not serious.
He had simply fallen victim to sunstroke. He would go great
distances in the heat without a shirt. All of us had lips
parched from the heat. Some were even bleeding.

This little Jewish village, where we spent two nights, was
like a tonic for us. We took turns going to the station to see
if there was a train for Koristin, from where one might get a
train to Kiev. This was a minor junction, however, and it
was difficult to find out precisely when a train would arrive.
Nevertheless, we had to have steady contact with the station
in order not to miss a train. We were relatively comfortable
in this little village, for we ate cooked food and Mel felt
better.

Suddenly one day when our hosts were cooking lunch for
us, one of our friends came running: "The train is leaving!"
The Jews at whose house we lived were disappointed. Sad-
eyed, they gazed at us sympathetically, as if they felt that
soon the same fate awaited them. Everyone quickly gathered
his things, even though there was really nothing to pack. We
ran to the station, and our hostess rushed after us with the
pot of food. We just managed to jump onto the train, while
she, poor soul, remained standing there gloomily with the pot
in her hands.

We found ourselves in a baggage or cattle car. The heat
was murderous, and the metal walls, which had baked for
hours in the sun, were sizzling.

More dead than alive, we arrived in Koristin, where everything began anew. No one knew when the next train would
arrive. This time we decided not to budge from the terminal.
We were chased out, but some of us squatted and others lay
down in the square outside the terminal; such squares were
typical in the Ukraine. My husband sat down on a bench, I
rested my head on his knees, and thus we spent the night.
At dawn it began to rain and we had no protection. We
covered ourselves with papers and leaves. When it became

lighter, we noticed a hut on the other side of the square and entered it. Just then the rain ceased and the sun came out, but we could not rest there because almost every hour, and even at shorter intervals, there was an air-raid alarm. We experienced these alarms throughout our entire journey. If just one plane was visible some kilometers away, they sounded the alarm in neighboring regions.

Finally, several hours later, we heard that a train was leaving for Kiev. We gathered up our belongings and pushed our way into the train. No one asked us for tickets. Apparently the train had already been machine-gunned by a plane, for now a Soviet plane flew watch overhead the entire length of the journey to Kiev.

Exhausted by hunger, the crush, and the heat, we arrived in Kiev after a twelve-hour journey. From the station I phoned the Hotel Continental and asked for my daughter.

"She and her husband left last night for Moscow," said the manager. I wondered what to do but then decided that Kiev, after all, was a big city and we did have some acquaintances here. We drove up to the Actors House. The remodeling they had mentioned a year ago had probably been postponed, for the same lack of order reigned at the entrance. Here I learned that several people I knew had already left the city. Those I spoke to were afraid of saying this explicitly, for creating panic was prohibited. However, Mel and I sensed that they wanted to get rid of us.

We checked into quite a nice hotel, with clean rooms and beds. I felt good; even the alarms no longer bothered me. Still, the panic several hundred miles from the front amazed me. I did not really want to leave my room. While waiting out an alarm, I would meet several of our friends in the corridor, and this made me feel somewhat more tranquil. I tried to convince myself that perhaps we could remain here longer, but the panic grew from hour to hour, and it began to affect our calm mood. Since we were running short of money we went to the office of the Society of Authors, for I had some

LEFT: Ida Kaminska at age four in Odessa, 1903.

RIGHT: Ida Kaminska with her mother, Esther Rachel
Kaminska (1870–1926), in St. Petersburg, 1908.

ABOVE: Ida's father, Abraham Isaac Kaminsky (1867–1918).

RIGHT: Esther Rachel Kaminska in the title role of *Mirele Efros* by Jacob Gordin, with daughter Ida playing the role of her grandson, Shlomo, in Warsaw, 1905.

Ida Kaminska as Esmeralda
in a dramatization of Victor
Hugo's *The Hunchback of
Notre Dame* in Lodz, 1925.

BELOW: Ida Kaminska, her husband, Meir "Mel" Melman, and their son, Victor, in Moscow, 1946.

ABOVE: *Meylech Freylech* ("Jolly King") by J. Preger, produced and directed by Ida Kaminska in Warsaw, 1958.

LEFT: Ida Kaminska and Meir Melman in the 1965 Yiddish
State Theater production of *Mirele Efros*, in Warsaw.

Scene from a 1953 Lodz production of *Meir Esofovitch*, adapted by Ida Kaminska from the novel by Eliza Azheshkova. Kaminska translated and directed the play.

ABOVE: Ida Kaminska and Joseph Kroner in *The Shop on Main Street,* the prize-winning film which won her a 1966 Academy Award nomination as Best Actress.

BELOW: Arthur Miller with Ida Kaminska when he visited her theater in Warsaw in 1964.

With Gregory Peck in Hollywood, 1966.

ABOVE: From left Jan Kadar (director of *The Shop on Main Street*), Francis Lederer, Ida Kaminska, and Julie Christie in Hollywood, 1966.

RIGHT: The Swiss dramatist Friedrich Dürrenmatt and Ida Kaminska in Warsaw, 1967.

From left: Golda Meir, Yosef Kaminsky, Ida Kaminska, Ruth Kaminska, and Erika Kowalick (Ruth's daughter), backstage after a performance of *Mirele Efros* in Tel Aviv in 1968.

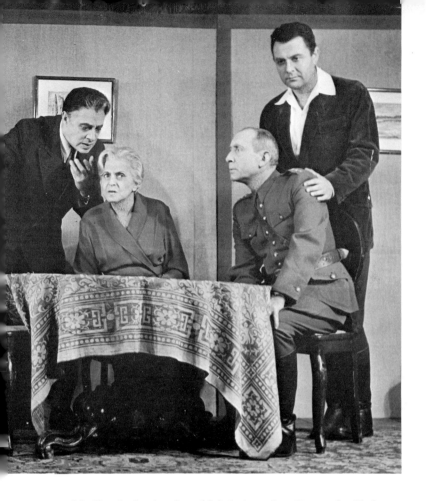

ABOVE: Ida Kaminska (at the table) in her play *Cover the Shelters*, Warsaw, 1964. At far left is Meir Melman. Chevel Buzgan, one of the noted Yiddish actors in their company, is speaking to Kaminska.

LEFT: Gravestone in Warsaw for Esther Rachel Kaminska, the "Mother of the Yiddish Theater."

Four generations today (New York, 1973). From right: Ida Kaminska, Ruth Kaminska-Turkov (her daughter), Erika Kowalick (her granddaughter), Amaris Kowalick (her great-granddaughter). On the wall is a picture of Esther Rachel Kaminska. (*Photo by Isaac Berez*)

royalty due me. They inspected the books and found my contention correct. They said, however, that they could only offer partial payment. I took what they gave me. Later I learned that prior to the evacuation, hundreds of thousands of rubles had been burned in that office, money from which not one author benefited. Here in Kiev, through various ways, all of the sixty-two people who had been in Rovno gathered. We decided that henceforth we would not be separated and would travel as a unit.

The panic among the local population was unimaginable. The stream of thousands of people fleeing from the city grew continually. We decided to travel farther and were advised to take a ship to Odessa. Sixty-two of us went to the port and waited there a day, but getting aboard a ship was a wild dream. Hundreds of people preceding us had booked all the ships. We almost boarded one ship, but it removed its gangplank before sailing time and pulled away. Several days later we found out that this ship had been bombed just before reaching Odessa and everyone on board had drowned.

At night we returned from the port to the city. We slept in the Actors House. We were admitted by an old friend, Shimon Weissman, the only person there. (Everyone had fled.) Shimon was the son of Gershon Weissman, the noted actor. When we woke up, Shimon had also run away. After experiencing one more air-raid alarm, we decided to make our way to Darnitza, a train junction near Kiev. We were told that from there we could make easier connections for eastbound trains. We wondered how to get there. Finally we took a trolley fully packed with refugees to the edge of the city. The ride was a perilous one, and in my state of pregnancy I felt the crush especially.

We then had to cross the bridge over the Dnieper River and continue on foot until we arrived at Darnitza. There were no through trains. The only possibility was to proceed to the next station and from there trust in Providence. I maintained we should take the local triain and thus keep moving from station to station. However, Zaiken, who by now had joined us, said that we should wait here for a train to Kharkov. We obeyed, patiently sitting on the ground. Finally I said I would wait no more. I would enter the first train that came along.

When a train arrived, I made for it with Mel. Immediately the entire troupe followed. We entered the baggage wagon. After a short ride we had to leave the train. Thus we made our way day by day, from train to train, until we reached the larger city of Poltava.

In Poltava all of us were brought into a huge hall, where we lay down on the floor to sleep. The next morning the entire group ran to the beautiful Poltava River to bathe, actually just to wash. On the beach we suddenly met the two deserters who had left us stranded behind Novgorod Volinsk and fled with the truck. They recognized us and ran away. After remaining several days in Poltava, we were informed that there was a train to take us farther. With this train we reached Kharkov.

22

From Kharkov to Baku and Beyond

I N Kharkov we met the troupe of Djigan and Schumacher, who showed us much friendship. Djigan took us into his room, for there were no empty rooms in any hotel. Here again we were surprised. We were hundreds of miles from the front, yet the fear, the terror, was great. People were evacuating; they possessed a kind of rare intuition or perhaps the mass psychosis of sheep—probably more the former than the latter.

I went to a hairdresser for a haircut. The barber, a Jew, asked me where I came from and if the Germans were really so horrible. I had the feeling that this man would not budge from his place. I told him that I had spent only three weeks among the Germans.

"Yes?" he asked, continuing.

"One cannot imagine anything worse. Whoever can, should flee."

This was the first time I had violated my principle of not giving advice. After several days in Kharkov we went to the railway station to see if we would have the good fortune of traveling farther. The Kharkov station, huge and crowded, served a city of a million people, but there was no train for us.

"There are no trains at the station," the railroad officials said. "One is forbidden to go there."

So, then, where to? That they did not know. Some of our group discovered there was an empty train that was heading for Baku, the famous petroleum center.

"Well, then, let it be Baku," I said. "Anything, as long as it's farther from the Germans." The train was empty. Clean wagons, third class. Here I felt the baby moving for the first time. I remembered that my daughter Ruth was probably feeling the same thing now. Both of us were wanderers, I thought, and I began to cry softly. I wrote letters and sent telegrams to all sides to let Ruth know where I was and that I was on my way. Of course, I could receive no reply. In any case I informed her we were heading for Baku.

Upon arriving in Baku, we were told it was forbidden to leave the terminal. There was an edict against refugees coming into the city. We entered the terminal, encompassed by the terrible heat of the south. The temperature was about 120 degrees. We were a pitiful sight.

The director and the administrator of our theater went to the city authorities to request permission to admit us temporarily. They came back with a refusal. What were we to do? Return? Where to? With what?

"I'm going to the Hotel Intourist," I told my husband. I knew about that hotel, for Ruth had written me that she had stayed there.

"What are you doing?" Mel said. "You know it's not permitted."

Without even hearing what he said, I ran to the trolley car and asked the conductor if he was going to the Intourist Hotel. He said yes, and I boarded the trolley. When I came to the hotel, Mel, to my surprise, also emerged from the trolley. He had jumped in after me, on the rear platform.

I approached the clerk to ask for a room. Just then the manager came and asked me if I had been at the hotel before. I replied that my daughter and her husband, Addy Rosner, had been there.

"Oh, my! How you resemble your daughter! You look so

much like her I thought that you were she," the manager said. Then he added, "You probably don't have too much money, so I will give you a fine room very cheaply."

I turned to him and said, "At the terminal sixty-two people of my theater are waiting, exhausted. Among them are several pregnant women and some old and sick people. Can you help them?"

"I can give them only two large rooms, but I'll get in touch with another hotel to see if we can arrange lodging for them. However," he added, "they must come over immediately, for the trolleys stop running soon, and in the evening it is forbidden to be out on the streets."

I phoned the police officer at the terminal. I begged him to do me a favor and immediately call the director of the Lemberg theater troupe to the phone. Zaiken came and I told him, "Don't ask anyone any questions, but get everyone immediately to come to the Hotel Intourist."

They all arrived shortly thereafter. Meanwhile, I had entered a magnificent room with a luxurious bath. The view through the window was superb; Baku had a somewhat oriental style. After a fine cup of coffee with fresh rolls, I began to cry. My accumulated experiences had suddenly overwhelmed me.

Mel returned to the station to gather the remaining members of the collective and brought them back to the hotel, where all of them were set up for the night. Despite our awareness that it was forbidden to enter Baku, we had come into the city. The hotel had an excellent restaurant where everything one wanted was available. Then another "miracle" happened. We were told that Baku had been blacked out until yesterday and that today the city was illuminated again for the first time. This lasted only one day, for the next evening the kindling of lights at unblackened windows was prohibited again.

The next day we went out to see the city. Yiddish actors, now residents of Baku, who had heard of our arrival came running. They embraced us and kissed us and asked what we needed. We went to the actors union to ask for their help in getting us a permit to remain in Baku. They promised to help but were unfortunately not successful. Suddenly a telegram came from Ruth that she and Addy were in Omsk, Siberia. My joy in finally establishing contact with Ruth and her husband was unimaginable.

Baku, as petroleum center of the Soviet Union, had a very strict set of regulations for refugees. The local actors union provided theater tickets for us, and we rested up for several days, but there was no chance of remaining in the city.

For several days the local authorities tactfully tried to tell us to leave. "You dare not remain here," they said. "It is against military orders." We thought our reply that we would not leave the city would suffice, but several days later a military patrol came, took our passports from the hotel clerk, and under guard led us across the city to the port.

The heat was unbearable. At the port we saw thousands of people crowding one another. Only because of our military guard were we permitted to go through. We boarded a ship where our group was given good places on the top deck. Representatives of the actors union and the Ministry of Cultural Affairs came to bid us farewell. They justified themselves by saying that they had no choice and that, while others would have to crowd themselves uncomfortably, we were given "choice" places on board (sleeping on deck).

Now we would be heading for the other side of the Caspian Sea, for the port city of Krasnovodsk, which was in Asia. From there we would be able to travel farther.

The name Krasnovodsk made me shudder. I remembered the name from novels and from conversations about the criminals who used to be sent there. But what choice did we have? It was July 20, my daughter's birthday. I sent Ruth a telegram wishing her well and informing her of our destination. I added we did not know where we would go after Krasnovodsk. I asked a polite young man from the Culture

Ministry to send the telegram. He promised he would and kept his word.

We lay down on the deck of the ship under the open skies. The moon shone down on us, but the horns were pointing the other way, as in Arab ornaments. By the light of the moon we sailed for the frontier between Europe and Asia.

It is difficult to describe our arrival in Krasnovodsk. First of all, as we disembarked from the ship, we saw bare, slate-colored mountains that alone could have driven one to depression. From the port we were taken to the railway terminal. Along the way we already felt a heat the likes of which we had not experienced during all our wanderings. We thought we were walking across glowing coals. There was no water to drink. Later we were told that drinking water was imported from Baku.

So we "occupied" the waiting room of the railway terminal. I half reclined on a broken sofa. It was impossible to go out into the city. I thought that here my end would come. After much anguish we finally got something to eat, bits of dried cheese that the Turkomans, the local residents, produced in a primitive fashion. When we saw the Turkomans' large fur hats the size of buckets, we wondered how they could wear them in such heat. Then we discovered that these hats were a protection against the sun.

We remained under these conditions for several days. Zaiken came to me and said, "Pluck up your courage. Come with me to the city commandant. Perhaps you can convince him to give us a wagon on a train for us to travel on."

I went, overcoming the horrible heat. I put our request to the city commandant. He replied that there were thousands of evacuees in Krasnovodsk who were waiting to travel farther. Nevertheless, I argued that we were actors with a long journey behind us and that we could find work in the next town.

"Where, then, do you want to go?" asked the commandant.

"To Ashkhabad."

"Impossible!" he said. "That's a closed city."

"Well, then, where?"

"To Tashkent."

"How long does it take to get there?" I asked.

"Nowadays, about forty-eight hours."

We agreed and were given a separate wagon on a train. It normally held thirty-six people but now contained sixty-two. The journey was insufferably difficult. Several of our people fell ill with dysentery. The heat was so intense that when we came to a station Mel would run for cold water and cover me with wet towels. Thanks to the intervention of Zaiken, I was admitted for a short while into a so-called soft-seated wagon. This car was also full, but its seats were more comfortable. Unfortunately, I had to leave it because high Soviet officials entered with reserved tickets for those seats.

We kept traveling deeper and deeper into Turkestan. The panorama changed continually: deserts, camel caravans, the Orient. I remember a characteristic joke. One of our colleagues from Warsaw was sleeping. We woke him and called out, "Look, look! People on camels! Look at their costumes! Look!" Half awake, our colleague, not even willing to look through the window, replied, "I'd like to see all of this, but at the Stylowy Cinema," one of Warsaw's most popular movie houses.

After we passed Stalinsbad, Samarkand, Bokhara (where Zaiken had a sister and brother-in-law), our journey came to an end. And so we arrived in Tashkent.

However, once again we were not permitted to leave the station. No amount of intervention helped. Depressed, we sat at the terminal. Suddenly people who had learned of our arrival started coming to us, including members of our theater who had somehow succeeded in arriving here before us. Most of our colleagues returned with Zaiken to Bokhara; the rest remained with us. Our friends suggested that we leave the station and we took their advice.

Without asking questions, we took the trolley car to the center of the city. We arrived at the Hotel National, but getting a room was impossible. We met some well-known actors there, members of the Miniature Theater of Lemberg. One of them took us to his room (he did not have to pay); others of our group somehow managed to settle down on their own. On the third day I began going to various offices requesting permission to stay in Tashkent. I made use of my document that I was a deputy of the Lemberg City Council, but after a polite reception I was refused.

In Tashkent I met the famous operetta star Clara Young, an old friend of my mother's. She had fled here from Moscow. We also met Shlomo Mikhoels and his Moscow Yiddish Art Theater. Djigan and Schumacher, directors of the Little Art Theater, were in Tashkent, too, with their troupe. In our hotel resided my brother's old friend Henryk Warshavsky (a noted composer, today he lives in Hollywood and is known as Henry Wars) with his wife and children. Incidentally, it was his wife who sneaked me into the hotel. But none of these people was able to help us remain in Tashkent.

Unexpectedly, a telegram came from Frunze, capital of the Kirghiz Republic, from our friends Sigmund Tonetsky and A. From, who had worked for the Cultural Affairs Department in Lemberg. They had both been on vacation in Moscow and could not return to Lemberg, where they had left their families. They had been sent to Frunze, "where the climate was surely a good one," and suggested that we come immediately to Frunze. Accompanied by Didya Epstein, one of our actors (formerly of the Vienna Opera), we decided to go to Frunze.

23

Two Births in Frunze

ARRIVING in Frunze, I saw a beautiful boulevard lined with palm trees that led from the terminal to the city. Mountains were visible from the distance, and the surrounding greenery was striking. We went to the best hotel, the Kirgistan, which had small but clean rooms. A bath was available for a ruble. The room was now twenty-five rubles per day—more expensive than in days gone by.

We were at the point where we had to begin selling some of our belongings to pay for the hotel bill; I sold a gold watch, and my husband, a diamond stickpin. At the market everything was available at low cost. After all our wanderings this surprised us. Fruits, meat, sugar, all in plenitude. Before the war this had been a center for the production of sugar, and the peasants, even the members of the *kolkhoz* (an agricultural cooperative), used to get sugar as wages. Now they brought it out to market and had few customers for it.

I decided that instead of us traveling to Omsk, where famine raged, Ruth should come to Frunze, if only for the fruits. There still were very few refugees, so everything was cheap.

We were told that there were eight-eight Jews in Frunze —so few that there was no interest in them. While returning from my first visit to the market, we met a handsome Ukrainian who was just slightly inebriated. When we sat down on a bench along the boulevard, he approached us and, looking at our western manner of dressing, declared, "Foreigners!" He sat down next to us and told us that he had been a farmer in the Ukraine with much land and had been exiled to the Kirghiz Republic.

According to the Ukrainian, a horrible anti-Semitism was spreading in Frunze. He lived on the outskirts of town, and his daughter had married a Jew, a teacher in a village.

Before his daughter's marriage, everyone had liked him, the Ukrainian declared. Now people avoided him and, of course, his family as well. Soldiers were returning from the front, the Ukrainian continued, who had spent only a short time in German captivity—released sooner because they were wounded. Before being sent home they were indoctrinated, which meant that they were told the Jews were responsible for everything. These former soldiers came en masse to the bazaars and spread the word that the Jews had brought on the war and were responsible for everything evil in the world.

This was one of the invidious activities of the Nazis. They agitated in various ways. For example, a few weeks later we heard that in Kirghiz the native-born population would say at the marketplace: "Wait, wait! As soon as the Germans come, we'll slaughter all the Russians along with the Jews."

My husband boldly said to a Kirghiz, "Well, I can understand your attitude toward the Russians [who were hated as the ruling masters] but why the Jews? You don't even know them."

The Kirghiz was dumbfounded and did not know what to say. He merely repeated the words "the Russians and the Jews," like a well-learned lesson. That is how the Nazi propaganda worked. It left its traces for decades and was later nimbly exploited by the ruling regime. The people were confident that Hitler would occupy all of Russia, along with the Asian republics.

One morning I received a call from a woman who was the director of the Philharmonic. In the Soviet Union this is an institution that organizes concerts and performances. She introduced herself as Espira Yefimovna Zyelonaya, a Jewish woman. She had been exiled to Frunze during 1936-37. She lived here with her husband, who was now on the front as a soldier. One year later I found out that they had been sent here for the crime of Zionism.

Since Zyelonaya was very capable, she advanced in her post. The artistic director was a man named Fere, a German Communist who also had been exiled to Frunze. After a period of imprisonment—he was a very talented composer who had helped establish a Kirghiz opera for which he composed music—he became the artistic director of the Philharmonic. Both Zyelonaya and Fere treated us with rare friendship.

Tonetsky and From, the two men from Lemberg who had convinced us to come to Frunze, worked in the Kirghiz Republic Arts Section. They tried their best to help us and sought jobs for us. Zyelonaya did the same. In fact, she immediately organized a concert for us in the municipal park, where there was a huge, unwalled, wooden structure with a stage.

The concert was fascinating. We actually performed for Kirghiz, Russians, and a *minyan* of Jews. My pregnancy was already visible, and I had no costumes; but it just so happened that I had with me a very colorful Japanese robe. I put it on backward to make it look original. The Japanese decoration on the front pleased the audience, for they had never seen such a dress before. Nothing in our recital interested the Kirghiz and the Russians, but the few Jews present wiped tears from their eyes upon hearing Yiddish spoken. The Kirghiz and the Russians gradually left the park. The little songs that Didya Epstein, who had a very fine voice, and I sang warmed up the Jewish audience. There was no striving for artistic success here, and only a small remuneration. Most important was that we be recognized officially as members of the Kirghiz Philharmonic, which had certain benefits. Later, for instance, we received ration cards, without which one could not live. These enabled us to get a kilogram of bread per day for each of us, a large amount that we exchanged for other products at the bazaar, the Frunze marketplace.

I wrote to Ruth and asked her to come to Frunze. The winter was short and not severe (we had no warm clothing with us), and in general getting food was easier here than any place else. She quickly made up her mind to come. The trains from Siberia did not operate regularly, but still I waited for her. I prepared all sorts of fruits that were unavailable in Siberia, even some kinds I had never eaten before.

When I met Ruth at the station, I saw the great change that had come over my daughter. Large and puffed up, she was hardly recognizable. When she entered the hotel room and saw all the fruits, she literally threw herself upon them. We could not tear her away, for it had been so long since she had seen fruit.

My "rich" daughter (compared to me) not only did not have any fruit in Omsk but could not obtain even a bit of flour. Living conditions were also bad there. She and Addy had slept on a chest. Indeed, she came to Frunze with money for which she could buy nothing in Omsk.

Ruth and I had to begin looking for an apartment immediately, for our hotel was too expensive. It was almost impossible to get an apartment in the middle of town, but apartments in the outskirts had clay floors, and we didn't want to live in this fashion. Finally we found a large apartment with a kitchen and a small corridor. It even had a wooden floor. Except for a chair and a table, there was no other furniture, and we had to order everything. We bought various items with funds realized from our sold possessions and with the money Ruth had brought with her. We settled down with the thought of being as comfortable as possible and with hope for the two babies who would soon come into the world. Our visitors, both local residents and refugees, considered our apartment well decorated and talked much about it.

However, soon a rumor spread that Ida Kaminska was very rich and that her daughter too had brought much money with her. After all, how many other refugees had settled down in such fashion? Ruth had endless ideas on how to beautify the house and make it more livable. For instance, she was able to convert simple mattress beds into sofas, and she had other innovations as well.

In the little corridor we placed a water barrel we had purchased, and poor Mel had to go fill it every morning, carrying the wager jug, summer and winter, from a well that was more than three hundred yards away. Mel carried it according to the local custom, on a yoke from which two large barrels were suspended. Thanks to this, we were able to draw water all day long, as though from a well.

Soon Ruth and I went to a gynecologist who determined that we would give birth at approximately the same time—within a period of two weeks—but that I would be first. I was due in about six weeks. The night after the examination I felt I was lying in a pool of water, a sure sign that I would soon give birth, despite the doctor's prediction. I became very frightened. We decided to call for first aid. My husband ran two miles to use the phone at the Hotel Kirgistan.

When the first aid squad came, the lady doctor said she couldn't help me. I had to go immediately to the maternity hospital, where my daughter and I had registered. I told the doctor we had signed up for a later period, but she insisted that we go there first. So in the middle of the night we traveled to the maternity hospital. My husband accompanied me and, according to hospital rules, took with him all my personal belongings. They gave me a short nightshirt of rough linen and began to examine and tap me as though I would soon give birth.

I maintained it was much too early but still they took me to a room adjoining the delivery room. Suddenly I became an eyewitness to the pains and sufferings of other women in labor. I had no pains. The flow of water had ceased. I was convinced I would soon return home. When the hospital's gynecologist (her husband, Professor Vidrin, the head doctor, was an evacuee from Minsk) came to me, I told her that I felt quite well and would like to go home, for I didn't like hearing all this groaning about me. She replied, "Well, you can remain here overnight. Tomorrow morning we'll examine and release you."

The next morning Mel came. He was not allowed to visit me, so I wrote him a note that I would have to stay one more night and would return home the next day. That evening I again had pains but still felt I was not yet due. The pains intensified, and at dawn, in my seventh month, I gave birth to a baby boy.

The next morning Mel came with a letter stating that our house was being painted that day. If I wished I could remain another day in the hospital, but if not he would welcome me with open arms. Meanwhile, someone in the waiting room congratulated him: "You've become a father."

"You're mistaken," my husband replied. "My wife isn't due yet." Just then Mel received my note that I had given birth to a little boy. He ran home immediately, in tears, to tell the news to my daughter. On his way he met Fere of the Philharmonic, a tall, good-looking man, who asked him why he was crying.

"My wife just gave birth to a boy," said Mel.

"Then why are you crying, my good man?" Fere asked.

"But it's much too early. She was only in her seventh month."

Fere began laughing. "Look at me. Do I look like some sort of premature child? I, too, was born in the seventh month." This calmed Mel somewhat.

The birth occurred during one of the most difficult days of the war, October 16, 1941. Moscow was almost completely surrounded. A massive evacuation of hundreds of institutions created a depressing atmosphere in the entire land, even thousands of miles from Moscow. In Frunze people were already whispering, "Tomorrow we'll already be hearing German from Moscow."

The mood such words created need not be described. I even heard these rumors in the hospital, where on the following day I was already moving about. I would sit in the room and communicate with Mel through the window. Once I even showed him the baby—stealthily—for this was strictly forbidden.

I remained in the hospital ten days. During this time my husband would keep sending me notes with news. He would also bring me delicacies that Ruth had prepared. Once he and Ruth wrote to ask what name we would give the baby, for he had to be registered. I replied, "How about Victor?" for I had in mind the victory we all longed for. My husband and daughter agreed.

Mel would regularly come to visit me after 5 P.M. One day he left the house earlier and decided to wait in a square until five. He sat down on a bench and wrote me a letter. As he was writing, a nearby loudspeaker suspended on a telephone pole broadcast a communiqué from staff headquarters concerning the military situation: that on October 16—the day my son was born—the Red Army had repulsed the German tanks from Moscow. While Mel was writing this happy news a Soviet policeman came up to him, put his arm on his hand, and took the letter from him. "What are you writing?" he asked.

"A letter to my wife in the hospital," my husband answered.

"Why were you writing during the broadcast, when they were giving the communiqué?"

"Why should I bother writing it when this news is being heard all over the world?" Mel joked. "It's no longer a secret."

"Don't give me any of your alibis," the policeman replied sharply. "You're coming with me immediately. Just follow me."

Mel followed the policeman straight to the NKVD. He later told me that he was led in and out of corridors, probably so he would not remember the way. The policeman made a report, and my husband was taken to an investigator. The investigator only wanted to know what kind of secrets my husband was writing in the letter and why he was writing precisely when the communiqué from staff headquarters was being broadcast. Moreover, the letter was written in Polish. Mel immediately replied in Russian, but it didn't help. For several days in a row he was ordered to come to that office at midnight. Finally the investigator declared that they had found out who he was and that the letter had been translated by a trustworthy translator. Only then was Mel cleared.

When Ruth came to take me home from the hospital, she brought a pillow made especially for Victor, but he was so tiny that he was actually lost in it. Nevertheless, the baby looked healthy and had a small, fine, expressive face.

During my stay in the hospital many refugees arrived in Frunze. They came from Poland, the Ukraine, and from deep inside the Soviet Union. Among them were many Jews, including actors from our Lemberg and Bialystok Yiddish theaters. They were happy that I had given birth, for this raised hopes that through me we could organize a theater. It also meant that the actors could get bread cards and be registered in the Philharmonic as employees, which was a very important thing.

Better news came constantly from the front; the Germans were being pushed back in many places. We breathed easier and began looking hopefully to the future.

Our apartment became very pleasant. With her own hands and ingenuity my daughter Ruth made it very European. It was a joy to live in such an apartment, even though we had to bring a newborn baby into alien surroundings.

The refugees altered the appearance of the city. Now not only Yiddish but Polish, too, was heard on the streets. We made plans to begin working. Since we had actors but no plays with us, I transcribed from memory about seven or eight plays, which, when compared several years later to the originals, were found to be faithful copies. Thank God, to this very day my memory serves me in like fashion.

Two weeks after my return from the hospital, my daughter

felt labor pains and I called Professor Vidrin. He came and determined that Ruth still had three weeks to go before her delivery, but her situation was similar to mine: pains at night and a call to the first aid squad. Mel accompanied her to the hospital and returned with her things but without any news.

The hospital was far off. There was no means of transportation except walking. It was impossible for me to walk the several miles, but I couldn't wait any longer. I left the baby with Mel and ran to the hospital, where I discovered that Ruth had given birth to a little girl.

I was stunned. I had never expected it to come so quickly. I sent a note to my daughter and anxiously awaited her reply. Her note came, which I read with dismay. "Mama, I'm cold. [It was November 5, and they still had not yet begun heating.] The baby is lying next to me, crying and screaming. No one attends me. I don't feel well, and they have not even sewn me up yet."

I was so angry I thought I would faint. I ran out through a rear door and entered a room where doctors were conducting an inspection. They paid no attention to me, but then I began to scream, "Why are you neglecting my daughter? Why is no one attending her?" As they left the room, Professor Vidrin's wife approached me with an angry look. Then I began pleading, for I knew that shouting would accomplish nothing. My tearful pleas helped. They asked me to wait at the main entrance, where I remained a long time.

Finally I received a reply both from Ruth and from the professor's wife, who calmed me: "Why did you raise such a fuss? Everything is in perfect order. The baby is well, and your daughter feels well, too." My daughter's note confirmed the woman's remarks. Ruth said they had attended her. She was now in a warmer room and the baby had been washed.

I returned home by foot, traversing the long streets, crying as I went. I frequently mention crying, because in these memoirs I may give the impression that I weep easily and often. Actually, I rarely cry, but each time I do I remember it well. I barely made it home, saw my baby, and told my husband that Ruth had given birth to a girl, who would be called Erika, after *E*sther *R*achel *K*aminska. He immediately ran to see Ruth at the hospital, where she remained for ten days.

I found out that Ruth had not given birth in the delivery room but, because of lack of space, had been placed on some cot. Suddenly she felt the baby coming out and at that moment noticed an empty bed. On her own she went to that bed, and before anyone came she herself delivered the baby. When Ruth saw that the baby had been born, something exploded in her and she began screaming, "The baby! The baby!" The hospital employees were afraid to approach her, for they were responsible for her having given birth without assistance. However, finally they began attending her.

I imagine what the situation would have been under other circumstances, in freedom, when my only daughter would have prepared herself for confinement, but the events justified everything. I would go to the hospital daily, stand before the window, and exchange a few words with her. When I brought Ruth home, we had two premature babies, both of whom were healthy. We would take the babies to a clinic for examination. Our children were pointed out as an excellent example of cleanliness and proper handling by the mother.

24

Life in Frunze

DURING this period we were rehearsing *Chasya, the Orphan,* by Jacob Gordin. The performance took place in the hall of the Philharmonic. It was not a large place, the stage was primitive, and we couldn't make any new decorations. We received the hall free of charge but bore the production costs. Backstage there hung a curtain with a painting of a Kirghiz man holding a banjolike folk instrument. During all our performances the Kirghiz with the banjo kept looking over our shoulders.

While performing in *The Slaughter,* I could no longer stand this Kirghiz hanging in the rabbi's house, so I sewed up the curtain to conceal the painting. The newly arrived actors were fine and experienced, and so we had no difficulty in producing the plays. We also had an audience, for the war had brought to Frunze refugees from Poland and all of Russia who were longing for the consolation of a Yiddish word.

When I appeared onstage, I witnessed a moving demonstration. Everyone stood, applauded, and wept. All of us onstage wept, too. Here stood audience and actors facing one another, homeless, persecuted, thousands of miles from our homes, where most of us had left our dearest kin.

The performance continued in a festive atmosphere, and the audience received us warmly. Nevertheless, we couldn't give frequent performances because the hall was not ours.

Once, however, we were successful in obtaining the Russian state theater, where we performed according to professional standards.

Meanwhile, as a result of the political agreement between the Polish premier, Wladyslaw Sikorski, who was in London, and Stalin, the so-called Polish delegations were opened in Frunze and other cities. These somewhat eased the lot of former Polish citizens, especially the children. We, too, registered and occasionally received various items, foods, and things for our babies. Still, our situation was not a good one. The money that we had was gone, earnings were minimal, and unlike others we did no business at the marketplace. At that time transactions at the bazaar were a national occupation.

About three months after we had given birth, my daughter's husband, Addy Rosner, came to Frunze. Our material situation improved. He gave successful concerts and had various connections. For example, as an economy measure, electric lights had been shut off along the entire street. Because of the babies, Addy got the electricity turned on in our house, causing envy among the other residents.

Soon my son-in-law and his ensemble departed, and Ruth was left with her baby at our place. My husband accompanied Rosner as stage manager. I wanted him to rest and regain his strength, as well as earn some money.

Once we all went to the children's clinic and were told that baby Erika had a slight case of nasal diphtheria. Ruth immediately took Erika home. There she discovered that someone had come from the epidemic hospital to see if the child was there. (At the clinic no one mentioned taking Erika to the hospital.) However, when Victor and I came home we discovered that Ruth and Erika had been taken to the hospital.

Simcha Natan, who was visiting us, told me what had occured. (Simcha, who had come to us in Frunze and performed with us, had left in Lemberg his wife, Natalie, and his daughter, Ida, who had recently given birth to a boy.) Because of his great longing for his only grandchild, Simcha Natan displayed unusual affection for my son and became attached to him. He would spend days playing with him.

Ruth had left a message for me that she had to remain with Erika. She gave me the address of a Jewish doctor from Minsk whom I should approach to insure better treatment for her at the hospital. So I left Victor with Natan, took a baby carriage which Ruth would need to bring the baby home, and ran to the hospital. There Ruth told me that she had to remain there with the child. She again gave me the name of a Jewish doctor from Minsk and told me to ask him to provide better treatment for Ruth. I left immediately.

By now it was already dark; the sun had disappeared behind the mountains. Suddenly I heard the lowing of a cow and saw the large-horned creature coming directly toward me. In my fright, I forgot that there was no child in the carriage and stood in front of it protecting it with my body. I screamed, for the cow was quite near. At that point, a youngster ran up and hooted the cow away.

Although I had a heart spasm, I continued running until I reached the doctor's house. The kindly man understood my feelings and immediately gave me a note to the head physician of the hospital. I thanked the doctor (I believe Halpern was his name), asked him if I could leave the baby carriage there overnight, and immediately ran to the head physician.

By now it was completely dark outside. The doctor had given me instructions about how to proceed in the darkness, but I couldn't orient myself and suddenly felt myself sinking in a swamp. I seized the trunk of a little tree and just barely managed to extricate my feet. Once again I felt a flutter in my heart. Finally I dragged myself to the house of the head physician. Locked! No one was at home.

I decided to wait. Suddenly I saw someone who looked like a nurse and asked her to help me find the doctor. Touched by my soft words and tears, she went to fetch the head physician. He gave me a note and even went out to show me the right path. At the hospital I heard Ruth screaming, for one of the supervisors had wanted to throw her out of the hospital. Since the door was closed, I began knocking and shouting. Ruth heard my voice. The door was opened for me and I flipped the head physician's note inside. Silence reigned. Wanting to calm me, Ruth said, "Everything will be all right now. Go home, Mama." I told her I'd return the following morning. On my way I crossed railroad tracks and went into a heavily wooded path which should have brought me home. But the events of the day affected my nerves and I began crying as I walked. Then, in the total darkness, I suddenly saw horses and riders galloping toward me and just avoided being trampled by them. Running again, I finally came home, crying and bleeding. There Mel calmed me. They washed the blood from my feet, and put me in bed.

On the table I saw plates and all sorts of foods that Ruth had prepared for me, for that day was my birthday.

When I visited Ruth the next day, she told me that conditions were unbearable in the room where she, her baby, and other children were located. She asked me to go to Sadayev, the secretary of Frunze's Communist party, which in the Soviet Union was the highest local position. He was Assyrian by nationality, a surviving member of an ancient nation that had settled in old Russia after fleeing religious persecutions in Turkey. Sadayev differed from other Russian party functionaries by his great intelligence and, as he himself stated, his great sympathy for Jews, whom he considered "brothers from whom we have separated." Thanks to Sadayev, Ruth's condition in the hospital improved. I received permission to visit her and found her in a beautiful, semiprivate room with good service and with special food. There my grandchild recovered very quickly and soon returned home.

Time flew by. We listened to the news broadcast from loudspeakers on the wall and on the streets. Up to the second half of 1943 the news was not good. Hitler's armies were deep inside Russia, which demoralized the population. Provisions, even in Frunze, so far from the front, were horribly low, but conditions were still better than in the European part of Russia.

The poison of anti-Semitism was spread among the local population by soldiers returning from the front who had been indoctrinated by German loudspeakers. Others agitated by saying that "the Jews had overrun Tashkent and Frunze and refuse to fight." A contrary view was spread by front-line soldiers who argued that "because the Jews on the front lines pushed themselves into the most dangerous positions we have to follow them and endanger our lives."

Thus, thousands of miles from the front lines, a campaign of agitation inspired by the Nazis was gradually accepted by the average folk. The populace behind the lines suffered, that is true. Want was widespread because of the lack of products, but at the same time speculation flourished at the bazaars. The women were most bitter of all. Their men were at war, and despite hard work they didn't have enough to provide for their children. In such an atmosphere it was easy to spread the wildest and most foolish lies.

We would get letters from friends and acquaintances who had settled in various towns in middle Asia. My chief correspondent was Grisha Rotshein, a childhood friend and colleague in our theater, who at that time was residing in Samarkand. (To this very day Grisha sends me news of Israel, where he has been living for more than twenty years.)

Grisha would write to me about conditions in Uzbekistan and in the city of Samarkand. According to him, conditions were much worse there, and speculation was much more widespread. Therefore, the Soviet police were arresting people indiscriminately, often innocent ones as well. In almost all of Grisha's letters there were names underlined in black, by which he indicated our friends and colleagues who had died in Samarkand and Bokhara. It was as though the plague had struck our group from Lemberg who had moved to those cities.

Among the deceased there once appeared the name of Karol Gimpel (a brother of the famous musicians Jacob and Bronislaw Gimpel, who now live in the United States). Karol Gimpel, a famous pianist and composer who worked with us in the Lemberg theater, was arrested in Bokhara for leaving his position as director in an Uzbek theater and traveling to Bokhara without permission. He wanted to reach the Polish army that was then being organized in the Soviet Union. Gimpel fell ill in prison and died.

At that time a spotted-fever epidemic raged in several central Asian towns. Most of the typhus victims were refugees from the western parts of Russia. In Frunze, too, there were victims of various forms of typhus.

Grisha Rotshein would also write about various persons we knew who had been arrested. One day I received a letter from him from jail. He, too, had been arrested. He didn't sit in jail for long but was living proof of the story that made the rounds at that time: "In Russia people live like riders in a bus. Some sit [meaning in prison], others shake in fear." Even in Frunze my daughter had told me, "Mama, I would rather die than be arrested."

These words later followed me like a ghost.

While describing my life in Frunze—actually the place where I saved my life—I must not forget that had I remained in Lemberg with the Germans, I certainly would not have survived the persecutions and humiliations which would have been far worse than our life in Frunze. The hardships and occasional tragic situations of which I write were a result of the overly zealous Soviet bureaucracy, which has no equal in the world. In those days the arrests took place because of exaggerated suspicion and petty misdemeanors like selling bread and food on the black market.

We remained in Frunze two years and eight months. Many people went through my apartment, including actors and friends who stayed with me for weeks on end and lived in the kitchen until they found other quarters. There were also strangers, Jews who knew that I lived here and who were told that I had a "good" apartment and was a "mother" for everyone. Very often such a guest had more in one pocket than I owned all told. They would ask only to sleep over and leave a few things in my house, which they pushed behind a bed in the kitchen. I never asked them any questions. I simply felt that if Jews came into my house at such a time and requested a night's lodging or to remain for another day, it was a *mitzvah* to accommodate them.

Unfortunately, people often took advantage of my good will, to the point where it could have brought me great trouble. Once, when I was ill and literally had no food to eat, an inspection team came into my house in the middle of the night. Two Russians entered, and one man, a Jew, remained outside. This was a terrible surprise, which hurt me. An inspection in my house?

When the inspection was over, one of the officers told me, "Since we have begun our inspections in various homes, we have not yet found such poverty. Do you want to know why we came to you?"

"Yes," I replied.

"A Jew informed us that you have lots of suspicious and smuggled merchandise in your house."

It was an awful thing to hear. Now I realized the contents of the packages that had been left under the kitchen bed. This was the thanks I got for keeping an open house for people from whom I never asked a penny, God forbid, for lodging.

There were other difficult moments. Mel returned from the trip with Addy Rosner because he had to be with me, but he began losing his strength. He didn't eat but gave the best part of everything to Ruth and me and exchanged some of the ration cards for milk for the children. All this reduced this strong, healthy man to a state of complete weakness. Carrying water several times a day made Mel lose 40 of his 180 pounds. He simply fell off his feet. When I noticed this, I took the last of my possessions, my Japanese robe and a pair of Italian slippers, along with some other lesser items, and went for the first time to the bazaar. There I sold them all and bought butter, eggs, and other food on the black market. I placed Mel in bed and didn't let him get up until I noticed an obvious improvement in his condition. From then on, I no longer permitted Mel to eat alone in the kitchen. He had to eat with me so that I would see that he was indeed eating. We all shared what we had. Sometimes we had more, sometimes less, but in any case I didn't permit my husband to starve himself purposely.

There were incidents that affected me and continued to haunt me. I would see little drunken children on the streets. In general, I am very sensitive when it comes to children because of my great love for them. Once I saw two drunken children, one eight, the other nine. One was more intoxicated then the other, and two girls were supporting them, just like wives leading their drunken husbands home. The boy was using foul language and cursing in a horrible fashion. I also saw children who smoked and begged for cigarettes from adults.

There were evenings when we would gather in our kitchen, especially in winter, when it was difficult to heat the larger room. There we would sit, usually with the Korlenders and the Perlmans, couples who were our closest neighbors. There would also be other visitors, among them our old friend the stagemaster, Chaim Goldzader. Everyone would bring something for the gathering and a bit of alcohol (actually ersatz alcohol). We would prepare potatoes and herring, if herring was available, or just simply potato pancakes, and we would talk and reminisce. We spoke of old Jewish Warsaw, its great Jewish personalities, the famous Polish actors, the little villages that we had visited on tour. The nostalgia was so great that we would become ill. Occasionally I even developed a fever, especially when I was waiting for Ruth and her baby, whom I missed very much. When Ruth left to sing with Addy's orchestra, Victor and Erika were eight months old, and now both were about a year-and-a-half.

Our living conditions improved. Ruth brought some money with her, and I had the children around me. My feelings toward little Erika were not grandmotherly; I actually felt as though I had another daughter. Ruth, too, responded like a mother to Victor. If was as if we both had two children. That is why, when we separated, our yearning was greater than normal, and when we would reunite, we felt very fortunate and overjoyed.

At that period many interesting things occurred. The Polish Delegation, previously much honored by the Russians, was ordered closed. It had been located in the comfortable Hotel Kirgistan, from which a Polish flag flew. The delegation would sponsor cultural evenings, and Soviet officials would attend. I, too, was frequently invited. Just before the closing, rumors began to fly that something would happen. Various Poles, as well as our actors, were called to the NKVD. Each one was told that he would be severely punished if he informed anyone of this interrogation by the secret police. Nevertheless, we knew. Each one was asked why he had registered at the Polish Delegation and was requested to inform on the others. I don't know who agreed and who refused. There were some, I am sure, who didn't submit, but I can't say this of all my colleagues. I happened to be the last one called. I was led through various corridors (according to their old system), and then a young man began the investigation with the routine question: why had I registered with the Polish Delegation?

"What do you mean?" I said. "There was an announcement that everyone who had been a Polish citizen up to 1939 had to register."

"But you are a Russian citizen," said the young investigator. "You have a Russian passport."

"Yes," I said. "I was a Polish citizen until 1939. If there will still be a Poland after the war, I will want to return to my home in Warsaw."

"What's the matter? Don't you like it here?" he asked provocatively.

I replied, "I'm in a strange land. The times are difficult. There still is not anything to like. And you—are you from Frunze?" I asked him.

"No."

"Then tell me, don't you feel the need to be where you were born and raised? I have no longing for the old Poland, but I hope that now there will be another Poland. Perhaps I will see ruins there. I don't know if I will find any of my family. Still, I am drawn there. Don't you miss home?"

"Yes, I do," he said, somewhat ashamed.

After our conversation the young investigator, visibly moved, took me to the door and kissed my hand, an unusual gesture for a Russian. He asked me when I would be performing, for he wanted to see me in a play. I invited him. Several days later he came to a performance and even sent flowers. In time he became a friend.

When the Polish Delegation was closed, I once again received a note from him inviting me to come to his office. This time he asked me, "What are people saying about the closing of the delegation?"

"Actually people are confused. Was it closed only in Frunze or in other cities as well? There are various opinions, but no one knows anything."

"Can't you write down what they're saying?" he asked.

I was shocked and angered. I didn't believe my ears. "The last time I was here you said, 'I wish all the Poles were like you.' Now you want me to become like the others who were here? You want to make me an informer? Young man, you could have been my son. How dare you talk to me like this?"

"What do you mean?" he said, enraged. "This is important work for a Soviet citizen. This is the second time you are betraying the fatherland—first when you registered and now when you are refusing my request."

"Please don't scare me," I replied immediately. "The most

you can do is send me into exile, but here in Frunze I am *already* in exile. So what can you do to me?"

"Come here on Saturday."

"I won't come," I replied. "I am disappointed in you, as I am in other things."

"Then I'll come to you."

"Fine. I'll brew you some tea. More than that I can't offer you."

"I'll come, but I don't want anyone else to be home," he concluded.

"Do you want me to quarrel with my husband? But all right, that I promise you."

I left, broken. I had a long way to get home. The streets were empty. Dogs barked. I felt confounded and depressed. I felt humiliated to the depths of my soul. As soon as I got home, I told Mel everything. However, the investigator never came, never called, and caused me no harm.

There were two other tragicomic episodes from Frunze.

I had accumulated a quantity of flour, which we received from our ration cards. I didn't need it and planned to sell it. One of our actors helped me carry the flour to the market. On the way he met a friend with whom he had more lucrative business, and so he left me. (Perhaps he was dealing in gold and other things.) I waited in vain for his return, then finally dragged the flour myself, hoping I would meet my lost helper at the marketplace.

At the bazaar I put the flour on the board, just as others did. I did not know what to expect. People kept coming up to me, asking how much the flour cost. I didn't know what to say. I heard a price from a Kirghiz man who stood near me. This same Kirghiz also weighed the flour for me. The scene of me standing at the marketplace, weighing flour and selling it, made me laugh. I kept smiling. The women who bought the flour looked suspiciously at me, wondering why I was smiling.

I soon sold almost all the flour. I pictured myself in a photograph selling flour among Kirghiz, Uzbeks, and Dungans (a mixture of Kirghiz and Chinese). Wearing a beautiful but quite shabby coat that I had brought from Lemberg, I was selling flour at the bazaar. People seemed to be looking at me, and although I had some flour left, I took it and abandoned my "stand." On my way home I saw the director of the theater department in the Kirghiz Ministry of Culture selling bread she had received on her ration cards. She didn't notice me, but seeing her calmed me. Such was the sort of world we were living in.

At the bazaar, which was the liveliest place in town, simple Jews gathered—porters and wagoners who had the folk wit of the Polish Jew. Once, when a Russian called a burly Jewish porter a dirty Jew, a fight broke out. The porter nearly beat the life out of the Russian. The police came, and both men were taken to the station house. The investigator was a young Jew who asked the porter in Russian, "Why did you beat him up like that?"

The porter replied in Yiddish in a Warsaw dialect, "I don't understand."

The investigator repeated the question in Russian.

The porter again said, "I don't understand."

Since the investigator did not want to speak Yiddish in the presence of the others, he asked everyone to leave the room. The only one who remained was my friend Chaim Gold-zader, who stayed with the accused, and he was the one who later relayed the entire incident to me.

Now the investigator asked in Yiddish, "Why did you beat him up?"

"He called me a dirty Jew," the porter answered.

"Oh, my!" the investigator said, "And you never heard such terms in Poland, huh?"

"But there I only paid two pennies for a roll," snapped the Jewish porter. This reply, pregnant with so much folk wit, meant: "Yes, I'm ready to go in rags; I'm ready to bear all sorts of hardships and not eat, but I want to be equal with everyone else. But if in Russia I have to hear 'dirty Jew,' as in Poland, then rolls should cost me only two pennies, as in Poland. There I didn't have to suffer so much, and I always had food to eat."

In Frunze I lived in a house where the windows were just above ground. Often poor people would knock on the window, begging for food. When members of our family were at home, we would always find something to give: some soup, potato, a piece of bread, or a couple of kopeks. I admit that we would never let them into the house, for during a period of epidemics it was dangerous to let people encased in dirt into a house where babies lived.

One morning I heard a knock on the window. I pushed aside the curtain and saw a monstrous figure. I couldn't even tell whether it was a man or a woman. It was a tall person, dressed in a tattered army topcoat tied with a bit of string, and feet bound with rags. There was no hint of any other clothing underneath the topcoat. The figure suddenly called me by name and spoke to me in a pure Warsaw Polish. Since it was freezing outside, I let this person into the kitchen, where I discovered that it was a woman, Dr. Helena Shtim.

Dr. Shtim knew my entire family and had gone to school with my sister, Regina, of blessed memory. I noticed that her entire body was swollen. First I gave her something warm to eat. Dr. Shtim said she had been a dentist in Warsaw and that in 1940 she had been sent to the Arctic regions with her two sons. This occurred during the period when the Soviets had sent into exile all refugees from western Poland who had come to eastern Poland and refused to declare themselves as Soviet citizens. After the agreement between Stalin and General Sikorski, the premier of the Polish government-in-exile in London, the exiled Poles were once again permitted to leave for the south and for central Asia.

Now Helena Shtim and her younger son lived in a village in the outskirts of Frunze. The older son had joined the Polish army, which had been recruited in Russia; he was later killed in the war. In the village where she resided and from which she had walked to Frunze, Dr. Shtim occasionally earned some money by pulling peasants' teeth with the few dental instruments she possessed.

Dr. Shtim remained with me until we left Frunze for Moscow. Within a few days she was a different person. Her swelling had disappeared. She wore clothes I gave her and became a pleasant, happy person who grew attached to our family. She also helped me considerably. When she went to the villages to pull teeth, she brought back some potatoes or other food. We helped her son enter an orphanage not far from our house, where he had food and clothing. After our departure she suffered again. However, a few years later we met her in Warsaw, where she was a doctor in a hospital, mourning after her elder son. (The younger one was studying in a university.)

My memories of Frunze are chaotic. We lived through the worst days of the war. When my daughter was with me, I had both children and I was happy, but when Ruth returned to her husband and took Erika, I felt a sense of emptiness around me. Moreover, each day was different. Sometimes there was no light during weekdays. Mel, who had returned from Rosner's orchestra, worked hard carrying water a quarter of a mile, and I cooked outside in the southern heat, unable to drive away the masses of flies.

When I learned that the Polish army would have a theater, I wrote to Wanda Vasilyevska, the famous Polish writer, under whose patronage the army had been organized in Russia. I knew her from Lemberg and wanted her to know that Mel and I would be glad to work for the theater. We also noted that we would want to take our child, Victor, with us. She replied warmly, by telegram, and informed me that when the time came she would call me. However, I received no further word, and perhaps this was indeed fortunate.

25

Moscow

IN 1944 Ruth and Addy were giving concerts in Moscow, where they intended to stay a long time. I could no longer remain in Frunze. My son-in-law got me the special permit needed in order to travel to Moscow, and Mel, Victor, and I left for Moscow at the end of March.

My Frunze apartment was taken over by Simcha Natan and another colleague. The newly founded Yiddish theater engaged Natan, and I left them several plays. Thus the Frunze theater continued its activity. The entire ensemble, as well as other friends, accompanied us to the train station.

The day we left was exceedingly hot. Victor, dressed only in short pants, and I traveled in a sleeping car, while Mel and Chaim Goldzader, who was going to work for Addy Rosner, traveled third class. The train journey took four and a half days. On the third day, somewhere near the town of Kuybyshev, I wanted to take Victor—as I usually did—out to the station. I looked around—snow! I rummaged in the valise and quickly removed some warm things for the child and myself.

Some stations later, by the edge of the Ural Sea, almost all the passengers rushed to buy barrels of salt, and when we drew close to Moscow, they began exchanging the salt for meat, chickens, butter, and other food. We arrived in Moscow on April 1, 1944.

Ruth and several other people awaited us. In Moscow lived my former schoolmate Doba Taubin, today known as Doba

Santatour. I asked Ruth why Doba was not at the station. My daughter replied that Doba would visit us at home. Later, at the hotel, Ruth explained, "Mama, I didn't want you to be shocked. Doba not only looks like your mother but like your grandmother. I didn't want you to be frightened of her. I wanted to prepare you."

It was now late at night. My husband and I received a single room in the large Hotel Moscow, where we lived during our first year in Moscow. (The Hotel Moscow could have swallowed up twenty Hotel Kirgistans. However, the mice and rats were proportionately bigger.) Meanwhile, Ruth and Addy were staying at another hotel until a special apartment at the Moscow would be ready for them. Mel remained in the hotel to unpack, while Victor and I went to Ruth's for supper, and we slept there. (Because of the war, people were not permitted on the streets after 10 P.M.). The meal surprised me because I didn't remember such food since prewar times. In Frunze I had yearned for an ordinary glass of tea with lemon and a spoon; there we drank tea from old tin cans. That evening after a fine bath, I felt again that I was alive.

For me, however, living is connected with work. We thought of what we'd do. The next morning we went to the Anti-Fascist Committee, where we met the actor Shlomo Mikhoels, the poet Itzik Feffer, and others. Mikhoels received me warmly. "Don't be afraid," he told us. "Everything will be taken care of. Everything possible will be done for you."

I remained in Moscow two and a half years. My husband met many acquaintances from Poland in Moscow, which was the seat of the Polish Patriots Organization, founded by Wanda Vasilyevska and other Polish leftists who happened to be in the Soviet Union. Meanwhile, my husband got a job as a Polish announcer on the Soviet radio. He presented eight programs a day and came home sometimes after midnight. He received a special pass that permitted him to be on the streets at night.

Mel was one of the founders of the Jewish section of the

Polish Patriots Organization. He discussed this with Berl Mark and David Sefard, and permission was granted to organize such a section. It was understood that there were many problems that could be considered only within the bounds of Jewish organizational activity. I was also a member of the presidium of this section.

Mel's salary was not high, but thanks to his position he had a residence permit in Moscow and excellent ration cards. We bought food in a special store managed by the friends of the Polish Patriots, where we were able to get many more products and of much better quality than in other stores.

Meanwhile, I looked for work in my own profession. I met Mikhoels several times at his theater. Intelligent and sensitive, Mikhoels had a well-deserved reputation. He was a small man, not particularly good-looking, and was called "the clever Shlomo Mikhoels." Nothing came of our discussions until I asked him openly, "I can do everything in the theater: direct, act, even be a prompter. I can also manage the props. Outside the theater I know nothing. I must earn some money, and I don't want my husband to support me."

He answered in Russian, the language he used most frequently. "Why are you talking to me like this?" he reproached me. "Don't you think we know who Ida Kaminska is? Rest assured we'll do all we can for you. Prepare an evening's performance. On Fridays we have no set schedule. We'll invite people from the Ministry of Cultural Affairs and do something."

Frankly, I had misgivings about his theater. I knew that we would come to no agreement. The actors' Yiddish dialect seemed too harsh to me (exaggeratedly Lithuanian), and I was not accustomed to their style of acting. Nevertheless, I was hopeful and waited. I saw them perform Sholom Aleichem (the first time I saw their theater was in Kiev), as well as Goldfaden. I can't say that I was pleased enough to call it the finest theater in Moscow.

I kept waiting for the promised Friday, but every Friday

their evening schedule was already filled. This happened once, twice, three times. I was never given a Friday. Once I had a visit from Sarah Rotbaum, one of the leading actresses in Mikhoels's theater, the sister of Yaakov Rotbaum. She was an amiable, pleasant woman, a member of the theater's board of directors. "It's regrettable that this evening didn't take place," she apologized. "But it will take place. Just have patience."

I trusted them and believed them. I once again made my preparations, but nothing ever came of it. To this very day I find it difficult to understand why. I no longer talk about this, however, for Mikhoels is a martyr whom the Soviets murdered in a most brutal fashion.

In Moscow I never went onstage and was not active as an actress. I went to see A. Holtzman, the head of the theater department at the Ministry of Cultural Affairs. I knew him from Lemberg, where he had been the director of the opera and the ballet theater. He received me cordially but sadly told me, "Madame Kaminska, you will not be able to act here. Gather up your troupe, which is still in Frunze or elsewhere, and go on tour through the provinces."

"No," I replied. "I performed in Frunze because fate brought me there. Since I am now in Moscow, I don't understand why I shouldn't perform here. Besides, I am tired of traveling around. I have a baby and can't drag him from town to town."

Holtzman couldn't help me. I didn't ask him to use his influence to bring me into the theater, but I thought that through him I'd at least have an opportunity of performing in Moscow.

In 1945 came the twentieth anniversary of my mother's death. This occasion was commemorated by the All-Russian Theater Society in a festive and noteworthy fashion. The affair took place in the hall of the historic society on Gorky Street. The hall was packed with a fine audience of culture lovers. The head of the society was the chairman of the eve-

ning, and various Russian actors performed. The actor Vasily Kachalov of the Moscow Art Theater was scheduled to
come but was prevented by a last-minute illness. We heard
remarks by the famous Russian actress Vera Yurienieva,
but the main speaker was Shlomo Mikhoels, who delivered
a magnificent speech. Known as an excellent orator, he pointed
to me as a worthy continuation of Esther Rachel Kaminska.
Everyone spoke in Russian except me. It turned out that in
this institution no one had ever openly spoken Yiddish. The
fact that I spoke in Yiddish, and the way I talked about my
mother, made a great impression. At the end of the com-
memoration people came and asked me why I was not performing. I couldn't give a satisfactory answer.

I had already become accustomed to my situation in Moscow. I kept busy by working for the Jewish section of the
Polish Patriots Organization. Dozens of former Polish citizens came daily into the offices from the entire Soviet Union,
seeking help, advice, and news from Poland.

Meanwhile, Mel worked diligently for the radio, both in
the news and in the arts departments. Occasionally I would be
invited to participate in the artistic programs of the German
and Polish sections of the Soviet radio. Thus passed the
more than two and a half years of my stay in Moscow.

I would often meet with my old friend, the great poet
Peretz Markish. We would visit each other's homes. I would
also meet with other Yiddish writers, such as David Bergelson and Shmuel Halkin, and I was invited to participate in all
the activities of the Jewish Anti-Fascist Committee.

My mother's old friend, the operetta singer Clara Young,
lived in Moscow at that time. She was very lonely because
her husband and only daughter had for many years resided
in New York. She often met with me and reproached herself for remaining in Moscow. Her successes were past her,
and she was unable to visit her closest relatives. (She died
two years later in Moscow.) Clara was very warm and amiable
to me. From time to time she advised me, "If you ever have
the opportunity of leaving Moscow, take it."

I often think of the clever poet Feffer, the sensitive writer Der Nister, and the nightingale of Yiddish literature, Shmuel Halkin. All of them treated me with great kindness. I remember them, victims of the last years of Stalin's rule, with great awe.

Now some words about Peretz Markish. Although his brother-in-law had been committed to a labor camp in 1937, Markish and his wife were great Soviet patriots. When I criticized the regime in Markish's presence, he always defended it vigorously. He was not alone in being such a patriot. Yet all these people were indicted in 1952 as traitors to the fatherland. Most of them were shot. What historical irony lies in their tragedy! The liquidation of the Jewish intelligentsia during that period sheds light on many things that happened in the regime both earlier and later.

In 1946 I received an invitation from the All-Russian Theater Society to give an evening performance. They were impelled to invite me because of the many letters they had received from Moscow residents. This made me very happy. They asked for pictures and reviews; I gave them everything I had. They informed me that the introduction would be given by Mikhoels. He invited me to his house to give him more personal details. I asked him for some props to help me in the evening's performance. He promised me everything. As we parted, Mikhoels said, "The evening's performance will be rendered in Polish."

"What?" I said, stunned. "I'm known as a Yiddish actress! Why should I perform in Polish in Moscow?"

When I returned home, I told my husband, "You'll see, the performance won't take place."

"Why?" Mel asked.

"I don't know," I replied, "but it won't take place."

And it didn't take place. When I went to the secretary of the All-Russian Theater Society to take back my material, I asked him why there had been no performance. He didn't reply.

"Tell me, is what I suspect true?" I asked. I assumed

Mikhoels didn't want to break precedent and suddenly have a Yiddish program at the All-Russian Theater Society.

"Yes," he replied.

My daughter's family life would occasionally cause me heartaches. My son-in-law, Addy, was very successful on the concert stage, perhaps too successful, especially among women. Frivolous by nature, he had various opportunities, and Ruth suffered. They found no common language. Still, Addy was particularly devoted to her, continually buying her presents, diamonds, and expensive furs, but this didn't make Ruth happy. On the contrary, it hurt her. Outwardly, Addy Rosner was very correct in his behavior and demonstrated special affection for me, Mel, and our son, Victor; nevertheless, my daughter's situation, of which I was aware, also hurt me.

But, my family was a great joy to me, especially the two little children, Victor and Erika, whom everyone considered twins. When Ruth and her husband went on tour, quite often for extended periods, I would again feel sad. However, we had friends in the hotel who were like a family to us, especially David Sefard and his wife, Riva. When the Polish Embassy was established, I was invited there quite often, and Riva lent me some clothes, for I didn't have a large wardrobe.

I frequently attended the theater. Moscow had very good actors and directors. The Moscow Art Theater, founded by Stanislavsky, had excellent actors of the new generation, but in general it gave the impression of being a museum; they staged no new good plays.

I attended other theaters as well, but the differences in those days were not great, for the classical repertoire was acted well in a traditional manner. The lack of a new repertoire prevented the display of any new styles. There were no searches for new forms between 1938 and the 1960s.

Still, the theaters were always full. The greatest success was had by plays in the classical Russian repertoire—Gogol, Tolstoy, Turgenev, and Chekhov—which had been produced years ago by the great masters.

My long stay in Moscow enabled me to get to know the city. Neither the two weeks I spent there in 1939—when the city was not the same as it was twenty-five years later—nor the couple of days I spent there in 1940 had given me this opportunity.

I noticed certain changes in Russia since my last visit. The Russian woman used to have a proud profile with smoothly combed hair and was elegantly yet modestly dressed. Now a standard was imposed upon all. Most women had dyed hair with permanents (I also noticed permanents on men), and their garb was terribly monotonous and shabby. Something had happened to the woman I had known from literature and from life before the revolution. We often spoke of this. People suggested that peasants now comprised most of Moscow's population. The peasants came to the city where there was work, and the village woman had not yet learned to adapt to the urban civilization.

In general the population was embittered, especially the veteran residents of Moscow. They were distressed because of the horrible dwelling conditions and because of lack of foodstuffs and consumer products, a situation that had lasted more than twenty years and had become intensified during the war. People were sick of the long waiting lines that had become a part of life. Despite the Russians' reputation for being good-natured and amiable, people were irritable and unfriendly. Every time I used public transportation, I heard arguments and squabbles, always accompanied by horrible curses.

One of the veteran residents of the Hotel Moscow was the famous writer Ilya Ehrenburg, whom I befriended and spoke with often. At that time he was very productive. He would make frequent trips to the front lines and return with many letters, some of which were written in Yiddish or Polish. His secretary would come to me and ask me to translate them into Russian. These letters were horribly authentic testimonies that told more about the Hitler terror than dozens of literary works. They were letters from children and people on the eve of their annihilation.

People also would come from behind the front lines and tell of their experiences. When I recall them and their reports, I realize that no play, film, or fiction can approach the truth of these autobiographical tales. Ehrenburg collected everything. Once a girl named Rachel, who had known Ruth, told Ehrenburg how her mother had sent her out of their flame-enveloped house. From the street below Rachel had seen her mother looking out the window, which was now surrounded by fire. Rachel said she had not cried then, but while telling this story to Ehrenburg, she choked back her tears.

Another girl from Bialystok had been sent away from the ghetto by her mother. Her mother had given her a diamond. When the girl approached the gate of the ghetto, the German guard asked her, "Where are you going?" and the child replied, "I want to live." The German looked at her, turned aside, and said, "Go." On the way she met a Polish schoolmate, who also asked her where she was going.

"I want to go to the peasants who used to bring dairy products to our house." Her schoolmate showed her the way. At the peasants' she spent several years in a hayloft into which snow seeped in the winter. When the Germans retreated, the peasant who had saved her came to bring her the news. She ran off, not knowing where she was going, and hid in a bundle of hay, where she spent the night. Suddenly she heard Russian songs. She then ran back to the peasant, pressed into his hand her one treasure, the diamond, and ran off again. The peasant's daughter sped after her and pushed the diamond back into her pocket.

The girl made her way to Bialystok, looking for relatives, but found no one. There she sold the diamond, bought some clothes, and befriended a Russian colonel, a doctor. One word led to another, and she discovered that he was her mother's brother. He brought her back to Moscow, where I met her. She remained in Moscow until the liberation and married a Polish Jewish officer. (Now they and their children reside in Denmark.)

Another incident concerned a woman doctor from the town of Pruzhany in Poland. She, too, came to Ilya Ehrenburg. She and her husband had been placed on a wagon that was on its way to a concentration camp, but her husband simply pushed her off. She made her way to a cloister, where she treated the monks. They dressed her as a nun and hid her until the end of the war. She told me how the Germans would ask her blessings when they were going to the front. She acted just like the other nuns, but instead of mumbling a prayer, she cursed them in Yiddish.

I would meet Ehrenburg on various occasions; he never smiled but to me he was always very friendly. Once he phoned to tell me that there was an open letter titled "We Polish Jews" from Julian Tuvim, the great Polish Jewish poet who had been in the United States during the war. "I don't know," Ehrenburg said, "if they will print this letter here."

When we met a couple of days later, Ehrenburg pointed to his chest pocket and said, "This is where I'm keeping the letter. Only Tuvim could have written it. I shall not remain silent, I shall not remain at ease, until the thoughts contained in it are presented in my articles or speeches."

To this day I read selections from this letter in my translation during public appearances.

It is well known that the war was a great destructive force, and it's also well known that the Jews suffered most. However, there were degrees of suffering, and the differences were very great. The sufferings of individual Jews during wartime who lived far from home or who had been exiled into the Arctic regions of Russia were great. Yet all these hardships combined could not be compared with the sufferings of Jews in places where the Germans set foot, especially in Poland.

I received my first direct reports about this from Lublin,

after the city had been liberated, in a letter from Jonas Turkov, brother of my first husband, and his wife, Diana. I read
this letter several times, unable to believe it could all be true.
The list of dead colleagues, relatives, acquaintances, and
friends was endless. With few exceptions, almost everyone
had perished. I shall never forget my first impressions after
reading this letter. Although we knew much of what had happened in Poland, this letter was the first testimony. The story
of the Turkovs and how they had sent their little daughter
to be hidden by Poles was later described in extraordinary
fashion in one of Jonas Turkov's books.

The end of the war was approaching, although it took nine
months from the time that Lublin was liberated until the
actual cessation of hostilities. Nevertheless, we were already
waiting to return home because the war's outcome was no
longer in doubt. Hitler's spine was broken from both east
and west. People even began registering for the return home,
and some of our Polish friends departed immediately after the
liberation of Lublin. There the Polish National Committee of
Liberation immediately formed the first government, despite
the existence of the London-based government-in-exile, which
was a continuation of the prewar regime.

In Moscow we daily awaited new communiqués from military headquarters concerning the occupation of various cities.
These communiqués were read by the popular radio announcer Yuri Levitan (incidentally, a Jew). We Jews heard
these broadcasts with joy but at the same time wept, knowing
that these cities were already without Jews. The day that
Levitan's beautiful voice announced, "Our military forces
have captured Poland's capital city, Warsaw," we were
stunned. Deepest joy and profound sorrow mingled, for we
knew we would meet no one there. We felt that the war with
its multitude of victims would soon end. Our sorrow had
consolation only in the fact that the greatest enemy of our
people, barbaric Hitlerism, was being destroyed, its strength
already broken.

Events literally flew by, one after another, and the sequence of events is difficult to remember. I do recall the moment in July 1944 when along with thousands of people we stood on the streets of Moscow and 96,000 German prisoners captured in White Russia were marched through Moscow's main boulevards. When this great parade came to an end, motorized street sweepers followed, cleaning up the streets. It looked quite symbolic, as though in Europe the filthy traces of Nazism were being washed away. Everyone was in an ecstatic mood. We were under the impression that with this war all wars among peoples would end and that an epoch of friendship among nations would commence. How sweet were these dreams and how bitter was the awakening a couple of years after the war!

At this point I also want to mention an interesting historical fact. In the years 1939-40 the distinguished Dr. Émile Somerstein and the wise and witty Leo Finkelstein were among the many to be arrested. The former was a veteran deputy of the Polish parliament, an attorney from Lemberg, and the latter an essayist, critic, and cultural activist. In 1941, after the agreement between General Sikorski and Stalin, many thousands of arrested persons and former citizens of Poland were freed. Among them were Somerstein and Finkelstein, who came to Moscow and joined the Polish Patriots Organization.

Somerstein would rarely appear, but Finkelstein was at the office almost daily. Since both lived at the Hotel Moscow, we met often and became close friends. In 1944, after the Soviet army had occupied a part of Poland, the two went to Lublin, where the first Polish government was founded, composed of the Polish National Committee of Liberation. (This was an opposition government to the government-in-exile in London.) Before the departure of the group that was to have been the government, Stalin arranged a reception for them in the Kremlin, at which Émile Somerstein, who had been taken into the government, was present.

Somerstein came home from the banquet at 3 A.M. Although

we had already said good-bye—since the officials were leaving for Lublin the next morning—Dr. Somerstein called us at 4 A.M. He apologized for calling at that hour but wanted to tell us something very important before his departure. Because one of us had to look after our little son, Mel went alone up to Somerstein's apartment. A long while passed before he returned. When Mel returned, I saw he was still under the impression of his talk with Somerstein.

Somerstein apologized to Mel for waking us up and regretted the fact that I was unable to hear what he was saying. He didn't know how long he would live and he wanted to have someone remember his statement. (Like Finkelstein, he had suffered in the Soviet concentration camps and his health had been impaired.)

Somerstein said that at the banquet he had sat opposite Lazar Kaganovitch, the only Jew in the Politburo, who at the time was one of Stalin's closest colleagues. "Kaganovitch," Somerstein said, "never removed his glance from me." Somerstein, with his white beard, looked like a patriarchal figure. "Perhaps I reminded him of his father or his grandfather, and that was why he had tears in his eyes," said Somerstein.

When they said farewell at the end of the banquet, Somerstein reported, all the guests went up to Stalin one by one and thanked him for the reception. When Somerstein approached Stalin and shook his hand, he told Stalin, "The fate of our people lies in your hands. Our people must have a homeland, and you can be of help."

Stalin replied, "We shall take revenge for the sufferings of your people. Be at ease, your people's fate and their land is in sure hands. This I promise you."

All of this Somerstein narrated to Mel in a festive tone and concluded: "I beg you to pass this on when you feel it is necessary. I want others to know of this."

I would often know about events before people read about them in the newspapers. In his capacity as a newscaster,

Mel would receive prepared materials. If there was something interesting, he would phone and ask me to tune in at a certain hour. Many times they were articles or commentaries not published in the Soviet press, yet they were broadcast in Polish as counterpropaganda.

On May 7, 1945, I experienced a great moment with Ruth. Mel called me: "Be sure to tune in at eleven!" At eleven he read the news that Germany had capitulated, that a cease-fire agreement had been signed. Moscow knew about this only at noon. We celebrated this joyous event at eleven, and then the people of Moscow poured into the streets to celebrate one hour later.

Since my husband worked in the Polish section of Radio Moscow, we both received Polish consular passports from the Polish Embassy much quicker than others who had registered to receive a document permitting their return to Poland. At the end of 1945, however, came an order that if former Polish citizens wanted repatriation to Poland they had to register with the militia for foreigners. The latest date for this was December 31, 1945.

Since Ruth and Addy Rosner were in Minsk at this time, I called and asked, "When and where will you register?" They replied that since they couldn't come to Moscow now, they would register in Minsk. This made me uneasy, for it was said that only families that registered together would be able to leave together. I informed Ruth and Addy of this and they promised to come to Moscow. Mel and I had to register with the members of the Polish Patriots Organization, all of whom were scheduled to leave as a unit. However, I decided to wait for my children until the final day of registration.

Some time passed and I had no news. At the end of December 1945 members of Rosner's orchestra, former Polish citizens, came and told me that whoever had wanted to register had done so but that Rosner and his wife had not. I had been certain that my children had registered—discreetly, so that no one should know. Finally my husband and I went to register.

Once again I phoned Minsk. Addy Rosner was afraid to talk explicitly about registration, but he assured me that concerning "that matter" I should rest at ease.

After January 1, 1946, my children arrived in Moscow. Addy said that they couldn't register because the party chief of White Russia, First Secretary P. Panamarenko, would have found out and this could have hurt him. Addy assured me in German, his mother tongue, "Mama, you'll see. I'll arrive there [in Poland] sooner than you." My intuition told me that this was not good, that new misfortunes were awaiting me and those closest to me.

At the end of 1945 or perhaps the beginning of 1946, rumors spread in Moscow that there had been pogroms against Jews in various Ukrainian towns, especially in Kiev. This was another blow for me. Pogroms in Kiev? In the Soviet Union? What was the reason for this? Facts were pieced together from stories passed from one Jew to another.

It seems that at the Kiev bazaar, the place for anyone who wanted to sell anything, an argument had broken out between a Jewish officer, a war hero decorated with medals, and another soldier, a veteran of the war. One word led to another, and the Ukrainian told the Jewish officer, "Don't brag about those medals to me. You probably bought them, because you sat out the war in Tashkent, far from the front."

The Jewish officer, feeling insulted, shot and wounded the Ukrainian. Immediately the word was passed that Jews were shooting Russian soldiers, and the masses then attacked Jews and destroyed Jewish homes. Some Jews were wounded.

Only toward evening, so the story went, did the security forces restore order. A bitter aftertaste remained for the Soviet Jews. This happened only one year after German Fascism had annihilated Jews and persecuted Russians and Ukrainians. People attempted to justify the fact with the explanation that this was the fruit of what Hitler had been sowing in Russia for three years.

Two months later came the shocking news that there had been a pogrom in the town of Kielce in Poland because of an anti-Jewish blood libel. Fifty Jews lost their lives—Jews who had survived the German slaughter. They were killed by Poles, whose nation was the first victim of the Nazi war, people who themselves were oppressed by the Germans and who knew quite well that when Hitler finished with the Jews he would begin with them.

I felt as though I had been stabbed in the back. During the six years of the German occupation of Poland people grew accustomed to the fact that a Jewish life was worth no more than two pounds of sugar, which at the beginning of the war was the Germans' reward for locating a Jew. (Later the populace brought Jews out on their own, without asking for payment.) The pogrom in Kielce and the lesser "excesses" in Kiev showed how difficult it was to remove the deeply rooted hatred against Jews that had been cultivated for hundreds of years.

My unrest increased from day to day. Long weeks passed. Mel was in no hurry to travel to Poland, for his work satisfied him and I was waiting for Ruth. Also, the infamous pogrom at Kielce made us tremble. A pogrom against Jews in the post-Hitler era!

In 1942, when we were still in Frunze, the Polish army was founded under the command of General Wladyslaw Anders as a result of Sikorski's visit to Stalin. There were many Poles and Jews, former citizens of Poland, who volunteered for this army. Half of Addy Rosner's orchestra joined. The actor Hersh Hart, who lived for a while in my house, immediately volunteered, too. After his return Hersh told us that the attitude toward Jewish volunteers was hostile; the Polish soldiers did not want to accept the Jews. To his good fortune, Hersh had chanced to meet a high Polish officer with whom he had served in the volunteer anti-Russian legions of Jozef Pilsudski, and so the Polish army accepted Hersh (in 1942), even though he was forty-five. Other volunteers for Anders's army were the two well-known actors of the Little Art Theater, Djigan and Schumacher. We still don't know which individuals in the Polish army turned the two over to the Russians, who exiled them to a labor camp.

Now, in 1946, Djigan and Schumacher were released. They came to Moscow and wanted to return all the quicker to Poland. They visited us and spoke at length about the labor camps, of which we knew, but to our delight they reported it, as was their style, from a comic point of view. Both Djigan and Schumacher were in communication with Lemberg, from which—since it was a large city of former Poland —a large repatriation of citizens was taking place. Like countless others who wanted to live in Poland and not in the Soviet Union, Djigan and Schumacher went through Lemberg on their way to Poland.

Those who found themselves deep inside Russia had to register for repatriation in their places of residence, but since the cutoff date of December 31, 1945, had passed, thousands repatriated themselves through Lemberg and Vilna. Apparently the Soviets were not too careful, for even many Soviet citizens departed. Addy and Ruth wanted to leave in the same fashion. They had proof that in 1939 they had been registered in Lemberg, which was the formal prerequisite for being repatriated via Lemberg. When I discovered Addy's plan, my intuition once again foretold that this was not good for him.

Addy wanted to exploit his formal right to return to Poland via Lemberg. Indeed, in 1939 he had been registered there as a Polish citizen, and this enabled him to apply for repatriation in Lemberg. He communicated with various people in Lemberg and later flew there with Djigan and Schumacher to complete the formalities. When Addy returned, he said that he had finished everything but it had cost him a fortune: twenty thousand rubles. Without this payment it could not have been accomplished. Now everything was in perfect order.

However, I had an awful premonition. Addy was going to go with a violinist from his orchestra (today a well-known composer, Adam Viernik) and with Chaim Goldzader. Prior to Addy's departure to Lemberg, I was not well. I lay in bed and spoke to my son-in-law till four in the morning, asking him not to go through with this plan.

"I don't like it," I said. "We'll have to find another way to leave. I'm afraid of this plan."

Addy replied, "They won't permit me to leave in a normal fashion."

"And I don't want you to risk an irregular route," I pleaded.

The next day Addy phoned Viernik that he would not go, but on the third day he indeed left. My daughter was thoroughly exhausted from all this but pleaded, "Mama, let him have his way. I have no more strength for these sudden changes of plans."

Then there came a moment that I shall never forget. Ruth's little daughter, Erika, was dressed in a fur coat and a fur hat. Ruth told her in Polish, "Come, you little border thief." This cut me to the quick, and I replied, "Ruthie, what sort of jokes are these?" for these had been my thoughts all along, thoughts that oppressed me. Ruth and Addy didn't want me to accompany them to the station, for they had let it be known that they were going to Lemberg for concerts.

They left and I walked up the hotel stairs; it was the first time in my life I had climbed so many stories. On the way I passed the hotel buffet. I asked them to give me a glass of vodka, which for the first time in my life I swallowed in one shot. I went into my room. The Russian maid, whom we had kept for Erika, came up to me, saw my state of mind, and suggested that since today was Friday it was a good day to tell my fortune with cards. She proceeded to do this and then called out, "What's this? Only tears and more tears?

The cards show that you'll have a good life, but here I only see weeping."

My husband and I were scheduled to depart on November 26, 1946. I called Ruth and Addy in Lemberg every few days, first in the hotel and later in the apartment. We spoke very carefully. "Taking a summer house" meant they would travel with a special train for emigrants; or "the premiere will take place on such and such a date." But this "premiere" was constantly postponed. I wanted them to go first so I would hear that they had already arrived. I couldn't postpone my cutoff date, but theirs kept changing.

Before our departure Addy told me that Erika had caught the measles but that this would not delay him. "My premiere is on the twenty-eighth." This meant he would leave Lemberg despite the child's illness. On November 26 I phoned to say good-bye. My heart was very uneasy. They were still remaining.

I bade farewell to Yiddish writers and actors I knew, not knowing that many of them would become victims of the terrible Stalin terror that lasted from 1949-53. I said most of my good-byes via the telephone. Ehrenburg's farewell was very warm; he wished me luck and added that I surely deserved it. I said good-bye to Peretz Markish, Shlomo Mikhoels, and Clara Young personally. They even promised to be at the station. Markish and Clara indeed came. Mikhoels did not. Others present were my old friend Verite, Doba and her daughter, and a new friend from the Hotel Moscow, Salo Flor, a grandmaster of chess in the Soviet Union, originally from Czechoslovakia.

We were amazed at the number of Soviet military personnel who traveled with us, but it was natural since the Red Army was already in Berlin and in western Poland. At Brest, the last station in the Soviet Union, nothing was available in the buffet, and yet ten miles farther, at the first Polish station, white rolls and hot salami were sold. We quickly bought some, for we were hungry and so was little Victor.

The Soviet soldiers were particularly eager to buy. We somehow felt more calm in traveling with so many Russian soldiers. After the horrible pogrom in Kielce we feared bands that, we were told, even dared to attack trains.

Evening fell. There was no light in the cars. The dark twilight stirred up thoughts about prewar Poland and what was awaiting us. The windows in the wagons were broken and it was cold. I wrapped Victor in a blanket and put him to sleep. We were traveling to Warsaw over the Polish earth, not knowing what was awaiting us. We didn't know whether we would be able to remain in Poland.

Through the broken windows we saw ruins. We entered Warsaw in a mournful mood, greeting the land that we had left under different conditions, when so many thousands of Jews had remained behind in every town and village. But the most important thing for me was to be reunited with Ruth, Erika, and Addy.

26

Back in Warsaw

IT was late at night when we arrived in Warsaw. My
heart pounded, and despite the darkness my eyes sought
something familiar in the outskirts of the city. In the dark
the ruins looked like fantastic forms in a nightmare.

The train pulled in at a provisionally built terminal in
the Praga section of town, located on the eastern shore of
the Wisla River. A few people awaited us. The first one I
recognized was Jan Gorsky, formerly Yaakov Ginsburg, an
actor who had been with my theater for several years but
was now a major in the Polish army. (In 1949 he emigrated
to Israel, entered the police service, and changed his name
to Yaakov Ginosar. He died in 1961.) Others at the station
were Feivel Gorenshtein, formerly a merchant and occasional impresario and now only the latter. There were also
representatives of the Jewish Central Committee with some
flowers for me.

Jan Gorsky took us in his car to the Central Hotel, one of
three that had survived the burning of Warsaw. Opposite the
hotel was the Vienna Terminal. When I looked at this "terminal," a pall of dread came over me. One's wildest fantasy
couldn't imagine the ruin before us: a mass of twisted
steel and stone that no human force could ever straighten.
My husband, astonished by this apocalyptic sight, said, "This
won't be rebuilt in our lifetime." Nevertheless, two or three
years later people removed this rubble and built a new station,
thus demonstrating man's capacity for genius and labor.

The nearby Hotel Polonia was entirely reserved for the diplomatic corps. We learned that Mita, the daughter of the famous Yiddish writer Alter Katzizne, lived there; she was now married to the Italian ambassador Eugenio Reale. Her parents had perished, and how she was saved is a story unto itself, rivaling the most fantastic film scenario.

Two rooms were reserved for us at the Central Hotel, one for Mel and me and the other for Ruth and her child, who, we hoped, would come tomorrow or the day after.

I asked the hotel manager to heat up the other room, as well as ours (they were heated with ovens), since my daughter had a little child with her. Although it was late at night, we asked for room service, for we were famished. Seeing the famed Warsaw kaiser rolls was like a breath of air of former times, before the hell of Hitler.

It's hard for me to express the feeling that overwhelmed me at the train terminal. There was nothing there to remind me of old Warsaw except the almost intoxicating air. I had promised myself that I'd try to restrain my feelings when I set foot in my hometown again; I'd remain absolutely calm until the arrival of Ruth and my grandchild. I wanted to cut off all my feelings, for I wanted to share them with my daughter. However, I wasn't successful.

Since we arrived in Warsaw at night, we couldn't see too clearly what it looked like. In Moscow, we had read eyewitness accounts of the utter destruction that had encompassed Warsaw. We learned that it lay under heaps of ruins, and that hardly any Jews had remained there. Now my heart trembled at this encounter with reality.

Friends took us across the destroyed city to the Jewish cemetery. We drove across a desert of dust, stones, bricks, and sand—the remains of the Warsaw Ghetto. Here our people had lived—our relatives and friends. Here had taken place the heroic uprising of those who with their bare hands stood up against the cannibalistic might of Nazism. Strangely, the cemetery gave the impression of being part of a living city. I visited my mother's grave next to the Y. L. Peretz mausoleum, and paid my respects to various others whose great names were eternalized there. I was oppressed by the feeling that only this had remained from the great Jewish city of Warsaw.

We were taken to a huge ruin that had been a prison before the war and a place of horror, cruelty, and death during the German occupation. There I saw thousands of tattered pages from Jewish books, many of them burned. Mel picked up a page on which he read the Biblical verse: "Man comes from dust and returns to dust." He put this fragment in his pocket and keeps it to this day as a relic.

Jews used to have a custom of visiting ancestral family graves. *We* had come to the grave of an entire people—but the graves were covered as though with a volcanic ash, with sand and stones.

We returned to the hotel—to life.

We took the grief with us in our hearts, but the people, the people who had withstood the seven measures of hell, the people lived!

The next day we were invited for lunch in a restaurant, which like other businesses was located on the ground floor of a bombed-out building. Many things could be bought in these ground-floor shops. At the restaurant the waiter replied to each of our requests with "Yes, madame, I shall bring it immediately." My little five-year-old son asked, "What is it, Mama? They have everything here!" In Moscow, Victor used to go to restaurants with us and frequently hear, "We don't have it." We all laughed. It seems that children have keen powers of observation.

After my return to Warsaw I immediately began thinking of work in the theater, but I was waiting for Ruth's arrival. We often visited Jan Gorsky, who lived in an undamaged, relatively comfortable house. The previous tenants had been German Gestapo officers who stayed until their last days in Warsaw. Now only German officers lived in the building. The janitors and maids were German women who had been captured and arrested after the liberation of Warsaw.

We were invited to the Jewish Central Committee, which was located in a beautiful building on Shienna Street, where the Germans had had a hospital. The entire week after my arrival I expected my children, but they didn't come. One day passed, then another. I began to ask various people if a group of repatriates had come from Lemberg. I was informed that a transport had arrived but that it was in the outskirts of Cracow.

My next question was did Ruth and Addy Rosner come, but no one knew. We phoned an attorney friend in Cracow, asking him to find out, especially since we knew that this had been the last transport from Lemberg. The next day the attorney called to say that after diligent inquiries he had learned that my children had not registered for that transport.

My sense of foreboding intensified. I could no longer eat or meet any people. I telephoned everywhere without results. Two days later, as I was leaving my room, the elevator opened on my floor. Two people stepped out.

"Are you Ida Kaminska?" said one.

"Yes," I said.

Before they began to speak, I knew that a misfortune had occurred. They told me my son-in-law had been arrested on November 27.

"And my daughter?" I barely managed to whisper.

"Your daughter and her child are in Lemberg. She was not detained. She is bringing him food every day."

I ran to the post office and phoned my friend Doba in Moscow, for there was no direct phone link to Lemberg. I told Doba, "Call Lemberg. Find out exactly what happened, and tomorrow I shall call you back."

The next day Doba, speaking in a kind of code, told me, "Yes, your son-in-law fell ill [meaning he had been arrested], and your daughter is bringing him food daily to the hospital."

"The extent of his illness?"

"We hope it will soon pass. Many others fell victim to

the same illness. Djigan and Schumacher, as well as Chaim Goldzader and others. Some people have already left the hospital."

I latched on optimistically to that last phrase.

I went to see various ministers. They consoled me and said this had not been the last transport and that my children would be able to come later. The next day, when I phoned Moscow, the news hit me like a thunderbolt. "Your daughter brought food to her husband. She, too, became infected and fell ill." This meant that Ruth had also been arrested.

In a choked voice I asked, "And what about the little girl?"

"Others are taking care of her," Doba answered. "The people in whose house they lived."

"One of you, either you or your daughter, should immediately go to Lemberg and bring the child home with you." I promised to send Doba as much money as was needed. I still didn't know where I would get the money, but I knew that I would get it and send it to her.

My state of mind after discovering this news is indescribable. I couldn't speak to anyone and I couldn't even cry. I was stunned, paralyzed. Later, in the middle of the night, tears gushed out of me; they ceased only when someone was with me. I didn't eat anything. Mel sat next to me with tears in his eyes and pleaded, "At least take a sip of coffee. How can you survive like this?"

I ran to various people who I thought had good connections and might be of help. I was advised to go to the cabinet minister Yaakov Berman. At that time he was the vice-premier and, with help of the Soviets, was *de facto* the most important man in the new government. We knew each other from before the war. Berman happened to be sick and invited me to his home. When I arrived, two doctors were with him. When they departed, he came out dressed in a morning robe. He greeted me amiably, but seeing my face, he realized that something terrible had happend.

I was just barely able to tell Berman about my tragedy, but he calmed me. "I'll try to do everything to help you." When my friends heard of Berman's promise, they concluded that everything was well because he was the only man who could have done anything. Berman told me to phone and to come, which I did ceaselessly. One time he told me, "I beg you, begin to work. Do something. It will be much easier for me to help you when people know who you are."

Only the fact that this could have helped my children prompted me to begin preparing a theatrical evening for myself and my husband. I have a very good memory, but at that time nothing stuck in my mind. I continually had to tell myself, "It's for my daughter. It's for Ruth and Erika and her father."

Our first recital was in Warsaw. After each appearance on-stage I tore the hair from my head. After Warsaw we toured with the program to several towns where Jews were living, but from each place I commuted back to Warsaw to go see Minister Berman and other influential people. Everyone promised to intervene. Everyone sympathized, and I even saw tears in the eyes of some.

I was also constantly in touch with my friend Doba in Moscow. During my first phone conversation with Erika, who was already in Moscow, my knees buckled and I collapsed in the phone booth, but I didn't faint. I heard various versions about the events surrounding Ruth and Addy, but not one of them was definitive.

I could not believe it. My daughter arrested? I remembered her words: "I'd rather die."

Later, during 1948 to 1953, at the height of the Stalin terror and the time of the Doctors Plot, when Yiddish culture in the Soviet Union was being destroyed, when they arrested and murdered innocent Yiddish writers and killed Shlomo Mikhoels, the president of the Jewish Anti-Fascist Committee, I thought, "Well, my daughter is a victim of a distorted interpretation of the law. They thought she wished

to betray the Soviet Union by wanting to return to her homeland [Ruth was born in Russia] Poland, where her mother
lives."

Thinking about the arrest of my daughter, my son-in-law,
and others, I began to understand the entire nightmare of arrests and gradual annihilation of Jewish intellectuals and cultural figures in Russia, many of whom were my friends who
always accented their Soviet patriotism.

Just at that period Mel and I received an official invitation
from the great Yiddish actor Maurice Schwartz to come to
New York. At such a time I certainly couldn't have enter-
tained the notion of accepting and traveling to New York and
being so far from my unfortunate children.

I regularly sent money from my earnings to Doba for my
grandchild in Moscow and also for Ruth and Addy, should
any news come concerning them. Soon Djigan and Schumacher, who had been arrested at the same time as Addy,
arrived from the Soviet Union. They consoled me with the
fact that soon, perhaps, my child would be released.

Finally a letter arrived from Addy stating that, according to
the trial that had taken place (*in absentia*, like other trials
at that time), he had been sentenced to ten years in a labor
camp and my daughter to five years' exile in Siberia, where she
would be able to work and move about freely; however,
she would have to report weekly to the local police. They
had already been in various jails—Ruth in Lemberg (Lvov)
and then in nearby Zlotchov, and Addy in Moscow.

Doba received word from Ruth that she was back in Lemberg in a prison hospital for seriously ill patients and that
from there she would be sent to exile. Ruth still wasn't sure
of the location. The letter from Addy was also sent via Doba.
After this news I ran about again, knocked on many doors,
but received help from no one.

Our series of recitals ended, and I had to begin a regular
cycle of work in the theater, directing and acting. I had to
send money for my grandchild in Moscow. This, however,

was not the easiest of things to do, for one dared not send money out of the country via a bank or the mails. To convey one thousand rubles I had to pay a private messenger five thousand zlotys and pay for his transportation, too.

Doba went from Moscow to the Lemberg hospital to see Ruth, who was already recuperating, and took her some money and food, which were useful to her prior to her long journey. Doba informed me after her return from Lemberg that a certain lawyer in Lemberg would undertake to free Ruth for five thousand rubles. I didn't have the money. I had only some earrings, diamonds, and a ring that my daughter had given me before her departure. I sold all of these, borrowed a sum, and sent this money away, but it did no good.

My state of mind at that time was terrible. I would even have hallucinations. For instance, once I was riding in a horse and buggy (in Warsaw they still had them). I imagined that from a distance I saw Ruth coming toward me in a buggy. However, when we drew closer, I saw that I had erred.

Sometimes during performances I would see her in the theater. I knew that this was impossible, but nevertheless I saw her. I saw the fine figure of a woman, and then next to her a little girl with blond braids.

My only consolation was my little son, Victor, who, even at his age, bore the brunt of some of my sorrow. At every one of my sighs—and there was no lack of them—he would look at me with his large black eyes, in which I would occasionally see tears.

Mel and my son helped me carry my burden, and thanks to them I was able to work more intensively to introduce new plays and learn new roles.

My husband saved every penny in order to send money to Erika in Moscow and also to my daughter. The first package I sent to Addy was returned. He had not had enough money to pay the duty. He did receive the second package. By then he was earning money, for he had formed an orchestra in the labor camp and even went on tour to other camps. The package he received came in handy, for it contained a suit that he used for his appearances. However, he informed us not to send him any more packages because, thanks to his artistic work, he lacked for nothing in the camp.

At this time we lived in Lodz and performed in a terribly primitive theater. A committee was formed to plan the construction of a better building. Here, I would like to mention a wonderful man, an American who came several times to Poland, where we became friends. I refer to Jack Greenbaum of New York, who from various Jewish organizations collected the first ten thousand dollars for the committee to begin constructing a theater. In those days this was a vast sum in Polish currency. Several years later we would meet Jack Greenbaum in various European cities. He would make special trips to see us when we were on tour in western Europe. His great ambition was to bring our ensemble to America. He maintained a steady contact with us via letter and telephone. Unfortunately, he was not destined to see our performances in New York. He didn't even see my film, for he suddenly died in November 1964 of a heart attack.

27

London

IN 1948, during the time my daughter was being led with
criminals to Siberia, experiencing horrible things along the
way, about which I learned later, I was invited to London to
perform in a new, beautiful theater. This took place after I
realized that all my efforts at freeing my children through the
Polish regime were fruitless. The vice-premier Yaakov Berman told me, "We have no right to deceive you or to create
false hopes. All our efforts are in vain. None of us can help."

After leaving Berman's office and thanking him for his assistance, I went into his secretary's room. The woman took
one look at me and burst into tears. She immediately knew
that this time I had departed without even the slightest hope.

At a loss about what to do, I went to Julian Tuvim, the
Polish Jewish poet who had returned after the war from the
United States. Although Tuvim received very few visitors, he
welcomed me immediately. I had hoped he might write to
Stalin. However, he told me that when he returned to Poland
he wrote to Stalin concerning his wife's brother and his best
friend, both of whom had been exiled into the Soviet Union.
His brother-in-law was subsequently freed, but when he in-
quired again about his friend, he received word not to dare
send any more such letters. Moreover, he told me that the
sister of Boleslaw Bierut, then president of the Polish People's Republic, had also been exiled and nothing could be
done.

In such a state of mind I went to London; nevertheless, I went gladly, for there my cousins lived and I especially wanted to see one, Henry Lister (formerly Liskowsky), who is like a brother to me. I recalled my mother's words: "My daughter, if you remain onstage, don't ever go for guest appearances to London or Paris."

After my mother's death Sigmund Turkov and I were in Paris, and we got to know some of the local conditions. However, we were never in London, even though we had had an invitation before the war.

When I arrived in London, where I was supposed to rehearse for two weeks and perform for six, the director (who had originally been a baker) suggested that I rehearse only one week. I told him this was unacceptable to me, and he left dissatisfied.

The theater was beautiful and the actors were quite capable, but I felt that conditions were intolerable, especially when the director asked me to stage a new play every week and also perform in a musical comedy. I broke the contract, went to the local actors equity, and asked them to pay me my entire salary for all my scheduled performances and also for round-trip travel expenses from Warsaw to London. It had been stipulated in my contract that I—and not the director—was to choose my repertoire; and, moreover, that he was to reimburse me for all my travel expenses.

The secretary of the actors equity told me to stay in London for the entire length of the contract and promised that they would take care of this matter for me. For three weeks I lived near the Alexander Theatre. Later, I moved in with my dear relatives, who surrounded me with rare love and devotion. During all this time I visited theaters and movies and became acquainted with people in the theater world. Receptions were arranged for me by various Jewish organizations, and a special party was given by the director Professor Herbert Marshall, now of Southern Illinois University, and his wife, Fredda Brilliant, a well-known sculptress. Also present at this reception were Dame Sybil Thorndike and her husband, Sir Louis Casson, the famous painter Felix Topolsky, and others.

When the period of the contract was over, I returned home to Mel and Victor, for whom I longed very much.

A few months later I received word from the London equity that the lawsuit against the director had taken place and that I had been awarded £365. My cousin sent me the money in merchandise, which was sold. I realized a fine sum, which I sent to Erika and to Ruth, who was then in the village of Kokchetav in Khazarstan, Siberia.

28

The Theater in Lodz

M Y friend Doba Santatour, her daughter, and my grandchild traveled to see Ruth in Kokchetav. The trip by train took more than four days.

I would like to mention here the good-heartedness of Doba's daughter, Lyalya Santatour, who had just finished her medical studies in Moscow. Because of her excellent grades, she could have remained in a Moscow hospital, but out of friendship for Ruth she purposely chose a hospital in the far-off village of Kokchetav in order to be near her. They all lived together for nearly two years. I was somewhat calmed by the fact that Ruth was no longer sitting in a closed place of confinement and that I could write to her directly and send her packages and money. This enabled me to work more intensively. Because the packages and money had to be sent through middlemen, I was occasionally deceived, losing both the packages and the money.

When I returned from London, I entered an apartment from which the acting family Lipman had departed. At that time there were two Yiddish theaters in Poland, one in the town of Wroclaw (formerly Breslau) under the direction of Isaac Turkov, Yaakov Kurlender, and Sheftel Zak (at the time of this writing, executive secretary of the Folksbiene Theater in New York), and the second one in Lodz, which I was asked to organize. It was in a primitive little theater on Yaracha Street. At that time we were attempting to find means to build a new theater, for which, as I've mentioned, the first ten thousand dollars was brought by Jack Greenbaum. The new building was planned for the same site as the prewar theater. After it had been bombed, the Germans wanted to enlarge it and build it anew, but they demolished it once they realized they would not remain masters of Lodz. A group of us undertook to ask the governmental and the local authorities for aid to conclude the construction of the new theater. This group was composed of the local Jewish committee, headed by its secretary, the attorney Anatole Vertheim; the chairman, Maria Feingold; as well as Mel and me.

Once I had the assurance that the government would build the new theater, I undertook to use temporarily the primitive hall, which could not even have been called an ordinary theater. All possible improvements were done to this old shack. We installed new upholstered chairs, replacing the long wooden benches. We built a foyer and made improvements onstage and backstage. When the audience entered the newly renovated theater for the first time, they did not recognize it. The money for all these improvements came from two simple Jews who trusted me explicitly and sought to gain nothing from their contribution. Once the theater began operating in 1948, we got support from the Jewish Central Committee.

Once while standing and watching a painter working on the stage decorations, Djigan and Schumacher happened to be at my side. They were already preparing to leave Poland. Schumacher remarked to me, "Have a good look. These are the last decorations that are being painted for Ida Kaminska's theater in Poland." He was mistaken. He was more than twenty years off!

At the time the appeal began to collect money from Jews to build the new theater, a great stream of emigrants went to Israel, mostly to join the Haganah. Now fewer Jews remained in Poland, but those who stayed contributed from their

monthly wages for the construction. After the black night of
Hitler, the Jews in Poland had a very strong feeling of Jewish
nationalism, and those who remained displayed great enthusiasm for Yiddish culture.

I opened the renovated theater in 1948 with my adaptation of Max Bauman's play *Glückel Hameln Demands Justice*. This was a festive performance attended by the minister
of culture, Jan Dybovsky, and his assistants, who made a
special trip down from Warsaw. After the performance the
minister came to visit me backstage. Since there was only
one chair (there was no room to place another), Dybovsky
stood. Naturally, I asked him for help for the new theater,
which was now being built, and he promised concrete aid.
When someone asked Dybovsky, who was a plain, down-to-
earth man, why he was standing, he replied, "If an artist like
Ida Kaminska can sit in such a dressing room, I can stand for
a while."

Two weeks later I visited him in the ministry in Warsaw.
I told him about my misfortune with my daughter, and he
said he would help. He immediately picked up the receiver
of the special governmental telephone and called Marshal
Konstantin Rokossovsky, the commander of the Soviet army
in Poland, whose headquarters were in the town of Lignitz.
(Later, because of his Polish origins, Rokossovsky was appointed chief of the Polish army.) Just as Minister Dybovsky
was quick to make the call, so did I notice that during his
talk his face lengthened with sorrow. When he ended the
conversation, I told him, "I understand everything. You don't
have to tell me anything." Then he stood, fell on my neck,
and began to cry. Dybovsky was a good man, but since he
was not a party Communist, he was soon replaced by the
cunning and clever Wlodzimierz Sokorski, a chameleon who
adapted himself to all situations.

With this small Lodz ensemble I produced several plays.
It was an average group, strengthened by two actors, a husband and wife team named Chevel and Rivka Buzgan. They

had asked me to bring them over from Argentina—they had an only daughter and grandchild in Russia. The husband was a pillar of our ensemble, and his wife, too, was quite competent.

Thanks to the help of the government, which at that time treated the Jews well, and thanks to the aid of the Joint Distribution Committee, which had not yet been expelled from Poland, the theater prospered. During that period the Jewish Central Committee was urging Jews not to emigrate, for this would weaken the rebirth of Jewish culture, which had flourished in Poland before the war. I didn't agree with this attitude, and the many actors who wanted to leave for abroad received my blessings.

I remember a committee meeting in which they were agitating to delay people's departures. Suddenly one Jew stood up and called out: "I simply don't understand. We've finally achieved a Jewish state after two thousand years. So, then, who should go there? The goyim?" Out of fear—fear they had throughout their entire lives—no one applauded, but everyone laughed.

Jews left. Later the exodus was stopped, and the offices of the Joint Distribution Committee were closed. At this same time, in reaction to a memorandum from my husband concerning nationalizing the Yiddish theater, a decree was issued in 1949 that the Yiddish theater would indeed be nationalized.

I went to Warsaw to become acquainted with the new Minister of Culture, Sokorski. I wanted to introduce myself, and I thought that at the same time I could raise the question of my own personal misfortune concerning my daughter. We had a rather lengthy talk, and during our conversation I had an opportunity to determine his personality. He was intelligent and clever but had a weak backbone and hence was a bad man. He probably didn't like Jews too much, I noticed, but his attitude toward me was polite. Of course, before I began speaking about my private troubles, I spoke about the theater. Suddenly Sokorski asked me about the Soviet Union and how Yiddish state theaters operated there. I looked at him in amazement.

"What do you mean?" I said. "Don't you know what's happening in Russia now?" I began to tell him—rather cautiously, for I still didn't know the sort of person I was dealing with—how the Yiddish theaters had been shut down. It was obvious that Sokorski hadn't heard this before and that he realized that Jews were not such a great "bargain" in the Soviet Union. I also noticed that he was not displeased by this fact.

I decided then and there not to raise the question of my own private concerns with him.

Nevertheless, while Jewish culture, along with writers and artists, was being liquidated in the Soviet Union, it flourished in Poland.

29

The Yiddish State Theater

WHEN Yiddish theater was nationalized, the two Yiddish theaters in the country, in Lodz and Wroclaw, were united because for the few Jews in Poland it was senseless to support both of them. My husband was appointed the administrative director and I, the artistic director. Meanwhile, the construction proceeded on the new theater that was to be our company's permanent home. Since we couldn't perform every day—the theater was very big but there were few Jews in the city—and since we also had to tour other towns, we permitted the building to be used by the Lodz Polish theater (the New Theater), which was directed by two enthusiastic young men, Kosimir Deimek (today a famous European director) and Jonas Varminsky (today the director of a Warsaw theater). Only young people performed in the New Theater.

Here, too, in 1951 I celebrated my thirty-fifth anniversary in the theater. This was not only a festive occasion for the close circle of celebrants, the Jews, but also for the Polish artistic world. The main speaker was the great Polish director Leon Schiller. Added to the awards that I would occasionally get was a National Order. On a flower-bedecked stage were representatives of various Polish theaters and high government officials.

If I were to say that complete peace reigned among the members of the Yiddish State Theater, I would be lying. At first there was strong antagonism between members of the Wroclaw and Lodz groups. Then various little factions were formed of which I could write at length, and even though these difficulties disturbed me, they were nevertheless minor matters that have long lost their meaning.

Later, however, a more serious situation developed. A plot was instigated by the group from Wroclaw, who had fine apartments in Wroclaw, and even a rather fine theater that had been built by Jewish communal funds. Through the Jewish Culture Organization they appealed to the regime, stating that the Yiddish State Theater could not be led by two people who were married and that objective conditions were such that the theater should have its permanent place in Wroclaw.

The Culture Ministry grabbed at this idea, for they wanted to make room in the Lodz theater for the New Theater group which had achieved high artistic distinction. The Jewish Culture Organization wanted to do the ministry a favor and used the argument that in lower Silesia (of which Wroclaw was the capital city) there were more Jews. Thus the idea of bringing the theater over to Wroclaw was accomplished.

Mel was relieved of his post as administrative director and, keeping the same salary, served only as an actor. I requested to be released from the position of artistic director, stating that I wouldn't leave the theater but would help as director and adviser. But under no circumstances did they want me to leave this post. Mel's removal from his position caused much sorrow among some of the actors and almost all the technical and administrative staff. To replace my husband they appointed a man who had no experience whatsoever in the theater. His sole qualification was that he was trusted by the party and came from Wroclaw. It was with him that the actors from Wroclaw and the leaders of the culture organization accomplished their plot against Mel and me. A short while later, however, this same man became a friend of ours and was totally dependent upon my husband.

The home base of the theater indeed became Wroclaw, but

Mel and I continued to live in Lodz. However, my determination to perform in Warsaw grew, for by the year 1953 it had been pretty well rebuilt. The rate of construction continued, and I understood that in time Warsaw would be the greatest center of Jewish residence in Poland and that performing in Warsaw would raise the level of the theater. I often traveled to Warsaw out of concern for my children's fate, on business in connection with theater, and to explore the possibilities of performing there. Even Mel was unaware of the latter, for everyone was pessimistic about performing in Warsaw.

When I raised this question in the Jewish Culture Organization, I received the following ironical comment from Shimon Zacharias (he was also a member of the Party's Central Committee and dealt with Jewish affairs): "There is as much likelihood for you to have Warsaw as a home base for your theater as there is for potatoes to grow on the palm of my hand."

This declaration was well-known in Jewish circles, and from it stemmed the absolute disbelief in the possibility of carrying out my plan to establish a Yiddish theater in Warsaw—a city that had the greatest tradition of Yiddish theater in the world. I also considered this a matter of pride. A Yiddish theater in Poland *had* to be in the city where Jews were martyred and where, in the Warsaw Ghetto uprising, they displayed their greatest heroism.

In conjunction with describing the general professional happenings of that time, I cannot omit my private feelings and sufferings. Ruth was freed from her forced exile in 1951, but then there began for her an even more difficult period, about which I learned in detail only two years later when we met again.

Although Ruth was released from forced residence in the village of Kokchetav, she was not allowed to live in any larger town, certainly not in Moscow, where her child lived and went to school. Ruth wandered from town to village, and even acquaintances turned away from her. This took place two years before Stalin's death. The letters and the money that I sent Ruth somehow often missed her. Finally, when in one village she did receive the money I sent, she called me for the first time in six years. It would be superfluous to describe what we both felt during this first conversation, especially since much could not be said out of fear of "eavesdroppers." From then on, Ruth would occasionally phone me whenever she had money. Then we would both encourage and console each other.

My daughter also took a forbidden trip to Moscow, incognito, to see her child. In Moscow she had many influential friends from the time when Addy was at the height of his career and when she had her successes as a singer. She wanted friends to help her get permission to remain in Moscow, where Erika went to school and where the standard of living in comparison to other towns was much higher. Many of Ruth's old friends were afraid of talking to her, but there were also people with compassionate hearts who demonstrated friendship through both feelings and deeds. It is very sad that after all these years I can't mention these people's names, for this may hurt them and their families.

Finally someone did come to my daughter's aid—Ilya Ehrenburg, who as a deputy in the Soviet parliament was able to get Ruth permission to remain in Moscow.

From 1949 the Yiddish theater in Poland flourished and developed artistically. Some of the premieres were presented on the large stage of the Lodz theater, but when we went on tour, we had to make the stage designs smaller and simpler. The reputation of our theater grew; it was considered among the better Polish ensembles. We would also be invited to participate in various festivals. At the 1949 festival we performed Ostrovsky's *The Innocent Guilty* and other Russian and Soviet plays, and at the 1951 festival we staged Irene Krzyicka's *Doctor Leshna* and other Polish dramas. At each festival we received prizes. I got them either for directing or for acting, and Mel, acting in the 1951 Festival of Modern Polish Drama, was accorded a special prize. I have all these awards in New York; they remind me of the entire past of the theater for which I had worked so hard.

In 1953 I was invited to represent Poland at a Jewish cultural conference in Paris. I accepted with pleasure, for just then my dear brother Yosef, concertmaster and occasional conductor of the Israel Philharmonic Orchestra, was scheduled to come to London with his orchestra. I called him from Warsaw and asked him to meet me in Paris so that we could finally see each other after sixteen years. I arrived in Paris, got my hotel room, but couldn't sleep all night in anticipation of Yosef's arrival.

The following morning I went to the conference hall. As a member of the presidium I sat on the dais for the opening ceremonies and constantly watched the people coming in. Perhaps my brother Yosef would be among them. Suddenly a man came up to me and whispered into my ear that someone was waiting for me in the lobby. Walking toward the lobby, I felt myself trembling and could scarcely open the door. At the far end of the lobby stood my cousin Henry Lister from London at some distance from my brother. I ran up to Yosef and embraced him. He put his arms around my shoulders; we didn't say a word for a long time. Not only were we weeping but also Henry and all the people who watched us wept with us.

Then, after a lengthy silence, we began to laugh. Henry approached us and joined the laughter. I returned to the dais and explained the reason for my departure.

During the three days that Yosef remained with me in Paris, we spent all our time in the simplest places of amusement. We laughed incessantly—in the quick snapshot booth, for instance—and enjoyed ourselves like children. I don't recall any other time which brought us back to our childhood as did these few days.

The following evening Henry Lister left for home. As he departed we saw tears in his eyes, and our happy mood was shattered. I spent a little while at the conference and then, later that evening, Yosef said, "Well, Idele, now you'll come to my room and I'll play something for you after all these years." Tears choked me as he began to play. When Yosef concluded, he came up to me—his eyes were moist, too—and wiped the tears from my eyes. Then he brought me back to my room (we lived in the same hotel) and we talked some more. The following morning, after breakfast, we went out to look for a taxi. For a long time we could not find one to take us to the airport. My brother grew anxious, for he feared he'd be late for his concert in London. Finally, he got a taxi and I followed it with my eyes until it disappeared from view. It was difficult for me to part with Yosef, but the great joy in seeing him remained in my heart.

Our theatrical successes encouraged me in the battle to move our theater to Warsaw, which I considered a natural step. Once, when I was in Warsaw again, I went to see Vice-Premier Berman. I told him that my daughter had received permission to live in Moscow.

"I'm happy to hear this," he replied. "Tell me, do you live in Warsaw?"

"No, in Lodz," I said.

"Would you like to live here?"

"Yes," I answered.

I returned home, and the next morning I received a telegram from the prime minister's office informing me that I would receive an apartment in Warsaw, in the brand-new buildings that had recently been built on the prestigious Marshalkavska Street.

The telegram was signed by Premier Jozef Cyrankiewicz. Disregarding the fact that I didn't yet have a theater in Warsaw, I immediately began moving my possessions to the capital city. Living in Warsaw made my search for a theater there easier.

By the end of the war almost all the Warsaw theaters had been destroyed. However, the Theater of the Polish Army performed in a wooden structure on Krolewska Street. Toward the end of 1954 the grandiose Culture Palace was being finished, a gift from the Soviet Union that contained four theaters, several movie houses, a huge congress hall seating three thousand people, museums, and other institutions. Although, objectively speaking, it was a great asset for the capital city, many of the Polish citizens had little gratitude for this great "gift" because it was given by the Soviet Union, toward which, to this day, Poles have little sympathy. There was even a joke that made the rounds: "May you have an apartment with a view of the Culture Palace," which was supposed to be a curse.

The much-honored Theater of the Polish Army moved into one of the theaters in the Culture Palace. The building they had vacated was sought by several Polish theaters. How great was the surprise when this building was given to the Yiddish State Theater.

Hardly anyone knew about this. On the very day I received the certificate of agreement from the Culture Ministry, there was a meeting of the Jewish Cultural Organization to see whether the Lodz Yiddish theater should be given over entirely to the Lodz Polish theater because the Yiddish theater already had a building in Wroclaw.

I protested sharply: "At least sixty percent of the theater was built by money that Jews contributed. And besides," I added, "when our base is in Warsaw, the nearest town for tour will be Lodz."

"Base in Warsaw?"

The first to laugh was Shimon Zacharias, and after him others followed suit. I was tempted to pull out the official paper and display it, but at that moment I didn't want to hurt certain people. However, after the meeting I did show it to David Sefard, then general secretary of the organization, and he passed this news on to other members.

30

The Theater Finally in Warsaw

IT was not so easy to begin acting in Warsaw. We had to liquidate the assets of the army theater and receive some necessary inventory from them. Then the greatest difficulty began: finding homes for the actors in Warsaw. To keep them permanently in hotels was difficult for the budget and uncomfortable and complicated for the actors, especially those who had families.

I was granted an interview with Premier Cyrankiewicz, whom I considered an intelligent man. He had several apartments for the leading actors. (Every minister had under his control a number of apartments to distribute to whoever had need of them in Warsaw.) As time passed, almost all the actors and administrative and technical personnel gradually got apartments in Warsaw.

At the thirtieth anniversary of my mother's death in December 1955, the theater received the formal right and duty to call itself "The Esther Rachel Kaminska Yiddish State Theater." It was a great event for me, even though such a memorial was nothing new. Various culture centers are named after her, and in Tel Aviv a street bears her name. My mother had always dreamed of a community-supported theater; she never dared dream of a state theater.

The year 1955 was rich in events for me. In July, on the Polish national holiday, during which various state prizes are distributed for the best artists and scientists, I was awarded a State Prize. In addition to the honor, I was also given twenty thousand zlotys, which at that time was a huge sum. From it I was able to pay off debts and take a trip to Moscow with my husband, which I will describe later.

What was the attitude of Polish society to the Yiddish theater? Of course, not everyone was pleased that in the finest place in Warsaw, not far from the Tomb of the Unknown Soldier, there stood a building inscribed in large letters in Polish and in Yiddish "The Esther Rachel Kaminska Yiddish State Theater." Certainly it made eyes pop, but no one dared raise the slightest protest. During fifteen years no one damaged or threw rocks into the glass showcases in front of the theater that displayed huge photos of Yiddish plays.

Many Poles, especially the intelligentsia, had a sympathetic attitude toward the theater, which they attended as regular theatergoers. In fact, there were some among the leading governmental circles who considered it a moral duty toward the Jews, who had suffered so much and lost so much during the German occupation. However, there were some who felt that it was good for propaganda that Poland was different than the Soviet Union and that it made Poland popular in the world, especially after the abortive antiregime revolt in 1956.

Our tours abroad, which began in 1956, brought us recognition and friendship in many circles all over the world. Nevertheless, we would often be neglected at various occasions. For instance, at the annual gatherings when Culture Minister Sokorski summarized the year's activities, I would have to remind him openly that there existed a Yiddish theater that had not been mentioned at all. He would apologize but repeat the omission again at the very next opportunity. This also happened in the yearly reports in the journals. I always corrected these "errors."

No Jewish actors were used in Polish films, except in mass scenes or in minor episodes when Jewish types were needed. In a period of twenty years I had not been asked to participate in a film. I made my first postwar film, *The Shop on Main*

Street, in Czechoslovakia. When, after the unusual success of the film, I was asked in Poland why I had not yet appeared in a Polish film—the question was asked by a Polish Jewish director—I replied, "Because most of the Polish film directors are Jews and so they're afraid of hiring Jewish actors." He admitted that in a certain sense this was true. My reply spread among members of the artistic world as a *bon mot.* Many of them in private conversation agreed with me.

Over the course of two years it was shown that Warsaw had the greatest number of Jewish theatergoers. While audiences in other cities became smaller after 1957, the number of productions in Warsaw grew. It soon became evident that from all points of view my stubbornness in bringing the theater to Warsaw was absolutely correct.

Among my Warsaw productions the most successful was my dramatization of *Meir Esofovitch,* a novel by the famous Polish author Eliza Azheshkova. The adaptation, the direction, and my portrayal of the hundred-year-old grandmother of the Esofovitch family prompted universal recognition and interest. Since the novel, which the progressive Polish writer had written about the Jews, was an obligatory text in the secondary schools, dozens of classes came with their teachers, and they enthusiastically followed developments onstage. Occasionally we would also have discussions with the young audience after the performance.

Meanwhile, I had twice been notified by the Culture Ministry that I had been nominated as a member of a theater delegation to Moscow. My joy was indescribable. Finally I would be able to see Ruth and Erika. Unfortunately, both times I was notified that they "regretted" to inform me that the list of the delegates had not been approved.

In the Soviet Union all the Yiddish theaters had been closed by 1949. I received hundreds of private letters from the Soviet Union asking me to go on tour with our theater, but how could the Soviet consul in Poland have permitted an official visit by the director of a Yiddish theater in Poland, especially the daughter of Esther Rachel Kaminska, who was literally a symbol for the Jews in Russia? In this case, however, the consul was not the one to decide; the decision had been made in Moscow on the highest level. My requests to travel to the Soviet Jews with the entire theater were always denied.

The knowledge that Ruth was in Moscow, where Addy had been amnestied after Stalin's death, and that I couldn't go to see her after nine years literally made me sick. I would suffer from liver and gall-bladder attacks. The doctor said that these organs were healthy, and it was a case of nerves that affected them. I decided to do everything I could and travel incognito to Moscow as a tourist.

I had an audience with the representative of the Soviet ambassador and told him about the fate of my children, about my illness, the result of not being able to see them—and it worked. I received a visa for myself, for Victor, who was then fourteen years old, and for my husband. We even sent my son two weeks earlier, and then Mel and I took the train. The journey took forty-eight hours, and I kept quite calm. As we approached Moscow, I felt that my strength was ebbing. My knees collapsed beneath me. I can only imagine what a sight I must have been, for the conductor of the sleeping wagon asked what was wrong with me.

I first saw my daughter Ruth from the window of the sleeping car. She looked young, beautiful, somewhat worn. With her were Addy Rosner, Doba and her daughter, Lyalya, and my son, who was accompanied by a big girl with a radiant smile. Ruth's daughter, Erika (Erele), was almost fourteen years old; she had been five the last time I had seen her. Ruth was terribly nervous; she continually pleaded with me, "Mama, be calm. Don't cry. Be calm." I just barely managed to reply "I'm calm. Just you be calm."

During my stay in Moscow I first learned that Ruth had separated from her husband. Addy had withdrawn the permit that would have enabled Ruth and Erika to come to me to Poland. I talked with Addy and convinced him to go to the proper authority and declare his consent to the departure of Ruth and Erika. This was the most important thing I accomplished in Moscow, but before the trip could take place, there followed a long chain of formalities.

Only now did I become aware of what my daughter had gone through during her imprisonment and during her journey to Siberia. After her arrest she kept asking where her daughter was. For weeks her jailers didn't tell her, though she had frequent visits by investigators who wanted to get details from her regarding her husband's "espionage." Ruth continuously demanded a reply regarding her child. Since after many long weeks she received none, she began a hunger strike and reached a point where she stopped speaking, seeing, and hearing. Only then did they inform her that Erika was in Moscow at Doba's house. She was taken to the hospital, and when she regained her strength, she was returned to her old room in the prison. She had changed so strikingly that her fellow prisoners didn't recognize her. Parts of her young head of hair had become gray.

It had been nine years since Mel and I had seen Moscow. In the center of the city not much had changed, but there had been much construction in the suburbs. Hardly any change had come over the people, however. They were still under the psychosis of the Stalin era. Their economic state had probably not improved. Externally, for instance, their clothing had not changed much since the years we lived there.

Once a taxi driver who heard us speaking Polish asked, "Are you forced to steal as much as us?" Then he added angrily, "I'm sick of stealing, but I have to provide for my family, and I, too, want to dress a bit better."

Jews were in a depressed state, and no wonder. In 1956 it was barely three years since the great holocaust of Jewish culture, when its finest representatives had been murdered: Shlomo Mikhoels, Peretz Markish, David Bergelson, Itzik Feffer, and many others. Many died after their liberation;

Shmuel Halkin and Moshe Broderson had been tortured in the concentration camps.

My "incognito" notwithstanding, many Jews were aware I was in Moscow and would tell me these horrible stories, adding, "Let the world know." All of this was taking place less than forty years after the revolution had preached such a mighty ideal. How great the gap between preaching and the true implementation of ideals in life, I very well now know.

Once when I was walking with my husband along the main street, named after Gorky, a Jew came toward us. He had a long beard, wide-set eyes, the appearance of someone who was a combination of a prophet and Job. We looked at him with friendly curiosity. He assumed we were not Jews and shouted to us, "What are you looking at? Yes, yes! I'm a Jew, and I am still alive!" He walked away quickly before we had the opportunity to calm him and say a few kind words.

It was very difficult for me to say good-bye, first of all to my daughter and grandchild and also to so many friends: Doba, Lyalya, and a cousin who also called himself Kaminsky (although his real name was Karlos), a former actor in Mikhoels's theater. Despite the hardships of separation, I was impatient to leave the Soviet atmosphere and be once again in Poland, where, conditions notwithstanding, one was able to breathe freer. Back in Warsaw, I felt somewhat better, expecting the return of my daughter and grandchild, with whom we would often speak via the telephone.

31

Our First Tours to Europe, Israel, and Australia

TO my great satisfaction, our theater established itself to the extent that most of the performances were given in Warsaw. One of the happiest days of my life occurred in 1956 when my daughter and grandchild finally arrived from Moscow. Ruth appeared confused from the radical change of atmosphere, but she was truly happy. A few months later she joined our ensemble as an actress, and in a short while she achieved a front-rank position, even though she had not been performing in the theater since 1939. Erika attended the Russian secondary school connected with the Soviet Embassy. She did this for two reasons: first, she was still a Soviet citizen, and second, she knew no Polish. She attended the school till her graduation and thereafter attended a Polish university.

In the fall of 1956 our theater had an experience that was like a beautiful dream. For the first time we went on tour to Paris and Belgium. The enthusiasm was great, and the Jews, especially those who had come from Poland, received us warmly both in the theater and outside of it.

In Brussels we had a rare guest, the Queen Mother Elizabeth; she was the late king's widow, an unusual patron of culture.

Before our troupe arrived in Brussels, I went there with a representative of the Polish Culture Ministry, Stanislav Dobrovolsky, to oversee preparations. Dobrovolsky, a person of high culture and sensitivity, was our escort. During the German occupation of Poland he had been chairman of the Save the Jews Organization in Cracow, and after the founding of the state of Israel, he served as chairman of the Poland-Israel Friendship Society.

We were invited to see the Polish cultural attaché at the Polish Embassy to discuss the arrangements for our performances. Among other things I was shown a list of invited guests.

"Why hasn't Queen Elizabeth been invited?" I asked.

Everyone laughed, but I replied, "I'm not certain she'll come, but she should by all means be invited."

When I came to the theater on the eve of the premiere, I was informed that the queen had stated she would attend. However, she would remain only for the first act because she couldn't stay up too late. We performed *Meir Esofovitch.* During the first intermission someone came to tell me that the Queen was waiting for me in the reception room and that I could take anyone I wished with me. My only means of getting there was through the theater, where the audience was gathered. I didn't like to go through the crowd in my makeup and costume, but since the Queen had bidden, I complied.

The Queen was very endearing. We posed for a photograph. She was so interested in the play that she remained to the end, at which she applauded heartily.

The next morning the picture appeared in all the newspapers. Since I was wearing a headcovering that looked like a crown, a joke made the rounds in Brussels: "Which one is the real queen?" The following day we received a huge bouquet of flowers from her and a telegram expressing her gratitude.

On tour in Paris, Brussels, and Antwerp, we performed *Meir Esofovitch*, which I had dramatized and directed, and

A Goldfaden Dream, directed by Yaakov Rotbaum.

Upon our return from Paris, we were witnesses to the so-called resumption of Polish socialism, which expressed itself in the tendency to be more independent of the Soviets. Just at this time I flew from Warsaw to Bucharest to participate in the celebration of the eightieth anniversary of the founding of the professional Yiddish theater by the father of Yiddish theater, Abraham Goldfaden.

Accompanied by Isaac Turkov, I took off, but I didn't arrive. We were detained in Prague. The anti-Soviet revolution had broken out in Hungary (October 1956), and one couldn't travel across that land. After several days we returned to Warsaw. My life was always intertwined with great political happenings in which I was not an active participant but which so often intruded into my private life.

In the spring of 1957 I traveled with the ensemble to London and Amsterdam. My theater began to be a world theater. When I was asked in interviews why I performed for the small community of postwar Jews in Poland, I would answer that our base was in Poland and that we were supported by the government. Moreover, I added that we were a theater for world Jewry, a fact that proved itself in later years, when we visited France four times, London three times, and Israel, South America, Australia, and the United States.

That same year, in October 1957, we went on tour with mixed feelings to East Berlin and Leipzig, upon the invitation of the East German government. To East Berlin came Jews from West Berlin, for at that time both sides of the border were still open. Our performances took place in Bertolt Brecht's Berliner Ensemble. We also made a special point of performing *Glückel Hameln Demands Justice*. Although the action takes place in the seventeenth century, it contains many allusions to the Hitler period in Germany.

In Berlin, after my performances, I fell victim to the epidemic of Asian flu. Despite my illness, I took a bus to perform in Leipzig. Upon my return to Berlin, however, I had to lie a week in bed, not stirring from my hotel. Our colleague Chevel Buzgan also fell ill, and his wife remained with him. They returned home first, and Mel and I followed later.

After the so-called Polish Spring, which took place in November 1956, when people thought that some form of renewal was taking place in the political life of the land—a certain liberalization of the system—events happened that prompted feelings of terror among the Jews. Concurrently with a new, truly liberal course in the regime, there surfaced a silent wave of anti-Semitism. The first to feel it were those who were in governmental positions. It began with the firing of the "unqualified." The first victims were Jews. Ironically, at this time the government readmitted into the land the philanthropic Joint Distribution Committee, which strongly supported the economic position of the Jews (by means of cooperatives) as well as cultural affairs through the Cultural Affairs Organization (a Polish-Jewish organization partially supported by the Joint Distribution Committee).

Nevertheless, it was strange. The Jews felt instinctively that if a liberal spirit was currently in the air and people were permitted to leave, then they should leave. Indeed, in 1956 one-third of the Jewish population, about fifteen thousand, departed Poland. This mood of emigration also caught about one-half of the actors in the theater. Before their departure they had to get the consent of the theater itself, that is, from me. From certain quarters pressure was put on me to deny the requests, but I permitted all to leave, even paying their wages to the last day. Later in various administrative offices I was berated for doing this. However, my conscience was clear, especially since I knew that most were traveling to Israel.

During the summer vacation of 1957 my long-standing dream of going to Israel was realized. My trip was supported both by the Polish government, that is, the Culture Ministry, and by the Israeli ambassador, who through the Foreign Ministry arranged beautiful receptions for me in Vienna, Rome, and Israel. My only brother, Yosef, was in Israel, and I had not seen his wife and son for twenty years. Mel's brother and his family, whom I had last seen in 1941 in Lemberg, were also in Israel. There were also many friends who waited for me, but I was most moved by my encounter with the land.

I made the trip with my son, Victor, and my granddaughter, Erika, who were not quite sixteen. In Vienna we were the guests of the Israeli Embassy, and from there we flew straight to Tel Aviv. This was my first flight with El Al, the airline of Israel. Jewish passengers from eastern Europe kept exclaiming, "My God! A Jewish airplane! Jewish pilots! Jewish stewardesses!" I understood them, but after all, what was there to wonder about? It could not be otherwise. I had never imagined that Jews would not be capable of running a nation, just like any other people. One only had to give them the opportunity and the means. During our history Jews served other peoples and nations and became famous, among them Benjamin Disraeli in nineteenth-century England, and Emil Rathenau in Germany, and Léon Blum in France.

At night all the passengers fell asleep except me. I couldn't believe that I would actually see Israel. I must admit I felt guilty that only now was I making my first trip to Israel. My only excuse was the great tragedy I had had with Ruth and the intermittent illnesses resulting from nervous tension. Now I was bringing my youngsters with me. I was going to show Victor and Erika that we have our land, built with our own hands.

Despite the fact that I had informed only my brother and my husband's brother of my arrival, many people awaited me at Lod Airport. I noticed flowers everywhere. Although according to eastern European time it should have been morning, here it was already afternoon. My eye caught my brother and his family, Mel's brother and his family, and many friends, acquaintances, and even strangers. I didn't expect to see them so quickly, and was not prepared as I stepped out of the plane. I was flustered but pretended that all was well. When I finally came to the waiting room, I saw that my two children, poor things, looked quite unwell.

As soon as I entered the hall, I saw my first husband, Sigmund Turkov. He had come to see me and his granddaughter, Erika, whom he had never seen before. After his first few words with her in Russian, he remarked to me in Polish, "I'm quite taken with her."

At customs the inspector, looking over the many gifts I had brought for relatives and friends, told me that the camera and portable radio could not be left in Israel but would have to be taken out. (Later, even though I wouldn't have been asked about it, I indeed did bring them back, out of courtesy to the laws of the Jewish state.)

My brother Yosef took us to a hotel near his apartment, which was not a luxurious one. Victor was faint with sleepiness, and Erika didn't feel too well. We were all fatigued.

The next few days we were surrounded with friends and acquaintances, but our first priority was Israel itself. I didn't have an opportunity to tour extensively, but I saw much. My impression of Israel was like that of all newcomers; the land of the Jews was a magnificent country. The first phone conversation I had on the day after my arrival was with Golda Meir's secretary. To my great joy I was invited to Jerusalem to see Golda Meir, then the foreign minister. The second call was from a member of the World Jewish Congress, who invited me to lunch.

Yosef, who noted that we had no opportunity to be alone, suggested that we go to the seashore the following day. We did, and that's where the tumult began. An endless number of people recognized me and greeted me, and that was the last time I spent a day by the sea.

My official visit to Golda Meir was a delight. It was an even greater pleasure to have her attend my concert. Afterward she told me, "What can I tell you? I love you!" I embraced her and we kissed each other like two old, dear friends. During our short trip I met this wonderful woman several times, and each time I had the feeling that I had known her for years and regretted that we both had so little time and no opportunity to talk at length.

I can't write enough about visiting this wished-for land. I only know that a twenty-four-hour day was insufficient. Moreover, I also had eleven performances during my stay. Actually they were not performances but beautiful experiences with people who took part in the official receptions during these special evenings. (In almost every town there were new people.) Happily, my brother and his son accompanied me on these evenings, and they took part in the musical interludes. This was very important to me, for I had not seen them for many years, and I would soon depart.

One of the speakers during these evenings was the talented critic and writer—who died at too early an age—Ber Malkin. Following his introductory remarks, the official representative of the municipality would speak, and only then would the actual concert part of the evening commence.

During my meetings with several officials of the World Jewish Congress, I suggested that they consider the possibility of bringing the Yiddish State Theater from Warsaw to Israel. At that time, I knew, the Polish government would not have opposed this. As a sign of friendship they might even have added a dowry: the huge wardrobe of costumes and other accessories mandatory for a working theater. However, after lengthy discussion I realized I would have to return to Warsaw and continue my activity there and, at best, come on tour to Israel for several weeks with the ensemble.

My short visit to Israel was a long holiday for me, which I always remembered. Adding to the festive mood was the visit of my dear friend and cousin from London, Henry Lister, and we were able to spend some time together. Another memorable occasion was the reception that the actors of the Habimah National Theater, headed by the beloved Hanna Rovina, gave for me.

I do not want to say that I was not well received in other lands, but this was my first visit to the Jewish state. I could write endlessly just about the things I saw in this colorful and fascinating land. Above all, I warmly remember the *kibbutzim*, who think not of taking but only of giving to the land.

Every holiday must come to an end, and my children and I had to return. As joyful as was my arrival, so was our departure difficult. Saying farewell to my dearest relatives was hard, but somehow I felt that we would soon see each other again.

On our return journey we stopped at Rome (my first time there) and Vienna. In the Israeli embassies I was warmly received, and I was shown the theaters and noteworthy sights of these two beautiful, historic cities. From Vienna we took the train back to Warsaw. My excursion had ended.

During the latter part of 1957 and the beginning of 1958 a part of our acting ensemble emigrated to Israel. This occurred after Gomulka's rise to power. At that time there was a large exodus of Polish Jews for Israel, but my activity in the theater did not cease for even a day. It was a difficult period for me, but performances continued and the audiences had no complaints.

Because of the reduction of qualified personnel, the theater experienced a period of crisis, but we managed to overcome it. At this very time there took place a repatriation of Soviet Jews, and among them were Yiddish actors. My husband opened in our theater a drama studio that trained young actors; others came to us from the Polish stage.

Along with the repatriates from the Soviet Union there came a famous actor, a fascinating man and witty writer, Abraham Morevsky. Unfortunately, he was not well, but he directed S. Ansky's great classic, *The Dybbuk*, and played his famous role, the *tzadik* from Mirepol, a role that he had created in the world premiere of *The Dybbuk* in 1920.

Regrettably, Morevsky didn't participate in any other plays, but he was a respected member of our ensemble. He devoted himself to writing his memoirs in several volumes, which he did not complete. He died in 1964. One year later his wife, an excellent pianist, died too.

In 1958 Ruth decided to visit Israel and see her father, Sigmund Turkov. Mel went with her to see his brother, whom he had not seen since 1946, when he found him, along with his wife and son, miraculously saved from the Hitler terror. Mel's brother and his family had lain concealed in a cellar for twenty months. The entire story of how they had been saved would make a separate volume.

Our theater visited Israel in December 1959 and January 1960. At this point I should mention my visit to the president of Israel, Yitzhak Ben-Zvi, which took place in Jerusalem at the end of 1959. He and his wife received our entire ensemble. The late President Ben-Zvi displayed much affection for us, posed for photographs, talked with us at length about various problems, and showed profound understanding for the reasons that we were maintaining our cultural work in Poland. It was an unforgettable experience.

When we returned to Poland, representatives of the Culture Ministry and the Jewish organizations awaited us with flowers. The Polish press reprinted our Israeli reviews and wrote about the visit with President Ben-Zvi. When all this is recalled today, one can see how radically things have changed.

In the spring of 1960 I received an invitation from the impresario Zilberberg to come to Australia with several actors. We accepted, and in mid-July 1960 Mel and I and Ruth and Karol Latovitch (whom Ruth later married) flew to London and then to Australia, where we had cousins and friends.

Australia was a distant and new land, but nevertheless we were anxious to meet with my cousin; with the beloved actor from the Vilna troupe, Yaakov Weislitz; with Mel's cousin;

and with my friend, the popular and excellent actress Rachel Holzer. All this gave us special impetus for visiting Australia. How great was our surprise when at the Melbourne airport a crowd of more than one hundred people awaited us, excluding our relatives and friends.

We immediately began rehearsals with the Australian actors, who, though amateurs, were quite capable. Our first play was *Mirele Efros*, and we presented it in an auditorium that seated three thousand people. We gave two performances, one of *Mirele* and one of *Trees Die Standing*, which is a chamber piece and hence very difficult to stage in a theater the size of a convention hall. However, the impresario was in a hurry to recover his expenses for bringing us such a great distance. Later, we performed in the hall of the local Jewish Culture Organization. After concluding our stay in Melbourne, we gave several performances in Sydney. The theater there was less than mediocre, but we had no choice. However, Sydney's beauty enchanted us.

In Sydney, Mel's cousin wanted to impress us with his wealth and at the same time impress his rich guests with the famous artists who were his relatives, and so he threw a beautiful party. In addition, my cousin, who was in more modest circumstances, arranged an intimate reception for us and our family, which made us all feel very good.

I was often asked, "How do you like Australia?" One answer could have been, "Every land has its beautiful aspects, and each person likes a land according to his degree of success." If someone is doing poorly, even the most beautiful land won't please him, but in Australia, a young country, I saw that people had settled comfortably rather quickly. Most of the Jews had come after the war, survivors of the holocaust. They had much initiative and skill, and they worked their way up to a comfortable status.

We were advised to make the return trip via Hong Kong, for it was an interesting city where many things could be bought inexpensively. When we got to the airport, however, they didn't permit us to enter the plane for Hong Kong because we had no visas. We protested in vain that we were only transit passengers. We had to gather up all our valises, return to the hotel, and depart the next day via Istanbul. Perhaps we could have obtained visas to travel via Hong Kong, but we were in a hurry. It was the eve of Rosh Hashanah, and on this holiday we wanted to be in Israel among our close relatives.

As I was leaving Australia, it dawned on me that I knew very little about its cities. An old proverb says that "a guest for a while sees for a mile," but because of rehearsals and performances and continual receptions for us, we didn't get to see very much.

In Istanbul we were to have transferred immediately for a plane bound for Israel. It turned out that on the eve of Rosh Hashanah neither the El Al planes nor those of any other airline could fly to Israel, for the airport was closed right after noon. What were we to do? We were transit passengers, and as citizens from "behind the Iron Curtain" we had no permission to go into Istanbul. We telephoned the Israeli Embassy (not the Polish one, even though we were, of course, Polish citizens), and a man from the embassy came to help us. We were permitted to leave the airport and check into a hotel nearby, a luxurious place, probably only for the very wealthy. We spent two days there, and although we were not permitted to go into the center of Istanbul, a chauffeur took us in an automobile and showed us many beautiful places in this interesting city. We saw the mosque that formerly had been the St. Sofia Church and a series of other fascinating sites. We also noted the contrast of the filthy and poor streets and lanes that already had the stamp of the Middle East.

Although we were staying at the hotel at the expense of Pan American Airways, we had to pay an added sum of quite a few dollars. The Turks know how to present bills. At the airport the same thing happened when the baggage was weighed again and once more we had to pay an added tariff. A couple of hours later we were already touching the soil of Israel.

Once again we were met by our closest relatives and many friends. This time we spent only three days in Israel, for we had to be back in Poland at a certain date. During these three days we met with friends and also attended the theater of the well-known actor Israel Schumacher. He and his partner, Shimon Djigan, were the leading satiric comedians in Israel. Their popularity literally spread all over the world. In September 1960, when I arrived in Israel, Djigan and Schumacher, after thirty-odd years of partnership, quarreled and separated permanently. I saw Schumacher in his last role on the stage (perhaps for the first time in a full-length play), in Sholom Asch's drama *Kiddush Ha-Shem*. He soon died of cancer.

Work in the theater proceeded in normal fashion. We introduced a new repertoire, including Shlomo Ettinger's *Serkele*, the finest Yiddish comedy of the nineteenth century.

The premiere of this play had taken place in 1923 with my mother, Esther Rachel Kaminska, in the title role. I, too, had performed in that play. In 1923 it was produced by Sigmund Turkov, and in 1962 I produced it in a stylized form and played the title role. In 1963 my husband staged a play about Spinoza, *Baruch from Amsterdam*, by Chaim Sloves.

With these two plays and with *Tevye the Dairyman* by Sholom Aleichem, we toured London and Paris in 1963. The press received these plays very well. I performed only in *Serkele*, but it was very important (and also very pleasant) to me, as the director of the theater, that the press received all these plays of our Yiddish State Theater warmly. I was also pleased that in these plays our actors excelled, especially Chevel Buzgan and my husband, Meir Melman.

32.

The Shop on Main Street

IN 1964 two directors from Prague came to Warsaw. They stopped in Warsaw on their way to Moscow, looking for an actress to play the role of a Jewish woman for their film *The Shop on Main Street*. The director of the Polish Artists Union, Stanislaw Siekierko, suggested that they visit the Yiddish theater and see me in the role of the grandmother in *Trees Die Standing*. They came, saw the play, and the next day informed Siekierko that they no longer had any reason to travel to Moscow, for I was the most suitable person for the role.

During my meeting with the directors they described the film and told me the role had to be played in Slovakian. I asked them to send me the script. Two weeks later I received it, with a letter in which the directors commented on the role. I wrote to them that in my opinion their interpretation was not quite correct. I had seen the character in an entirely different fashion. They wanted the woman to have a frequently comic aspect. I felt that she could elicit occasional cheerfulness, but in essence her character is a tragic one.

The woman in *The Shop on Main Street* is deaf. The horrors of the Nazi period do not reach her, and she does not know the reasons for what is happening. Her deafness, then, is a symbol. I wrote to the directors that I would not be able to play the role according to their interpretation, for the victims of the war were too precious to me. They agreed with me. In time the filming was completed, and *The Shop on Main Street* became an international classic.

The movie was first screened for international critics at the famous film festival in Cannes, France. Besides me, the two directors of the film, Jan Kadar and Elmar Klos, were present, as well as my partner in the film, Joseph Kroner (who was not a Jew). The film was selected for an award of distinction, and Kroner and I received certificates of merit. During the reception when my partner was somewhat inebriated, I said to him, "And for this I've gotten so dressed up, just like for an Oscar?" Kroner was a great laugher, especially when he had had a bit to drink. So he began to laugh, and they couldn't stop him.

The film was distributed in America, and its success grew from day to day. People streamed to the movie houses. I began to receive a deluge of awards, the greatest of which was that the film was awarded an Oscar and I, as the first woman from an Iron Curtain country to be thus honored, was nominated as Best Actress. And all this for a film with such an outspoken Jewish theme.

My granddaughter, Erika, who was spending two years in Chicago with my cousin, the actress Dina Halpern, and her husband, Danny Newman, a well-known consultant for theater management, joined me both times in Hollywood for the Oscar awards, in 1966 for the film award and in 1967 for the Best Actress nomination. Erika was grieved that I was passed over for the Best Actress award in favor of Elizabeth Taylor, but I told her: "I've had my satisfaction, my darling. I am a Jewish actress, and all my life the most important thing has been the stage, and I consider the nomination an honor for me personally as well as one for the Yiddish theater."

It should also be added that in 1967, on my way back from the United States, I stopped in Czechoslovakia, where President Antonin Novotny awarded me a state prize for my part in *The Shop on Main Street.*

It seems as if my whole life is devoted to traveling. One purpose of our tours was to meet Jews and tell them: "We're here and doing everything in our power to continue to exist."

During the year that I began to gather the spiritual fruits from *The Shop on Main Street* and after my trip to Cannes and Paris, I managed to visit South America. I met Mel and the entire ensemble at the Frankfurt airport and flew to Buenos Aires, where many people awaited us at the airport.

We immediately met Jews of the community as well as dear friends. One of them was Mark Turkov, Sigmund's brother, who had been living in South America since before World War II. Our meeting with Mark was a moving experience. Not only hadn't I seen him for so many years, but he is also an uncle to my daughter, Ruth, for whom he displayed much affection.

Our first days in Buenos Aires were devoted to preparations for our performances. This time I agreed to begin our series with a play in which I had no role, but in which the entire ensemble would be featured. The play was *The Dreamers of Kaptzansk*, adapted from Mendele Mocher Seforim's novel *The Travels of Benjamin III*, directed by and starring Chevel Buzgan. (He had been in Argentina for more than ten years before returning in 1948 to Poland.)

The preparations for the premiere lasted until 10 P.M., but the audience waited patiently until everything was ready. All these delays distressed us, but everything went well and we had a successful evening.

Our second production was the immortal *Mirele Efros*. The third was Arthur Miller's *All My Sons*, and the fourth, Alexander Kassona's *Trees Die Standing*. The last was very popular, for it had had a long run in Spanish when Kassona had lived in Argentina. The audience, the press, and even the Spanish actors who had played in the piece received our production favorably.

Our high spirits, however, were deflated when Chevel Buzgan fell ill and requested that he be transported back to Poland because he wanted "to die in Warsaw." Indeed, he returned to Poland and recovered. (He died in 1971.) *All My Sons* had been announced in several cities, and my husband and I quickly had to jump into the roles of both Buzgans, for Chevel's wife joined him when he left for Warsaw.

From Buenos Aires we went to Montevideo, Uruguay, for two weeks and then for one week to Rio de Janeiro and São Paulo, Brazil. Here, too, the scene reminded us of Argentina—friends, receptions in various communities and in the embassies. In a word, it was like old routine.

On our way home from South America, Mel and I stopped off in Sweden. I found it rather painful not to return home with the rest of my ensemble, but the Swedish television in Stockholm had invited me for a performance, so we delayed our return to Warsaw for a couple of days. These two days passed very pleasantly. The management of the Swedish television arranged for me to meet with writers and artists, and they took us to see memorable sights.

The television program consisted of an interview with me (accompanied by a Polish translator), followed by a recitation of Julian Tuvim's famous letter "We Polish Jews." The program concluded with scenes from *The Shop on Main Street*. This was the finale to my grand tour. We returned home, where my dear family was eagerly waiting for me.

I considered my work well done in the theater when I saw actors developing and growing. The theater can be beautiful and variegated only when one has excellent people to work with. In my theater I had good actors and bad actors, who occasionally spoiled a production. A weak actor might be a very fine human being, and one's sympathy for the person frequently clashed with one's dissatisfaction with his artistry. Often I would work hard with an actor to improve his style, and then I couldn't understand why, when he developed later, only the bad side of his personality was displayed. (Of course, not all reacted in this fashion.) Often actors would do things out of spite and then later come crying to me, apologizing and beating their breasts, reciting, "I have sinned."

Why do I mention this now? I want it to be known how

difficult it is to manage a theater where individual characteristics are so different, where ambitions are inflated, and where
actors' fancied talents are often much greater than their real
worth. However, I would never be obstinate. I would gladly
talk with actors, discuss their problems with them, and occasionally change my opinion. The actors of the older generation and the young ones who remember could certainly
confirm this. Of course, when one has the opportunity to
select actors from a much larger pool, one chooses those
with whom it is easier to get along. However, during the last
twenty years in Poland the choice was a very small one, and
I had to manage as best I could. Despite all my difficulties in
the theater, no one on the outside—in the Polish theater
world—knew of them, and both I and our Yiddish theater
were held in great respect.

33

The Six-Day War Begins

SUDDENLY, in May 1967, the news came that the Arabs had blockaded the Red Sea off Eilat. A rope around the neck of Israel in order to strangle the Jewish state. A clearcut call for war, which the Arabs were very likely prepared for. Is this what they wanted? The hearts of Jews all over the world, wherever they were and whatever their outlook, began to beat more quickly. And not only Jewish hearts, but the hearts of everyone who feared war, no matter where it broke out. Nevertheless, war came. It was a shock to all of us.

I told Mel, "There are so many of them and so few of us. They have much territory to fall back on, and we have only the sea."

We had seen what people with their own sweat and toil had made of a land where no grass had grown, no water had flowed, and where hyenas had run wild in the streets.

The non-Jews, those who didn't hate Israel, had no doubts that the Jews would win. On the first day of the war a Warsaw taxi driver told my daughter, not knowing that she was Jewish, "The Jews will teach them a lesson. They'll beat the hell out of them, and the war won't last long."

Ruth asked, "How can you be so sure? There are so many of them and so few Jews."

"Go on," the taxi driver said. "During World War II, I was in Palestine and in the Arab countries. All the Arabs know how to do is lie on their backs, belly up, but in Israel they know how to work. Every girl knows how to fire a weapon. What discipline they have! What technology!"

During the first two or three days of the Six-Day War, when news came of the Israeli victories, the reports on television, radio, and in certain newspapers were quite objective. The Jews were not yet called "aggressors," and the regime still had not begun to use the word "Zionist" as an insult. Nevertheless, it seemed that the official line had to sympathize with the Arabs, who were supported by the Soviet Union. The people, however, didn't hesitate to express their satisfaction and amazement at the Jewish victories, perhaps less for love of Mordecai (that is, Israel) than hatred of Haman (the Soviet Union). Even when the official anti-Israel incitement began in the state-controlled press, on radio and television, on the streets Polish people congratulated Jews, who were in a very good mood. No one attempted to conceal his joy.

Faces radiated pride. On the fourth day of the war, I was conducting a rehearsal. Someone came to notify me that a man was waiting for me; he had to see me immediately because he had to catch a plane. The door opened and into the theater came our old friend Zvi Netzer, who had been the first secretary of the Israeli Embassy in Warsaw and was now stationed in Moscow. Expelled from the Soviet Union, he was on his way back to Israel and had stopped in Warsaw. I broke off the rehearsal. We fell upon each other's necks, embracing, crying for joy. Everyone was moved. Zvi Netzer had to leave soon for the airport, and the rest of us, now greatly encouraged, continued our rehearsal.

Two days after the end of the Six-Day War the Israeli ambassador had been expelled in a most ignominious fashion, and all of Warsaw spoke of this. Hired hooligans, acting under orders of the Ministry of Interior, harassed and reviled the Israeli diplomats at the air terminal. These toughs tore the Israelis' luggage out of the porters' hands and shouted, "Let them carry their own bags." Honorable Poles said that such a deed was unheard of in a civilized nation.

There were also rumors that I was the only one who had accompanied the ambassador to the airport, which unfortunately was not so, for no one knew of this expulsion.

Various diplomats who had accompanied members of the ambassadorial staff to the airport had been witness to the vile treatment of the Israelis—and that evening an interesting demonstration took place. During the performance a long row of diplomatic cars parked in front of our theater. After having seen the disgraceful incident at the airport, the diplomats had come to the Yiddish theater to express in this fashion their disapproval and protest.

Immediately after the Jewish victory over the Arabs, there began a loud orgy of insults against Israel and the Zionists by the party leaders. The high point came on June 19, 1967, when the general secretary of the Polish Communist party, Gomulka, declared in a speech: "Poland will not tolerate in its midst a fifth column."

This speech was published in the press without the latter remark, but Gomulka's other statements were dispicable, too, and his facial expression and the prime minister's grimaces were repulsive, not only to a Jew, but to every honorable person. Nevertheless, the average Polish citizen asked, "What's a Zionist?" and everyone wanted to know, "What actually happened?" Jews, in reply, cited the story of the good cow who had given a full pitcher of milk and then knocked the pitcher over.

The morning following Gomulka's speech once again the beautiful limousines of various embassies were parked in front of our theater. Thus representatives of other nations were demonstratively expressing their solidarity with the Jews.

At that time the Swiss dramatist Friedrich Dürrenmatt was visiting in Warsaw. He had also come to our theater and to our apartment. We knew each other from the time when he had last been in Warsaw. He had visited the Polish Dramatic Theater, where I had done a guest performance in his *Frank V*, playing the role of Ottilia Frank. When the Swiss Embassy arranged a farewell banquet for Dürrenmatt, Mel and I were invited. After the recently begun incitement by Gomulka, I was not in the best of spirits. This was probably apparent in my face. Various people, foreigners and Poles, came up to me and expressed their sympathy, as though to protest the recently begun hate campaign. Dürrenmatt and his wife sat down with me alone, and we drank several glasses of cognac.

Then Mrs. Dürrenmatt said, "If anything happens, come to us in Switzerland. We'll receive you with open arms. You'll be our guests for as long as you wish." I was touched by this.

Later, as we began descending the steps to the waiting autos, in the company of the many people who were assembled there, Dürrenmatt suddenly approached and brought me two champagne glasses. He gave one to me and lifted the other and said in a loud voice, "Let us drink to the aggressors."

We drank, unconcerned with what was going on around us. I went home feeling grateful that there were people like Dürrenmatt. His name I mention happily, but others—Poles —I cannot mention, for I don't want to place them in a bad light with the Polish authorities. It would only hurt them.

Incidentally, after his return home to Zurich, Dürrenmatt delivered a magnificent speech to a huge audience, expressing his protest against the enemies of Israel in Poland and praising those Poles who sympathized with Israel.

On September 18, 1967, we celebrated my fiftieth anniversary in the Yiddish theater. This jubilee should have been celebrated on June 19, 1967. Fortunately, the celebration had been postponed, for just on that day Gomulka broadcast his despicable speech. Nevertheless, I didn't believe that in this atmosphere of incited anti-Zionistic (anti-Jewish) feelings, the festivities would take place. Perhaps the higher-ups were ashamed to speak up, and perhaps it was a political necessity prior to our New York tour not to call off this jubilee celebration lest it be interpreted as an anti-Semitic act. In short, on September 18, amid a joyous atmosphere, the celebration indeed took place. The attitude of the Polish theater world contributed to the festivities, as did the feelings of the Jews, who particularly at that time wanted to demonstrate their closeness to Jewish culture.

That evening the finest representatives of the Polish stage appeared in the theater. Unfortunately, there was no longer anyone from Israel, for they all had been expelled. The anniversary performance consisted of one act from *Mirele Efros*, several scenes from *Mother Courage* by Bertolt Brecht, and a scene from the film *Ida Kaminska and Her Theater*.

As soon as the performance ended, the stage was covered with flowers, wreaths, and bouquets. Then representatives from the Ministry of Culture, the Central Theater Organization, and various Jewish institutions that existed at the time took their places on the stage. The chief celebrants of the jubilee, the Yiddish actors, were all on the stage, in the middle of which, like a throne, stood an easy chair.

My beautiful daughter, Ruth, and the actress Ruth Kowalska, both of them magnificently dressed, brought me onstage and seated me on the "throne." Once more flowers and gifts from various organizations were presented to me. Then began the official addresses. First came the vice-minister of culture, K. Rusinek. In his speech, probably by order of the political authorities, he did not forget to attack Israel as an "aggressor." Following him were speakers from our ensemble, the Polish theaters, and representatives of the Jewish Culture Organization. When my turn came, I didn't want Vice-Minister Rusinek's remarks to go unanswered. After my address in Polish, I made reference to Rusinek's jibe by turning to the Jews in the audience and saying, "Not everything that I wanted to say can be said now, but in these fateful hours for the Jewish people you feel what I feel, and even if I say little, you will understand much." These few words elicited stormy applause. Later many Poles who understood my allusion shook my hand and congratulated me on my reply.

The next day a banquet was held in the theater for many

guests of the theater world. Once again so much honor was accorded me that even recalling it now moves me to tears. In honor of the jubilee, a book was published titled *Ida Kaminska—Fifty Years*. It included various biographical articles and assessments of my career written by theater critics, as well as illustrations from my many years of theatrical activity. Half the articles were written in Yiddish, and half in Polish.

The time was approaching when our theater would leave for New York, where our tour would begin in October 1967.

It was a difficult and unpleasant period. Every day we would hear of Jews fired from responsible positions and of pensions of elderly Jews revoked only because they dared to express their opinion that the anti-Zionist campaign was clearly anti-Semitic. However, people attempted to console themselves. "It will soon pass," they said. After all, there had been similar attempts to stir up anti-Jewish feeling among Poles in the past —for instance, in 1956—and that, too, had passed.

Nevertheless, everyone feared to utter a word of protest of any kind.

Among the Poles and among the hierarchy there were two people who dared to demonstrate that they wanted no part in such devilish politics. They were Foreign Minister Adam Rapacki and Polish President Edward Ochab. Some people thought that a form of Stalinism would take root that would look for victims. Others thought that the situation would return to the way it was. Nevertheless, when crystal breaks, one can no longer get the same clear tone out of it.

The Jewish organizations were asked for an open declaration condemning Israel as an aggressor. The negotiations between the regime and the presidium of the Jewish Culture Organization regarding the text of such a document dragged on for four weeks. Nothing helped, not even the members' resignations. Finally, under duress, they signed a declaration that was not the text they had collectively accepted but one that the regime wanted. This brought the signers only humiliation. The majority, wanting to rehabilitate themselves, emigrated from Poland.

Resolutions were required from schools, theaters, scientific institutions, but to our theater no such demand was made. When I learned from a television newscast that the Jewish Culture Organization had condemned the defensive war of Israel, I was shocked. I felt ashamed before my housekeeper, who calmed me with these words: "They probably had to do it."

We began to prepare ourselves for the trip to New York, which was a great undertaking for us. This would be our first appearance in the largest Jewish city in the world. Our debut on Broadway! I knew that in New York there were various types of people: those who wished us well and those who, because of hatred for the Iron Curtain regimes, might lose their objectivity and assail us. That is why we were somewhat apprehensive about our trip to this American metropolis.

Mel and I, along with our technical staff, preceded the rest of the ensemble by several days to New York. Many friends, as well as representatives of cultural institutions, were preparing a festive welcome at the airport. However, we did not arrive in New York. Because of bad weather, our plane landed in Washington, where we spent the night. Only on the following day were we able to fly to New York, welcomed by our closest relatives and the impresario Harold Leventhal. We were taken to the Hotel Shoreham on West Fifty-fifth Street, not too far from the theater where we performed, the Billy Rose, on West Forty-first Street.

As is usual when it comes to important events, I was fated to experience unpleasantries. In New York some malicious people had spread a rumor that David Sefard and I had signed an anti-Israel declaration in Poland. This was an insulting lie, for it was well known that for five years I had not been a member of the presidium of the Jewish Culture Organization and Sefard was at that time at a resort in Zakopane and first learned of the declaration from television, just as I did. Moreover, no names appeared with the declaration, just the words "the Presidium of the Jewish Culture Organization."

When I came to New York, I explicitly demanded at a press conference that the person or source of this libel be identified. Of course, I couldn't find out. Until the matter was cleared up and proved to be a fabrication, threats were made to picket the theater, but as the proverb says, all's well that ends well. The premiere took place before a fully packed house. Even the previews were sold out. Our sixty performances were almost completely sold out every day.

We presented Jacob Gordin's *Mirele Efros* and Bertolt Brecht's *Mother Courage*. We gave more performances of *Mirele Efros*, but there were many viewers who maintained that *Mother Courage* was the better production. I must add also that the impresario Harold Leventhal, a true gentleman, treated us extremely well.

Throughout our entire stay in New York we participated in various banquets given by various organizations: the American Jewish Congress, the Congress for Jewish Culture, the Yiddish Writers and Journalists Association, Actors Equity, the Yiddish Teachers' Seminary, the Hebrew Actors Union, as well as many others, all of whom received us very warmly. We simply had no time for ourselves. Besides all this, the Polish Embassy in Washington invited the entire company for a reception there.

I am reminded of the proverb: "It's good to be a guest, and especially an important guest." At every opportunity I was told (not officially): "Why are you staying in Poland? Come to us. We're rich; we'll give you a Yiddish theater just like the Polish regime." (Today, after several years in America, I can say, like the words of a song, "Oh, if it were only true!")

During our entire tour, which lasted more than two months (October 15 through December 18, 1967), we followed the situation in Poland. From the newspapers we learned that it had not improved. Nevertheless, I thought that we would decide upon our future destiny after our return. Our success and the enthusiasm of the audiences encouraged us to think that in America there was an audience that understood theater and wanted a better Yiddish theater.

Every day hundreds waited for me at the theater and pleaded, "Don't go back to Poland. Stay with us." This was pleasing to hear, but my family and I didn't want to be runaways. This was a question of honor. So we replied, "In the meantime, we'll return, and then we'll see what will be."

The unusual affection for us expressed by the English-language and the Yiddish press, together with the "voice of the people" and the exaltation we felt at every performance, truly heartened us at a time when we had to return to the atmosphere of rising anti-Semitism (labeled anti-Zionism) in Poland. Warm and endearing letters streamed in to us from all parts of the United States. Some complained about our return and asked us why we were going back to Poland. The audiences' attitude toward us was extraordinary. After every performance people would wait outside, wanting to greet us. The enthusiasm with which I was received both onstage and on the street, where most of the people would recognize me, was extremely touching.

One Sabbath morning several other actors and I were invited to visit the Brotherhood Synagogue. Since a representative of the Polish Ministry of Culture accompanied us—he also tagged along to keep an eye on our "*kashrut*"—he came to shul with us, too. The men put on yarmulkes and prayer shawls. The representative from the Culture Ministry, who was a gentile—one look at his face revealed his obvious non-Jewishness—also put on a tallith and a yarmulke. When we saw this, we could hardly contain our laughter. He remained for a while and then finally realized the grotesqueness of the situation and left the synagogue of his own accord.

Meanwhile, after the reading of the Torah, Rabbi Irvin Bloch delivered a fine sermon concerning the importance of my work for the Jewish people and then presented me with a beautiful silver-bound Bible. On this Sabbath there was also a Bar Mitzvah, and the young boy stated that he would always remember that Ida Kaminska was present at his Bar Mitzvah.

At the conclusion of our tour we returned to Poland. I flew via Copenhagen, where I remained for a day and bought a Volvo. Then I continued my flight to Warsaw, for the car was to be brought home to us by Karol Latovitch. At customs in Warsaw we noticed a different attitude toward us. It was not what it used to be. It seemed as though we were strangers.

Since we returned at the end of December 1967, our new theater season began this time in January. Several days later the news spread that one of our actors, Henryk Greenberg, had remained in the United States and requested political asylum. His interviews with Radio Free Europe were already being broadcast. Henryk Greenberg was not only an actor in our company but was also a noted young writer who had published several fine short stories (in Polish) that had received major literary prizes. His remaining in America was a bombshell. Officials from the Polish Internal Security office began phoning various actors, trying to find out if I had known that Greenberg would remain in the United States.

Finally, after speaking to everyone else, they called me. A young man spoke very gently with me and wanted to know my reactions to this defection. I told them that I couldn't be responsible for every individual, especially at a time when the leadership of the country had declared that whoever didn't like it here could leave. They swallowed this response as delicately as they could, and I suffered no repercussions because of it.

When we returned to Warsaw, we sensed that the attitude toward the Jews had not improved; it had become even worse. We performed—of course, not every evening—the same plays. The audience came and was pleased with us, but the reactions of those who heard the plays in translation through earphones reminded us of the difference between the festive atmosphere we felt in New York and the somewhat different mood here, at home in Warsaw.

We were under the illusion that today, tomorrow, there would come—as in former times in the Soviet Union—a declaration that everything that had been done against the Jews had been an "error" committed by "persons who perverted socialist ideology" and so forth. An old song!

Meanwhile, it grew worse from day to day. Student unrest, rising anti-Semitism. No contriteness was expressed by anyone. On the contrary, the situation grew more disgraceful and confusing, and so it has continued to this very day.

Our theater encountered new situations. First, we were given to understand that the contract we had made to perform in America in 1968 would not be honored. Furthermore, the suggestions that we visit the Scandinavian countries and East Berlin were "out of the question at present."

Suddenly, too, theaters in Upper Silesia that used to welcome us with open arms and present us with flowers found various pretexts not to rent us their theaters for any date that we proposed. Everyone to whom we turned for an explanation of this sudden discrimination replied in a hazy fashion that revealed nothing.

The construction of a new theater, begun two years earlier with funds provided by the Joint Distribution Committee, was halted at the end of 1967 with the excuse that there were insufficient laborers and no building materials.

I went to the presidium of the Jewish Culture Organization and told them that we dare not remain silent, that we should go to the highest governmental body and demand an answer to various questions. If no reply was forthcoming, that, too, would be an answer. But my words were in vain.

I decided to go by myself, if not to the highest authorities, then at least to one of my formal superiors. Unfortunately, I cannot mention his name, for I don't wish to harm this kind and honest man. He replied, with tears in his eyes: "It's bad for you. I don't mean you personally or your theater—I mean all of you. *You!* You," he repeated several times, "you who were always my friends and still are. What more can I say to you?"

I rose and left. That moment it became clear to me that my place was not in Poland, regardless of the fact that I would have to leave everything. The authorities didn't ask me to condemn Israel—they knew I would refuse and then they'd be in an embarrassing position about what to do with me. They would not arrest me; neither would they expel me —nevertheless, certain responses came that were directed against me.

One example concerned the Volvo I had bought in Denmark and brought into Poland. According to recent unwritten policy, the finance division of customs gave special consideration to actors who from their earnings abroad imported automobiles; they would either be freed from paying customs duty or pay only a nominal sum. When it came to me, however, they followed the letter of the law. I had to pay 45,000 zlotys, or more than a thousand dollars. Everyone was surprised at this, especially Polish colleagues, but the matter was clear to me. It was a tactic against Jews. Against me, because I didn't sign an anti-Israel declaration.

At the beginning of 1967 the Poles made a biographical film called *Ida Kaminska and Her Theater*. It never had a screening. The same thing happened to the film that was made celebrating my fiftieth anniversary in the theater in 1967.

Furthermore, in 1966, along with the very talented Polish actress Alexandra Shlonska, I made a television film called *The Black Dress*, based on a story by Stanislaw Wogodsky (now in Israel). It was a two-character film made by the excellent, unassuming director Stanislaw Mayevsky. When *The Black Dress* was shown at a Prague festival, it was judged by a jury that consisted of five representatives of the so-called socialist nations and two from the West. In Warsaw the press and professional film circles stated that the film had every chance of receiving top recognition, "especially because of Ida Kaminska." In Prague, however, only the director and the actress Alexandra Shlonska were singled out for accolades. Both Mayevsky and Shlonska avoided me after that. They felt ashamed for me and for the injustice done to me, but I wasn't upset, for I knew what lay behind the decision.

One day in 1968 both my films were to be presented as a double feature in a Warsaw cinema: *The Shop on Main Street* and the biographical film *Ida Kaminska and Her Theater.* People were amazed. "What! What does it mean? At a time like this?"

It turned out that at the very first scene there was a staged riot. Hired hooligans began yelling, "Get it off the screen, or we'll burn down the house." If they had been street hoodlums, they would have feared making such a demonstration, but these instigators felt quite secure.

The removal of Jews from higher and lesser positions under the pretext of calling them "Zionist agitators" grew to epidemic proportions. This even affected couples of mixed marriage.

Occasionally tragedies ensued. There was a couple, he a Jew, a colonel in the army, and she a Christian, a doctor, who were fired at the same time from their positions. For years they had lived together happily. Then suddenly came this slap in the face for both of them because he was a Jew and perhaps "a dangerous Zionist." They felt broken. In the evening they sent home their housekeeper, took large doses of sleeping pills, clasped their hands, and fell asleep. In the morning they were found. But a Jew doesn't even have the *mazel* of dying when he himself wishes to. His wife was dead, but he was saved. The letters that they had left to be given to friends, stating that they could not live in such an unjust world, were intercepted by the security forces before they reached their destinations—except for two letters that had been sent out earlier.

Under such conditions I maintained that my first obligation was to resign as artistic director and stage director of the theater. I wrote two letters, one to the City Council and the second to the Ministry of Culture. Then I patiently waited for an answer.

The events in Poland were distressing. The innovative and talented director of the National Theater, Kosimir Deimek, presented the classic drama of Poland's greatest poet Adam Mickiewicz, *Djiadi* ("The Spirits of the Grandfathers"), in a staging that was very close to the poet's intent. The play was a highly artistic protest against czarism, which had choked Poland more than a century ago. The Polish people received it with rare enthusiasm. The anti-czarist protest, however, could not be separated from the protest against the current Russian occupiers. The play recalled too much the present-day situation.

The theater, then, became an expression of political protest. The Polish authorities discovered this and, in fear of the Soviet overlords, removed this play from the stage. This led to huge demonstrations and strikes at all the universities. The demonstrations were broken up, and the authorities came up with a new false accusation: that Zionist provocateurs were the cause of it all. Hundreds of students were arrested, most of them Jews, who made up only about 2 percent of the student population.

I knew one young man, a student, who against the will of his parents also participated in the demonstration. When I told him not to do it for the sake of his parents' health—after all, he was an only son—he replied that he loved his parents but he had to express his solidarity with the convictions of his Polish colleagues who demanded freedom of artistic expression. The next morning this student was arrested for Zionism.

Before I submitted my resignation papers, I had been invited by the Czech Culture Ministry (during Dubcek's reign) to be a judge at the Carlsbad Film Festival. The president of the festival, Elmar Klos, made a special trip to Warsaw and through the Czech ambassador intervened with the Polish Ministry of Culture. Nevertheless, the Ministry of Interior (that is, the so-called internal security forces) denied me the proper documents. The Czech Embassy intervened a second time, to no avail.

My husband had a role in a Berlin film and in May 1968 was scheduled to conclude a scene and receive his honorarium of two thousand marks. This trip, too, was denied.

We were already on the "Zionist" list.

When we decided to request permission to leave, most of our friends asserted that the authorities wouldn't let us out, but others said, "The regime will be glad to see you go, for they know your position on certain issues [I would often state my nonconformist opinions] and they don't know what to do with you."

Ruth and Erika's husband (Yuri Kowalick, whom she had just married) went to the Dutch Embassy (they represented Israel in Poland) to get visa applications. They cited the names of all the members of our family. Seeing my name, the Polish secretary of the visa department asked, "Is this Ida Kaminska, the actress?" When Ruth said yes, the woman grabbed her head and exclaimed, "Woe, this is the end!"

Meanwhile, knowing that it was doubtful if permission would be granted, I began to tell everyone of our move. I would talk about my application on the telephone, under the assumption that it was tapped, and spread the news to people during both internal and international calls. In case my application was denied, I wanted it to be known why I hadn't left Poland, for I considered my emigration a question of human and Jewish national honor.

During this period the intensity of hate, insults, and vilification of Israel and the "Zionists" (meaning, of course, all the Jews) in Poland increased daily in the press and on radio and television. I couldn't believe that the television announcers were uttering such shameful words. During street demonstrations one could see signs saying "Moishe—go to Dayan." Calling the Israelis Nazis was a common phenomenon. Yet, at the same time, the television showed Jewish soldiers on Allenby Bridge tenderly carrying Arab babies who were either emigrating or returning to Israel-occupied Jordan. By calling these soldiers Nazis, these slandermongers were spitting in their own faces.

The lack of protest against this policy was terribly painful; so was the fact that decent human beings didn't rise against such lies. And no wonder. Just recently the students had been "quieted" by means of terror; writers had been threatened with punishment, and the best of them could no longer be published.

As previously mentioned, Poles asked, "What is a Zionist?" They simply didn't know. This question recalled an event that took place at the end of the war in the central Asian section of the Soviet Union. A Pole, an officer in the prewar Polish army, received a ten-year sentence from a Soviet court. He had been found guilty of not voluntarily joining the Polish army that had been organized in Russia (and later had gone to Iran under British command). When the verdict was announced to the officer, he asked, "What for?"

"For Zionism" was the reply.

The officer laughed. "But I'm a Pole. How can I be a Zionist?"

"None of your back talk," the judge replied. "You're guilty of Zionism, and that's that!"

The officer remained in jail until Stalin's death.

As grotesque and paradoxical as this story sounds, it illustrates the inane cliché with which the Communist agitation operated in its desire to convince the masses, who at meetings would listen apathetically to all the yammering about the new enemy: the Zionist.

The inscription "Moishe—to Dayan" reminded me of the prewar cheer "Yonah—go to war." The difference was that this "Yonah" indeed heroically went to battle for Poland and for Jewish honor. Thousands fell, not only in the ghettos but in battlefields all over Europe and especially in the Polish army.

The days dragged on. Once during an afternoon I fell asleep. (I used to take potent tranquilizers.) In my sleep I suddenly heard the cry *"Sieg heil! Sieg heil!"*—the hated Nazi motto. I had a vision that Hitler was standing off to a side, and before him marched his hordes with upraised arms. I awoke but continued hearing the words *"Sieg heil!"* I ran into the adjoining room, where the television set was on. There on the screen was Party Secretary Gomulka addressing the most active members of the Communist party. The audience was shouting, "Wieslaw! Wieslaw!"—Gomulka's pseudonym. In my dream this cry of "Wieslaw! Wieslaw!" had changed to *"Sieg heil!"*

Gomulka continued talking. He wanted to moderate somewhat his overly provoked anti-Semitic instincts. I thought that someone in this highest body of Communist party followers—composed of well-known people, intellectuals, students, and intelligent leaders of the factories and institutions—would stand up against this nationalistic hysteria, but I was naïve.

Gomulka's speech, which was supposed to tone down the remarks of an earlier address, was a disappointment to the audience. The faces recorded this reaction, and a murmur was one of its signs. This murmur soon spread into a full-fledged shout, a tumult. Gomulka attempted to still the audience. "Comrades," he shouted, "you don't know what I want to say!" The provoked mass, who were called Communists but in whom hooliganistic instincts had been awakened, cried out, "Bolder, Wieslaw! Bolder!" (meaning, come out loud and clear against the Jews, don't soft-pedal your remarks). Gomulka then probably skipped over his intended remarks and concluded with "Whoever doesn't like it here, the doors are open, and they can go," to which this group of "lovers of mankind" shouted back, "but right now! Today!"

In my life I have often had reasons for getting angry, but I always attempted to restrain myself, especially in my mature years. I just barely managed to control myself, ran into my bedroom, took a pill, and tried to contain my feelings.

Mel ran into the room and attempted to call me. I cried out, "Let's flee! Immediately! Otherwise, I won't be able to survive it."

Ruth, who had also come into the room, said, "Mama, what's the matter? Didn't you expect this? Be happy, for after a meeting like this we'll surely be given permission to leave."

I decided to keep my poise. The entire family then mobilized itself to make all the preparations for leaving, for we knew that after a person received the exit visa he had to leave the country within a month.

After my resignation and long wait for a reply, I finally got an invitation from the head of the Cultural Affairs department of the City Council, a man called Maksara. Present with him was his deputy. Maksara gave me a signed release. I was delighted with it, for I knew that in the conversation that would follow he would not attempt to restrain me from leaving the theater.

"Do you want to remain in the theater as an actress or director?" he asked.

"No."

"Do you want to work or direct in the *Polish* theater?"

"No," I said. "That would betray my links to my people, who are now in a difficult situation and for whom I have worked all my life."

"Well, then?" Maksara asked.

I interrupted him and said, "I certainly don't want to retire either, even though by rights it is due me. I still want to work for those I've worked for all my life."

"Well, then?" he asked again.

I replied, "From the highest tribune in this land it has been clearly stated"—I repeated Gomulka's words—" 'Whoever doesn't like it here can go.' I don't like it."

The head of the Cultural Affairs Department quickly stood. It seemed as though a stone had been removed from Maksara's chest. He kissed my hand, pressed it, and wished me well. He also thanked me for my great and beautiful contributions to Polish art. Maksara's deputy also shook my hand. There were tears in his eyes. I thought, how people must deny their own feelings and convictions if they want to remain in their high positions! The deputy soon became Maksara's successor, for Maksara was appointed cultural attaché in Yugoslavia.

Although my intention of emigrating was not a secret, I nevertheless assembled the executive council of the theater and announced that my family and I would leave Poland. Several people surely knew of this, but they pretended to be surprised. The reaction was: "Why didn't you tell us this before? Then all of us would have submitted applications to leave, and the regime would have given us the sets and costumes, and we would have departed as a fully equipped theater."

Of course, this was thoroughly naïve. It was only an argument to point out that I was leaving them at a time of trouble. The opponents of my emigration knew very well that had we made such a collective application it would have been considered an antiregime demonstration that could have had unpleasant consequences.

Furthermore, any individual who wanted to leave took the same steps as I. Actually, those who spoke up were simply waiting for the opportunity to reap the inheritance that I was leaving. Indeed, that is precisely what happened. They ran to the authorities and were squabbling among themselves about who would take over the little kingdom.

For most of the ensemble, especially the technical and administrative staff, my departure from the theater was a severe blow. However, since the regime had to show that it was not anti-Semitic but only anti-Zionistic, the theater was permitted to continue, even without its best actors, even without an audience. The costs—well, they had to be absorbed. The regime considered it worthwhile to be able to show the passing tourist in Poland that, contrary to common knowledge, they had *not* arranged an exodus of its last Jews between 1967 and 1969.

During this period I had a phone call from my London cousin, Henry Lister, who told me that the impresario who had wanted to bring over the entire theater was now prepared to bring only the actors in my family and form a troupe with them. Then a film agent notified me that he saw possibilities of a film for me in New York. And so it developed that our prospects after our departure from Poland seemed to be promising. My chief desire, however, was to flee from Poland, for I could no longer bear it there.

The American Embassy notified me that it had received a letter from two American Jews who requested the embassy to give all possible aid to Ida Kaminska and her family to help them leave Poland. If it involved extra expenditures, the two American Jews would cover it. The embassy even promised us visas, which we were to get in Vienna.

Meanwhile, a two-pronged campaign began in the press in Poland: on the one hand, articles against "the Zionist" and, on the other hand, articles and letters from various Poles stating how they had saved Jews during the German occupation. One might have gathered the impression from these letters that perhaps a million Jews had been saved by Poles during World War II. The intent of this campaign was "See how ungrateful the Jews are!"

The truth is that only about two thousand Jews had been saved by the Poles. Those who indeed had saved Jews didn't write letters because they considered such deeds their duty as human beings, which they did not have to advertise. Others didn't make this gesture public because they wanted to avoid being jeered by their neighbors and called "Jew lovers." I knew of incidents similar to the one in which Polish peasants who had helped save Mel's closest relatives asked Mel not to mention this in their village when he visited them.

The entire Polish people cannot be blamed, but the truth should not be covered up. During the German occupation there were Polish extortionists who blackmailed Jews, took their last penny from them, and when the Jews no longer had any money, delivered them over to the Germans.

The press, in informing its readers how many had perished during the Hitler occupation, would mention all the various nationalities except Jews, who were included statistically among the Poles or the Russians. The director of the Jewish Historical Institute, who collected everything that had any connection with the history of Polish Jewry and especially with the occupation period, submitted his resignation after the most important documents and valuable works of art were taken from the Jewish Historical Institute and transferred to the Polish Central Archives. Removed were objects that had been rescued by Jews after the occupation. In the Central Archives this Jewish material completely disappeared among thousands of unimportant exhibited objects, which were, incidentally, not designated for public viewing.

34

Permission to Leave

IN the beginning of July 1968, we received the necessary documents that permitted us to depart. I considered these papers contemptible. They certified that such-and-such a person was no longer a Polish citizen and was permitted to leave the land. People who had done so much for Poland and whose parents and grandparents had contributed to Poland's welfare, fought for its land, developed its economy, and made Poland's name famous through scientific or cultural accomplishments were suddenly robbed of their citizenship and literally thrown out of their homes. Yet, when we signed papers stating that we were relinquishing Polish citizenship, our hands did not tremble—for if they demanded this of us, then the mere signing was no extraordinary experience.

Stalin's insult against the Jews had come true. At the time of the so-called war against cosmopolitanism, he had called the Jews "wandering tramps without passports." Between 1948 and 1952 the regime destroyed Jewish culture in the Soviet Union and murdered its finest representatives, all under the pretext that this was part of the war against cosmopolitanism. (From 1967 on, these same "cosmopolitans" were labeled "Zionists.")

We quickly made all arrangements to depart, paying no heed to expenses. We had to spend the bit of cash we possessed anyway, for it was forbidden to take money out of Poland. No administrative obstacles were placed in our way. On the contrary, it even seemed that the regime wanted to get rid of us all the quicker, and not only because of the fine apartment that we had, for which "important candidates" were already waiting. I had to sell for Polish zlotys the Volvo I had imported, for they found a law that stated that an auto could not be taken out of the country prior to one year from date of import. The money we received for the car we literally squandered, for what use was it to us? I was even paid in zlotys for the twelve hundred dollars I had brought into Poland as royalties earned abroad, which, according to foreign-currency regulations, I could have taken back abroad. So, indeed, we had far more zlotys than we really needed.

When our impending departure became known, many Poles came to see me. Known and unknown, old and young, bade farewell to me with tears in their eyes. They begged me not to blame the Poles who disagreed with the regime's policies, especially their recent policy regarding the Jews. People from various levels of society came to me, people from the theatrical and literary worlds, and also white-collar workers and laborers. My chauffeur, who for several years had driven me in the auto that belonged to the theater (he is dead, so I can talk of him; now it can't hurt him), came to me with a worker I didn't know and asked, "Do not forget us. Come back as soon as things change." They themselves didn't know too clearly what would change, but at that time one could feel in the air the wind of renewal in Czechoslovakia, and masses of Poles were waiting for this. What a disappointment they must have encountered when several days later, in August 1968, the Polish military forces, together with the Russians, invaded the land of renewal.

Before leaving Warsaw, I bade good-bye to the grave of my mother. Our entire family looked for the last time at the famous Warsaw cemetery. One of the most honored places there was taken by the beautiful monument to Esther Rachel Kaminska, near the historic Y. L. Peretz mausoleum, where the writers Peretz, Ansky, and Dineson are buried.

Just one day prior to our departure Ruth's new husband,

Karol Latovitch, suffered a gall-bladder attack and that night had to undergo an operation. Obviously he couldn't go with us but remained in the hospital. My son, Victor, remained with him. They were to leave at a later date, once Karol had fully recuperated. Meanwhile, friends were still coming to see Mel and me, Ruth, Victor, and Erika and her husband. When we said farewell, these Poles all wept. My housekeeper, Bronya, who also was crying, said, "Leave already. You'll all drown here in the tears."

On August 21, 1968, at 5 P.M., we all were scheduled to depart on the train for Vienna. The apartment was almost empty, except for a large amount of furniture, clothing, and books. The dog, which we had given to our loyal housekeeper, wouldn't sleep during the last night at his usual place but stood guard at the door. Seeing the packed valises, the animal to which we had grown attached through the years was afraid that we would leave him and hence stood by the door.

Early in the morning on August 21 we received a call from our friend Yaakov Rotbaum, who had come from Wroclaw to say good-bye to us. In a calm voice he asked, "Are you definitely leaving today?"

"Why do you ask?" I said.

"Nothing special," he said with assumed calm. "This morning the Russian army marched into Czechoslovakia along with the Polish army. Since you're planning to go across Czechoslovakia, I was thinking that perhaps . . ."

My heart began to pound. "We haven't been notified as yet," I replied. "We're still waiting."

We listened to the radio, asked friends, and tried to get news at the train terminal, but no one could give us exact information about whether the train would leave. We were told that they had no order to cease train travel to Czechoslovakia.

Our phone rang throughout the day. People called to find out what would happen. No one had any concrete news. At 3:30 P.M. we left in several cars to go to the train station. My daughter preceded me. When I came up to the terminal, I already saw a host of Poles who were waiting for me with flowers. But when I came closer, I saw by the expression on Ruth's face that something was wrong. She signaled to me not to get out of the car. I understood. We were not leaving!

Suddenly all the strength I had amassed for this departure left me. I felt that I was simply collapsing. It's very hard to describe this, but I had the feeling everything was breaking within me, and pain was filling all my limbs from head to toe. I must have looked awful, for I heard someone saying, "Take her home immediately." I don't know who said this, for all the people and all the flowers blended into one mass before my eyes.

On my way home I didn't say a word. In the apartment I had just left, Bronya already knew what had occurred. She had received a phone call from the terminal. Immediately she placed me in bed, undressed me, gave me a cup of coffee, and for a while permitted no one to see me. Gradually, however, I began to feel better, and when I felt that the shock from this sudden change of plans was passing, I pulled myself together and was able to greet friends with a smile.

What would be? Would we have an opportunity to travel tomorrow through Czechoslovakia or perhaps go by another route? No reply to these questions was possible until the following day.

Early in the morning on August 22 we began to explore possibilities for leaving. It had become clear that the trains wouldn't be able to travel through Czechoslovakia for several days at least. The "friendly" help that the Czech people had received by means of tanks and occupying armies seemed to be permanent.

What were we to do? Erika's husband Yuri had connections with various circles and learned that it was possible to travel through Germany. However, we needed visas to cross through East Germany. (A West German visa was not necessary for transit.) When Yuri had arranged everything to travel by train with sleeping cars through both Germanys, the telephone rang. It was the Dutch Embassy, stating that they were sending out a specially chartered plane the next morning, which was coming from the Soviet Union to Hungary and Vienna. All our baggage, which was supposed to go by train, would be taken with this plane. The entire trip would take about three hours. Of course, we gladly agreed to this.

On the morning of August 23 not as many were able to accompany us to the airport as to the train. Nevertheless, about twenty people came to see us off. Most of them were Poles who had discovered when we would be departing. Meanwhile, Karol's operation was successful. Because of the postponed journey, Ruth even had time to see her husband. Victor came to see us off at the plane. There was no lack of tears, even though by now I was already quite self-composed and was waiting to be on the plane. Despite this, when a Pole whom I didn't know knelt before me and kissed the hem of my dress and said, "Do not judge us all," tears choked me, but outwardly I didn't cry.

During customs inspection the ambassador from Holland came and devotedly helped us, seeing to it that the contents of our valises would not be scattered about (a common occurrence). This was a great favor for us, not because we were afraid of carrying forbidden items but because we were spared the bother of gathering up our things from the ground and packing them helter-skelter in the valises.

The Dutch ambassador also informed us confidentially that a representative of the American Embassy would be waiting for us in Vienna. If we had to wait for a visa, this representative would provide a fine resting place for us, perhaps in Baden bei Wien, where we would be able to relax.

The plane took off. For a long time we didn't talk. The feelings we used to have while flying abroad for guest appearances coursed through us. In addition, there was another one: that of fleeing. It reminded us of our fleeing Warsaw from the Germans—may it not happen again! Of course, now conditions were entirely different; there was no danger to life. Nevertheless, we were departing, indeed in an airplane, but still because we were Jews. Perhaps Jews from Germany flew westward until early 1939 in this same fashion. It wasn't an exact comparison, for then there was fear of brutal extermination. In 1968 the reasons were more moral; we simply couldn't tolerate and endure the torture of the Jewish minority through the monstrous and cleverly manufactured hate campaign that "the Zionists were a danger to the land."

We breathed freely when the plane landed in Vienna.

35

The First Days of Our Emigration

IN Vienna at the airport there was no representative of the American Embassy waiting for us, but there was a representative of the Jewish Agency for Israel. The two men from the Jewish Agency were very happy to see us. Both of them knew me from Warsaw, where they had served in the Israeli Embassy. They took us to a modest hotel and promised to take care of us. Of course, I had nothing against this, but I couldn't understand why the representative of the American Embassy not only didn't await us as promised, but didn't even telephone.

As we set foot in the hotel, we began receiving calls from newspapers in various countries. The first was from a reporter from West Germany. He requested a television interview with me, which he wanted to take place on the streets of Vienna. For this there later came a group of technicians and cameramen from West Berlin. Articles and interviews soon appeared in various European countries and in Israel as well. On the fourth or fifth day after my arrival *The New York Times* called me from New York and arranged a telephone interview.

Since Victor and Karol Latovich had remained temporarily in Warsaw, we often spoke to them by telephone. Once my son told me that a letter had come from the film agent in New York concerning *Angel Levine*, a film that was to be made in New York. Without waiting for a reply, the agent called Warsaw, then reached me in Vienna.

Just then the director of *The Shop on Main Street*, Jan

Kadar, and his wife and mother-in-law were also in Vienna. They had come for a visit to Vienna before the Soviet occupation of Czechoslovakia, and now, like thousands of other Czech citizens, they found themselves abroad, not knowing what to do. Should they return or not? The majority of these people chose to remain wanderers and not to return to their oppressed land. Kadar and his relatives did the same. Kadar possessed a Czech multicrossing passport (unlike the usual passport that had only one exit or entry visa) and would often go to Bratislava, forty miles from Vienna, where he was directing and concluding the filming of a new movie. In fact, he was to direct the film about which the agent in New York had just phoned me.

All this while my friends from the Jewish Agency surrounded me with their devoted attention. Nevertheless, I was curious to know why the promised guardianship over me and my family by the American Embassy had not materialized. I sent my granddaughter's husband, Yuri, to the consulate to inquire. Upon his return I was no wiser, although now the consular officer invited me to come personally to him. Since more officials from the Jewish Agency had arrived—I had also known them from an earlier period—and suggested that we visit Israel in the meantime, I postponed the visit to the American consulate.

The trip to Israel was to be at the expense of the Jewish Agency, which was indeed a charming invitation for us. However, I had to make advance plans and ensure my return to Vienna, for we were still refugees awaiting American permission to enter the United States. We certainly had strong reasons for going to the United States. First, the possibility of making a film with Kadar became a reality; I also had an agreement with the impresario Harold Leventhal, who flew specially to Vienna to discuss my theatrical appearances. Furthermore, I had to conclude the contract with my publisher for my memoirs. In short, traveling to America was very important to my basic professional interests.

Thanks to the Israeli Consulate, the Austrian authorities

gave us special permission to travel to Israel and to return from there to Vienna. Four of us took this trip: I, my husband, my granddaughter, Erika, and Yuri. Ruth remained in Vienna, where she was expecting the arrival of her husband, Karol, and my son, Victor, from Warsaw.

The flight with the chartered airplane to Israel lasted several hours longer than expected, and the large number of people who waited for me at the airport slowly dispersed in the evening; nevertheless, more than a score waited until 5 A.M., among them representatives of the press and television, as well as my brother Yosef and Mel's brother and their families.

It was my fourth trip to Israel but never before had my arrival made such an impression upon me as this time. Perhaps the sorrowful days prior to my leaving Poland affected me; perhaps it was the feeling of amazement after the Six-Day War that shone over the land like a halo. My six weeks in Israel belong to the finest memories of my life.

At the airport at dawn Israeli television conducted an interview with me. My meeting with friends and close relatives was a very moving experience. Later we went to a fine hotel with a view of the sea. Everything appeared to be festive.

On the second or third day of my visit I was already swamped with suggestions for appearances, which I had not expected and for which I wasn't prepared. They asked for *Mirele Efros*. "Oh, Mother, Mother!" I thought. I was reminded of her words: "My daughter, you'll have performed a lifetime and you'll have presented more than a hundred different plays, but you'll still have to endlessly repeat *Mirele*."

We had no costumes with us. Ruth had them all in Vienna, where they were packed, along with a new wardrobe of costumes for *Mirele*. We called Ruth in Vienna and asked her to bring these costumes. Incidentally, she also was to appear in the play.

We made no special set designs for *Mirele* but used various decorations already prepared, which we carefully chose. A fine and diligent ensemble of supporting actors was chosen, and in a few days *Mirele Efros* was ready for production. Three of the central roles were performed by Ruth, Mel, and me. Thanks to the ensemble, who studiously accepted my directions, we had a beautiful production, which was successful both esthetically and financially.

When we performed in Jerusalem in August 1968, the president of Israel, Zalman Shazar, and his wife attended the theater. After the performance he came backstage into my dressing room. He expressed his satisfaction with the production and said, "If you want to stay, we will take you with open arms; if you have to go, go in good health, life, and peace, and do your work for Jews, for us all. May our blessings go with you."

We kissed him and his wife and they departed. A crowd of people milled around both inside and outside the dressing room. Since it was full of actors and the technical and administrative staff, the newsmen couldn't hear what President Shazar had said. When a reporter asked the impresario who had engaged us, "What did the President say?" the impresario answered, "They should stay here with us." Of course, that is the way it was reported in the newspapers.

We performed during the hot *hamsin* days. The theaters were actually cinemas that occasionally housed stage shows. The acoustics were very poor, and the dressing rooms were badly located, either one flight above or below the stage. My daughter and I would frequently have to dress in some corner onstage, which was not suitable for serious theater.

All these drawbacks were offset by the warmth of the audiences and the receptions arranged by various institutions and societies, including one by the Organization of Polish Jews. The one held for me by the Habimah National Theater had a beautiful atmosphere of its own. My family and I were especially moved by the guests, headed by the beloved Hanna Rovina, one of the founding members of Habimah.

At the end of my stay in Israel a special party was given me by Golda Meir in her private home in Ramat Aviv. I had first met Golda Meir in 1957, when she received me in her office in Jerusalem (she was then foreign minister). We felt very close from the very first moment we met; it was love at first sight.

Despite all this, I had several unpleasant experiences. My speeches (I always had to perform because of these receptions) would be misinterpreted, and my words twisted, which was almost an insult to me. For example, one report of one of my speeches quoted me as saying, "Wherever I'll be better off, that's where I'll remain." (By this they meant America.)

Whoever knows me only casually will obviously not believe this! I had not even wanted to perform in Israel, for I was too exhausted from the latest experiences in Poland. The Israeli impresario and his associate wanted to impress me and said, "You'll get five hundred dollars per performance." I replied, "Just make sure that it's a good ensemble. We'll talk about the honorarium later." Later, after the performance had already been advertised, the partners came to me and shamefacedly said, "Regrettably we won't be able to pay five hundred dollars. At the most, three hundred," meaning that if I bargained with them I'd get four hundred. I calmed them and said, "Let it be three hundred, and if you can't afford that, we'll settle amicably anyway." The result was that they made out very well, which pleased me.

In 1956, when I was in Paris, an American (non-Jewish) impresario came to me with a French Jew and offered me a sum for one year that I could not have earned in Poland for ten. However, I declined because the theater that I was directing in Poland was very dear to me. Once again in 1967, when I was in Los Angeles in connection with the Oscar for the film *The Shop on Main Street*, I was offered fourteen hundred dollars for an evening, but I would have had to sign a contract for several months. I didn't accept this offer either because my own theater was more precious to me than money. My reply to those who made me such offers was that I would come only with my entire troupe.

"What for?" they replied. "Why drag along so many people, sets, and costumes? And why do you have to remain in Poland altogether?"

I would often be asked this question, but unfortunately I couldn't explain to everyone that the Polish Yiddish State Theater had grown and developed under my direction, that indeed in Poland it had a small audience, a Jewish one, but that it had much governmental support—and that all this was my life's mission.

So the words "Where I'll be better off, that's where I'll remain" were never uttered by me. I had had offers from the Jewish Agency to select one of three theaters in Israel. Two of them were unsuitable little halls, and the third, a full-fledged (but not a good) theater, was to be available for performances three times a week after September 1969. None of this changed my decision of returning to Israel as soon as I fulfilled my obligations in America. Yet, I said, if the American Jews would gather the material means, I would not refuse to organize a Yiddish theater there, which could serve both America and Israel. I told them that while I was in the United States in 1967 with my theater I was told, "Don't leave. Stay here. We'll create better conditions for you than you have in Poland." I must admit that I was gullible.

I had assumed that I would be able to engage the finest actors from Israel and America and that I would be able to perform with this troupe for several months in Israel and several months in America. Although it would not formally be a state theater, it would fulfill that function by having the necessary material subventions.

That is why before my departure from Israel I called a press conference in my hotel, in the presence of various cultural activists, and outlined my plans. For all this one of the journalists snapped, "If you leave now, then there is no need for you to come back."

Surprisingly, no one reacted to that remark! Only Ruth jumped up to defend me.

I returned dejected to Vienna, where I met Victor and Karol Latovich. Victor and Erika's husband Yuri worked part-time for the HIAS, under whose aegis we spent the two months that we still had to remain in Vienna.

My plans to appear in the film *Angel Levine*, based on the story by Bernard Malamud, were realized. The director, Jan Kadar, was in Vienna, and the scriptwriter flew in from New York. The script was reworked in Vienna, but Kadar was still not satisfied with it. Occasionally he would have to interrupt his work on the script to complete his Slovak film in Bratislava.

We were soon called to the American Embassy, where we were well received. They knew about me, but they had to proceed with the formalities of the interview. We would have to wait, we were told, but the visas would surely come. So we waited.

Meanwhile, invitations had come from various Jewish communities in Germany—Berlin, Munich, and Frankfurt. We had heard from these places while in Poland, but the regime didn't permit us to travel to West Germany, for there were no diplomatic relations between them. Although we were now in Vienna, traveling to West Germany was still a problem. We had no passports that attested to our citizenship. In order to leave Austria, we would have to get a visa based upon our so-called traveling documents, which stated that "the possessors of these documents are no longer Polish citizens." However, after much effort and thanks to the intervention in Germany of Heinz Galinsky, the very energetic head of the West Berlin Jewish community, we received the necessary papers.

First we flew to Berlin. We felt strange there, literally unable to cross to the other side of the street, blocked by the Berlin Wall. On the other side were so many good friends of ours, and we couldn't even telephone them. Now, on this side, we understood better the situation of the city, which came as a sort of divine punishment upon it.

Audiences in Berlin, Munich, and Frankfurt received us

very enthusiastically. Nearly half the resident Jews there were Polish, who at every step displayed their affection for me. Although this was moving, I thought, why are these Jews here in Germany, where just twenty-five years ago the nest of our murderers and hangmen was situated? It was a historical paradox!

Once again the impresario Harold Leventhal came from America. We discussed our plans for New York. Our suggested repertoire was one of three pieces: *Mirele Efros*, which Leventhal wanted very much; *Trees Die Standing*, by Alexander Kassona, which needed fewer actors than *Mirele*; or a theatrical concert like the one we had done in Germany and Vienna. Leventhal had to make up his mind which to choose.

Finally we received the American visas, and we were scheduled to leave for New York on November 26, 1968, on a charter flight arranged by the HIAS.

Prior to our departure from Vienna we gave an evening performance in the beautiful Kameralin Concert House, which was completely sold out.

36

Arrival in New York

AT 5 A.M. we were told to go to a place in Vienna from where we and our baggage would be taken to the airport. The plane was supposed to take off at 9 A.M. We went through all the necessary formalities and began to wait—10 A.M., 11 A.M., noon—and we still didn't know when the plane, due from Israel, would arrive. We spent the entire day there until 10 P.M.

Exhausted, we finally boarded the plane and took off, stopping only for one hour in Paris. Although we were tired, sleep was very difficult. We were entering a new epoch in our lives: a new land, which comprised an entire continent, and people who were only casual acquaintances, although among them were many friends. We were flying to a country whose sea of people would be our compatriots. All of this aroused thoughts in me, and I couldn't fall asleep. Thinking of our future, I remembered an old anecdote that my mother had told me a long time ago.

Once there was a Jew in very poor circumstances who didn't succeed at anything. He decided to go to the *rebbe* for advice. The *rebbe* suggested that he move into another apartment, for the Talmud stated that change of place brought change of luck. The Jew obeyed the *rebbe* and went home full of hope. He told his wife, "We're packing," then went up to the attic and rummaged about among the old rags and junk. While so doing, he saw the personification of poverty

in a corner of the attic leaping for joy. "What are you jumping for?" asked the poor Jew. "What do you mean?" Poverty
replied. "I'm coming, too."

I thought of this in the plane, and here in America, too,
this anecdote often comes to mind, when I seem to discover
that it is not poverty that persecutes me so much in this land
as ill luck.

Finally at 4 A.M. we landed in New York's Kennedy Airport. Only those people closest to me, including Simon and
Cesia Federman, as well as both my impresarios, Harold
Leventhal and Henri Goldgran, were at the airport. They told
me that many more people had been here but that the plane
had arrived eleven hours late.

We moved into an apartment in the Hotel Wellington that
had been prepared for us. Erika was already in the late months
of her pregnancy and virtually collapsed with tiredness. (Her
husband Yuri had remained behind in Vienna for several
weeks, for his parents were also expected to arrive from
Warsaw as emigrants. For twenty years the Kowalicks had
served the Polish regime as high-ranking officials in the Foreign
Ministry. They had worked in Polish embassies in other nations, and yet their fate was the same as ours: emigration.)
We, the older people, still had time to talk a while on the
threshold of the unknown tomorrow. We went to bed, but
the difference between the European and American time somewhat disturbed our normal sleep.

The following morning was November 28, 1968, Thanks-
giving Day. We went to visit our friend Jay Wells—he had
already sent an invitation for dinner to us in Vienna—and
just like the Pilgrims of old we gave thanks to the new earth
upon which we stood.

After the holiday I began to interest myself in the film that
was to have been my first artistic endeavor in New York.
Kadar, the director, had already arrived in America, but it
turned out that the film script had been rejected and had to
be entirely redone. My spirits were lifted somewhat by the

English-language and the Yiddish press, which warmly welcomed our arrival in America. My picture and an article about my arrival appeared on page one of *The New York Times*. The *New York Post* also published a long interview with me. The atmosphere was ripe for me to make both artistic and commercial fare out of my coming here, but the film was not ready for shooting and my impresarios did not know when to start with my appearances.

Leventhal, meanwhile, had gone on a business trip. Time flew and the expenses in the hotel were mounting, so I suggested to the impresario Goldgran to make use of the publicity I had received and to arrange an evening performance like those we had had in Vienna and Germany.

Finally Goldgran rented Carnegie Hall for February 9, 1969. The advance sale for this evening was very good. Chances were excellent for a great success. (At this point I remind myself of the anecdote about Poverty and the poor *shlimazel*.) But on February 9, the day of the concert, there began a blizzard that, the papers reported, New York had not had for several decades. It was impossible to go out on the snow-covered streets. Some subways ceased operating. No taxis were seen on the streets. From the Hotel Wellington to Carnegie Hall was no more than a two-minute ride, but it took us more than fifteen. Despite such weather, a thousand people came to the theater. Many people who had tickets couldn't come. The results for the impresario were disastrous, and for us they were not too good either. In a word, *shlimazel*.

The newspapers suggested that we do a repeat performance at another time, but arranging this was very difficult.

That evening other actor friends joined me, including Molly Picon, Yaakov Kalich, Joseph Buloff, and his wife Luba Kadison. I should also note that the late drama editor of the *Jewish Daily Forward*, Herman Ehrenreich, was brought to Carnegie Hall in a wheelchair because he couldn't walk. He did not live too far from the theater, but he had to be carried down the stairs in the wheelchair. The following day he wrote a wonderful review titled "Not Just Great Theater But Great Art."

Participating with me that evening were my husband, Meir Melman, my daughter, Ruth Kaminska, and Karol Latovitch. The performance took place during a night in February, but how can I skip over January 31, 1969, which is a very precious date to me? That day my granddaughter's daughter was born, my first great-grandchild. It was a great joy for me to become a great-grandmother. Erika's little girl was named Amaris. She was my *naches* in all my free moments and is so to this very day.

37

My First Work in Films and Theater, 1969

BY February the script of *Angel Levine*, starring Zero Mostel and Harry Belafonte, had finally been completed and production began. At the same time rehearsals began for our upcoming tour of *Mirele Efros*. How was this possible? Indeed, it was impossible, as I learned later. My day was something like this. At 7:30 A.M. a limousine was waiting for me that took me to the studio. There I worked till six at night (sometimes later). After returning to the hotel, with scarcely any time to eat, rehearsals for *Mirele* began in a specially rented room in the Hotel Wellington. Rehearsals would last until about 10 or 11 P.M. This was my schedule for more than three weeks.

My work in *Angel Levine* was so planned that all my scenes would be made one after another. I would only have to participate for about a month. Just then I completed my rehearsals of *Mirele*, and the next morning we set out for Montreal, where the premiere would take place.

Our theater there, the Maison Neuve, was a magnificent one with fine acoustics, the best I had had in North America. For the production of *Mirele Efros* the impresarios hired a very good ensemble, and sets were designed by the well-known and talented painter Sam Lev. When I arrived, Sam Lev, along with a brigade of stagehands, had already built the set. A hope gleamed in me that with people who had good will and interest in the theater much could be accomplished for the renewal of the Yiddish theater.

Disregarding my fatigue, I was caught up with the work at hand. I sat in the theater consulting with Sam Lev about the lighting we installed for the performance. We discussed all the details with Julius Adler, an actor who agreed to serve as stage manager and performed the task with understanding and love. After completing the stage preparations, we went through our first dress rehearsal in high spirits. That evening we came to the theater for our premiere, and there I encountered once again the same *shlimazel*.

When the second bell rang, announcing the opening curtain, we were informed that we would not be permitted to perform because a delegate had come from the French Actors Union and declared that we could not proceed until the Montreal impresario who had organized the local productions had paid a certain debt. Indeed, there was no performance. All the actors, including me, removed their costumes and makeup and returned to their hotel. I felt a sense of humiliation and anguish. This was the first time that such a thing had occurred in my theatrical career.

For many years after each premiere it has been my custom to invite the entire ensemble, along with the administrative and technical staff, for a banquet. This time the banquet had been arranged in my apartment in the hotel. Despite the disappointment over the premiere that had not materialized, we all gathered for the festive meal. The members of the ensemble expressed their sympathy, and I attempted to conceal my feelings.

The next evening, a Saturday night, we offered the premiere in a mood of celebration. Sunday there was a matinee and an evening performance and on Monday an evening performance. All this taxed me physically, especially after my exhaustion during the making of the film, my rehearsals with *Mirele* in New York, and the cancelled premiere.

Perhaps this was the reason that after my fourth perform-ance on Monday night I developed a frightful headache. A doctor was called who gave me an injection that made me feel better, and I fell asleep. Dr. S. Barskey, a responsible and experienced physician, came again the next morning and took an electrocardiogram. He knew that I would have to perform that evening, as well as during the coming days. Dr. Barskey stated that he would return toward evening. After examining me again, he stated, "Your body is sending you a warning signal. Perhaps you will be able to perform tonight, perhaps even tomorrow, but this cannot continue for a longer period of time."

Even before he finished, I told him, "I'll go to the hospital." I felt I had the strength to continue performing, but I was afraid of the coming days. I felt a deep fatigue; however, I didn't feel ill. I was carried down in a stretcher even though I thought I could go on my own two feet. I was placed in the hospital ambulance. Ruth accompanied me in the ambulance, and Mel stood with tears streaming from his eyes. During all our years together he had never seen me in such a helpless state.

The next morning I received a phone call from Harry Bela-fonte in New York. "What the devil are you doing there?" he asked.

"I don't know myself," I said, for I felt quite well, prob-ably because I had cast away the yoke of work.

It turned out that I was indeed overworked. That is why the three weeks I spent in the hospital were like a rest period in a sanatorium. I was inundated with so much sympathy and friendliness. Dozens of telegrams, letters, and telephone calls came from Montreal and other cities. I was always surrounded by a garden of fresh flowers, which had to be removed from the room because they took up too much air.

I had a private room, and all day long Mel and Ruth would sit with me. When I remained alone, I watched tele-vision, which I controlled from my bed. For the first few days a special nurse sat with me upon Mel and Ruth's insistence, but the nurse herself did not know why she sat there.

Lying in bed gave me time to think. When I wished to avoid this, I would turn on the television set. What would I watch? Shooting, murders, tortures. I saw people who ran away from home and people who were beaten—all performed by excellent actors. To my consolation, "justice always triumphed," but until it did, dozens of people were killed, both guilty and innocent.

Of course, many masterworks of cinematic art have been created in America, but these are overwhelmed by the waves of brute-force films, especially on telvision, where a good movie is shown only years after its initial release. In the meantime the tens of millions of viewers whose only diversion is television are being reared with only one side of the diverse art of the cinema.

These are some of the thoughts I had while I lay in the hospital and watched television, thoughts that recur to this day. Perhaps I should not criticize because as a new immigrant to this country I have no right to do so, but does one need a special right to react intellectually to various things? I'm not offering any advice, but I see a treasure chest of great acting and directing talents, and so it disappoints me that for the sake of money they make films that I am sure their artistic sensibility rejects. However, I don't want to give the impression that I approve only of plays and films that make one's mood gloomy. Not at all, for I do like good comedies.

My convalescence in the Montreal hospital proceeded smoothly. The young doctors who visited me always told me I was healthy. They said that my stay in the hospital was only preventive medicine and that I would surely be released and be able to perform. The careful Dr. Barskey, however, said that after leaving the hospital I would still have to rest several weeks. Nevertheless, I felt that I could immediately resume performing. This feeling was actually prompted from the outside.

Once when Mel came to visit me I noticed he was carrying

a secret within him. If something plagues him, he cannot conceal it. Strolling in the hospital corridor, I asked Mel what was the matter, had something unpleasant occurred? He hesitated and then told me that the impresarios, without waiting for my release from the hospital, had canceled all my scheduled performances, not only in various American cities but also in New York, where I was scheduled to begin performing in six weeks.

This irritated me considerably. First of all, I had worked hard to create a fine show with a good ensemble. Second, I also had to begin to earn money to pay for my stay in the hospital. Moreover, the fact that Mel and Ruth had remained so long with me in Montreal had also cost us a huge sum of money.

Angered, I told my husband that we should take the stage sets, come to an agreement with the members of the ensemble, and on our own organize the performances. Then Mel told me the main secret, that the impresarios, unwilling to take the stage sets back to New York, had ordered them to be broken up. Why? Because they had been brought from New York with special permission from the Canadian customs, under the condition that they would be transported back within a month. The impresarios had to show that there was nothing to return to New York. Destroying the work of artists and craftsmen that could have been used for an audience's pleasure I considered an act of vandalism. However, for the impresarios financial considerations are uppermost.

Besides the emotion that all this prompted, I had another thought. The cancellation of all my appearances, despite my ability to perform, and the destruction of all the stage sets (which I could have made use of without the impresarios), severely damaged my possibilities of earning a living during the next few months. Then would come the summer months when I couldn't perform, and so I would have no livelihood for almost a year. Mel attempted to calm me. "It's too late," he said. "We have to adapt ourselves to the new conditions."

Indeed, for a long time we did nothing, and then later

with my family ensemble we made several appearances in concert form in various cities.

In the middle of the summer of 1969 the secretary of the American Jewish Congress informed me that some people had invited me to a meeting. The subject was the creation of a theater supported by Friends of the Ida Kaminska Theater. I was very pleased with such an initiative, which demonstrated interest in us and in the Yiddish theater.

Only a small group of close friends attended this meeting. Where were the hundreds of Jews I had met on various occasions who assured me that they yearned for serious Yiddish theater and would help support such a venture? Well, let it be that way, I thought. This was only the beginning. At this first meeting they decided that I should be given help to create a theater; they also decided to call another meeting.

Mel and I immersed ourselves in work. First we had to find a suitable theater. The Hebrew Actors Union aided us in this task. After several searches and visits to various theaters, we finally choose the Roosevelt Auditorium on Union Square and Seventeenth Street in New York City. The location was good and the hall was a fine one, but it only had a stage and no backstage. There were no dressing rooms at all. This meant that we would have to do some construction onstage, as well as other things, to convert it to a functioning theater. We got in touch with people who were good stage-hands, and everything was built. The cost ran to several thousand dollars. We also hired an ensemble of actors, and in a rented hall in the Hotel Wellington we made preparations for the season. We ordered stage sets, hired press agents for the Yiddish and the general press, and made arrangements for the necessary publicity. Advertisements in various newspapers cost no little sum of money. We rented an office where the manager and secretary of the theater were doing their jobs.

Our first production was *Trees Die Standing* by Alexander Kassona. My experience with this play was extensive; I had performed it with great success in many countries, including

Israel. Critics had written about my role in this play not only in newspapers but in books devoted to the theater. Besides, I purposely wanted to begin with a play that did not have a specifically Jewish character but deep general human content. It was a good theatrical play in which there were many interesting roles.

Enthusiasm for the soon-to-be-opened theater was very great. Many orders came in for tickets, but they were insufficient to cover the initial costs. I was waiting for organized material help. Once we were already deeply involved, the owner of the theater announced that we would have to have a deposit before we could begin to perform.

At this point I discovered that my husband had been writing checks from our joint checking account. "You've begun to pay?" I told him. "You'll end up paying until the very end." I intervened with the beloved secretary of the American Jewish Congress concerning the promised aid, but he declared that the original meetings were only supposed to create the proper organizational atmosphere for the eventual collection of funds.

We were already too deeply immersed and had to continue on our own responsibility. We organized a corporation with shares. Several friends joined us, and more than ten thousand dollars was collected. Of course, according to the projected budget, this was not even a third of what was needed. Perhaps others in our place would have broken off activity immediately, paid the necessary debts, and called a halt to the project, but for us these were new conditions and we had ambitions not to stop something we had already begun. We decided to continue with our efforts, even though we knew we would earn nothing by this. Our hope was to cover the original investments and our continuing expenses.

Our premiere took place October 6, 1969. It turned out that, despite microphones and loudspeakers, the acoustics in the hall were poor. We ordered new equipment, which improved the acoustics considerably. Moreover, we installed a simultaneous translation system so that with one ear a person could hear the language onstage and with the other listen to a word-for-word translation. We had thought that this would attract people who did not understand Yiddish. The rental for these units cost us five thousand dollars, while our receipts from the audience were no more than seven hundred.

Rumors spread that the acoustics were poor, but everyone we spoke to who attended the theater said they were good. So what was the cause of the difficulty? Yiddish theatergoers were either old people who were hard of hearing or those who didn't understand Yiddish well. I recalled the anecdote concerning the man who had a bad telephone and couldn't hear well until one day a friend suggested, "Why don't you try changing your telephone?" and henceforth he heard well. Unfortunately, such a suggestion cannot be given to those who are hard of hearing or don't understand Yiddish.

The premiere was a success, and the press reviews were very favorable. We hoped for a successful run. However, in our theater we could perform only on weekends and Wednesday matinees. Even this would have been good, but our contract with the landlords of the theater, the Amalgamated Workers Union, stipulated that when they needed the hall for union meetings we would have to cancel performances. Thus we lost several weekends. During the month of December the weather was very bad—rain and snow—and this also affected the attendance.

We concluded our season at the theater according to our contract on January 4, 1970. We ended with a severe financial deficit, not having earned a penny for our efforts for the entire season. This experience, my first independent attempt at theater ownership in New York, reminded me of a story that had taken place years ago.

At one time playwrights would bring their plays to the theaters to read them in front of the assembled actors. Although this was the custom in the Yiddish theater, the actors didn't like to listen to a play. Once, prior to such a reading, the actors conspired to play a terrible practical joke on the playwright. Since the author was going to read his play from the stage, they placed his chair precisely over the stage trapdoor, which was controlled by a press of a button. Just as the playwright opened up his manuscript folder and was about to begin to read, the floor opened up beneath him and he took a ride down beneath the stage. The actors were convulsed with laughter. When the playwright was raised again onstage, he took his manuscript and, in departing, said, "You think that I'm the one who fell, huh? It's *you* who have fallen." The laughter disappeared from the faces of the actors.

I remember that whenever my mother saw one person laughing at the expense of another she would narrate the above story.

Why do I mention this here? When the actors prepared to lower the playwright beneath the stage, they didn't know whether the play he was about to read would be good or poor. They simply didn't need any new plays. For them the old plays they had been performing for years and, occasionally, revising sufficed. Or they would present their own version of vaudeville comedies they had seen elsewhere. But to listen to a new play and seriously consider it—what for?

So I began to think, perhaps here they didn't need another theater, they didn't need me and my "bargains." That is to say, I knew that there were many people who wanted such a theater, but they were perhaps in the minority and had little influence. Certainly there were quite a number in the above category among the 23,000 theatergoers who in a short period had visited the Roosevelt Auditorium.

The applause and the frequent curtain calls were signs that the performances were favorably received, although not by the entire audience. A Polish proverb states that the man who can satisfy everybody is not yet born. Once, when I left the theater after a performance, two young men in their mid-twenties were waiting for me. They seemed to be fine, intelligent young men. They apologized for stopping me and expressed their warm thanks for the performance, which stimulated much feeling and thought in them. At the same time my husband emerged from another door. An old lady met him and said, "Are you a member of this company? Then I must tell you that you've shown us a terrible play and we didn't understand a thing." Two extremes.

After the closing of the theater I decided that I would no longer push myself forward with my *idée fixe:* that in a land with millions of Jews there had to be a good, permanent Yiddish theater in which the actors would not earn too much and for which philanthropic supporters would provide a small subsidy but not lose too much money, God forbid.

A theater of this sort one couldn't ask from Israel. To Israel one has to give because it gives us so much. In America, however, resources had to be found to support an authentic Yiddish theater that would serve America *and* Israel. I was prepared to do everything if my artistic cooperation was needed. If they wouldn't understand me, well, too bad.

One thing I knew. Various complaints would be leveled against me, but I wouldn't reply to them. I would remain silent.

The only truly joyful, happy experience I had was my great-grandchild, Amaris. The dear, loving people around me are happy only when I am happy, but during the period I am describing I certainly was not. I'm sorry, because I know that Americans love to read about satisfied, joyful, and happy people.

I must admit that I have had many successes in my life. I have always been surrounded with much love, and I have intensely loved the people around me and life itself. I have had many severe blows in my personal life and suffered all sort of general catastrophes, especially in recent years. I have experienced wars, changes of regime, and changes of official policy regarding my people. All have had their effect upon me directly and indirectly. I don't have to mention again these events, during which cruelties and murders were committed by normal and abnormal people, all of whom were a danger to humanity. Not only in the distant past but even during my own lifetime there were many witnesses to historic events and broken hopes and illusions.

There was a time when one did not have to lock one's doors, and now one has to think up all sorts of clever devices and alarm systems—a sign of an advanced culture! All these examples can be multiplied ad infinitum.

The worst thing is when children say to parents, "You're from another generation." Yes, another generation, another world. Perhaps from the ethical point of view not an exemplary world, but a more beautiful one, it seems to me, from an esthetic point of view. If civilization is amenable to acquainting itself only with outer space and neglecting the earth below, such a world will surely go under, and it will deserve to.

Why am I writing now in this fashion? I know there are many writers who have considered this matter more profoundly and can depict it more interestingly. However, my great-grandchild Amaris is still naïve about what is happening around her. Someday her beautiful, innocent eyes and her ears that respond so well to each musical sound will begin to see and hear everything that is seen and heard in the name of "freedom of creativity." The truth is that the concept of "freedom of creativity" is misused and transformed into filth and inelegance. I regret that such a pure little flower will lose the radiant innocence that even now illuminates my difficult life.

I know that I will be labeled an old conservative. Throughout my life I have been progressive, and I remain so even now. In the name of human progress I would wish everyone, including my great-grandchild, a better and more beautiful world. Perhaps these are two sides of the same coin.

Someone might interpret these statements about my difficult

life incorrectly, thinking that perhaps I lack food or that I live in unsuitable conditions. If so, I would like to state that I have a beautiful apartment in which I lack nothing, except that I am not working. And that is difficult. I am not able to accomplish my life's mission. This may be a delusion, but that's the way I feel.

How do I conclude a book about myself, a book of memoirs concerning things that happened to me and around me?

As in a kaleidoscope, events follow events, unexpected and sudden. Certainly people more competent than I will write about all these happenings. That is why at the very end of this book I would like to say something that has important meaning for me.

I have not found any repose of late, but I have no regrets whatsoever about leaving Poland, which I considered a necessity. In Poland I had been fully convinced that the finest ideals, if realized by means of evil, dishonest people, become degraded to an empty formula that in the end must go bankrupt. It is distressing that stupidity and dishonesty are victorious over uprightness and honesty.

On this planet there exists Israel, a small, anguished little state that has bled much, and it is difficult to understand why it is surrounded by so much hatred instead of wonder. Not a day passes when this little land is not mentioned in the press or on radio and television, not always favorably. Even favorable mention often serves only as a pretext somehow to berate the land.

The world's technological and scientific accomplishments, along with its moral decline that surrounds us, are colossal in scope. And here I am with my complaints, feelings, and opinions, which are of so little significance.

I consider all of this, but too late.

Protect us, O God, from general woe and all-encompassing sorrow, and let everyone be aware of every other person's sufferings and joys.

Amen!

Index